The New Chinese Economy

The New Chinese Economy

Dynamic Transitions into the Future

Edited by

Elias C. Grivoyannis

palgrave
macmillan

First published in 2012 by
PALGRAVE MACMILLAN®
in the United States—a division of St. Martin's Press LLC,
175 Fifth Avenue, New York, NY 10010.

Where this book is distributed in the UK, Europe and the rest of the world,
this is by Palgrave Macmillan, a division of Macmillan Publishers Limited,
registered in England, company number 785998, of Houndmills,
Basingstoke, Hampshire RG21 6XS.

Palgrave Macmillan is the global academic imprint of the above companies
and has companies and representatives throughout the world.

Palgrave® and Macmillan® are registered trademarks in the United States,
the United Kingdom, Europe and other countries.

ISBN: 978–0–230–11567–5 (hardback)
ISBN: 978–0–230–11568–2 (paperback)

Library of Congress Cataloging-in-Publication Data

Grivoyannis, Elias C.
    The new Chinese economy : dynamic transitions into the future /
Elias C. Grivoyannis.
        p. cm.
    ISBN 978–0–230–11567–5 (hardback)—
    ISBN 978–0–230–11568–2 (paperback)
      1. China—Economic conditions—2000- 2. China—Economic conditions—
1976–2000. 3. China—Economic policy—2000- 4. China—Economic policy—
1976–2000. I. Title.

HC427.95.G75 2012
330.951—dc23   2011036343

A catalogue record of the book is available from the British Library.

Design by Newgen Imaging Systems (P) Ltd., Chennai, India.

First edition: March 2012

10 9 8 7 6 5 4 3 2 1

Printed in the United States of America.

Contents

Figures and Tables

Figures

Acknowledgments

Many people contributed to advancing this project. Laurie Harting, Executive Editor, Business, Economics, and Finance, Palgrave Macmillan, extended the invitation to write a book on China, after meeting with me at academic conferences where I presented papers on this subject. My teaching assistant at New York University, Dr. Shenghao Zhu, introduced me to his scholar friends in China that changed the initial proposal for this project of my being its sole author. My wife, Prof. Beth Grivoyannis, read chapters 1, 6, and 9, Dr. Nuria Quella read chapter 5, Allan Warner read chapters 2, 3, 5, 6, and 8, Jared Rechnitz read chapters 3 and 8, and Hahim Mahir Gamzo read chapters 2 and 6. Their editorial contributions are greatly appreciated. Sam Hasey, Editor, Tiffany Hufford, Editorial Assistant, and Kristy Lilas, Assistant Production Manager, Palgrave Macmillan, along with Deepa John and Samita Narain (copy editor), Newgen KnowledgeWorks, greatly improved the readability of the text with their editing comments, and helped ensure the smooth production of the final manuscript.

To the givers of the seed,
with thanks,
the fruit is dedicated.

Elias C. Grivoyannis
Yeshiva University
New York City, December 20, 2011.

Contributors

Binkai Chen
Assistant Professor,
School of Economics,
Central University of Finance and Economics, Beijing, China.

Ben Duan
Research Scholar,
Pohang Mathematics Institute,
Pohang University of Sciences and Technology, Pohang, South Korea.

Mingzhai Geng
Dean and Professor,
School of Economics,
Institute of Middle-China Development,
Henan University, Kaifeng, Henan, China.

Elias C. Grivoyannis
Associate Professor of Economics,
Yeshiva University, New York City, NY, USA.

Xiaomei Ji
Associate Professor of Mathematics,
College of Applied Sciences,
Beijing University of Technology, Beijing, China.
Research Fellow,
Department of Mathematical Sciences,
Yeshiva University, New York, USA.

Kaixiang Peng
Professor,
School of Economics,
Henan University, Kaifeng, Henan, China.

Bingtao Song
Associate Professor,
The Center for Yellow River Civilization and Sustainable Development,
School of Economics,
Henan University, Kaifeng, Henan, China.

Rudai Yang
Professor,
School of Business,
Xiangtan University, Hunan, China.

Chao Zhang
Editor,
Natural History,
Chinese National Geography, Beijing, China.

Hao Zhou
Associate Professor of Economics,
Institute of Industrial Economics,
Jinan University, Guangzhou, Guangdong, China.

Acronyms

ABC	Agricultural Bank of China
CBRC	China Banking Regulatory Commission
CCP	Chinese Communist Party
CI	Confucius Institutes
CIRC	China Insurance Regulatory Commission
CISBU	Confucius Institute at Stony Brook University
CPC	Communist Party of China
CPI	Consumer Price Index
CSRC	China Securities Regulatory Commission
DIY	Do It Yourself
FDI	Foreign Direct Investment
i.i.d	independent and identically distributed
IT	Information Technology
LCDs	Liquid Crystal Displays
MPC	Marginal Propensity to Consume
MPS	Marginal Propensity to Save
PBC	People's Bank of China
PISA	Programme for International Student Assessment
PKU	Peking University
PPC	Pay-Per-Click (internet search engine)
PRC	People's Republic of China, mainland China
PSBC	Postal Savings Bank of China
Q&A	Question and Answer
R&D	Research and Development
RCC	Rural Credit Cooperatives
ROC	Republic of China, commonly known as Taiwan
ROSCA	Rotating Savings and Credit Association
SBU	Stony Brook University
SEZs	Special Economic Zones
SOEs	State-Owned Enterprises
SSE	Shanghai Stock Exchange
TFP	Total Factor Productivity
WTO	World Trade Organization

I

A Historical Background of China's Economy and Lessons from Its Globalization

Elias C. Grivoyannis

In 1978, a reform and opening-up policy was introduced in the People's Republic of China (PRC) known as "Gaige Kaifang." This policy had a tremendous impact on China's output growth and volume of trade with the rest of the world. Twenty-three years later, China's openness to the world economy was officially recognized by its entry to the World Trade Organization (WTO) in 2001. These were the beginnings of the new Chinese economy that have since had significant economic implications for the rest of the world.

1.1   The Old China

From the second millennium B.C. until the early 1900s, China was ruled by dynasties. The three most recent ones with characteristic economic developments during their period were the following:

The *Yuan Dynasty* ruled China and Mongolia from 1271 through 1368 and was demised, among other reasons, because of the neglect of irrigation systems that destroyed the agricultural economy. This forced high taxation on starving peasants in an effort to raise public revenue during periods of high inflation because of food shortages.

The *Ming Dynasty* ruled China between 1368 and 1644 and was responsible for enormous public works. They built a vast navy, restored the Grand Canal and the Great Wall, and established the Forbidden City in Beijing. Prior to the collapse of the Ming Dynasty, the country experienced an economic crisis caused by money shortages, natural disasters, and political inability to manage the bureaucracy. Shortage of silver, the official medium of exchange, made it impossible for peasants to pay their taxes in currency. At the same time, the ecological phenomenon of the "Little Ice Age" shortened the growing season, reduced agricultural production, and did not allow peasants to pay their taxes in agricultural commodities either. Earthquakes and epidemics exacerbated the impact of money and food shortages, and imposed a devastating burden on the ruling class and the country.

The *Manchu Dynasty* ruled China from 1644 to 1912 and established the Empire of the Great Qing. During this period, trade with European countries started and cultivation of peanuts, corn, and sweet potatoes was introduced from the Americas. The trade with foreigners increased the inflow of silver, and money supply in China, and expanded the domestic markets. Economies of scale along with the income benefits from trade and political stability induced high population growth. Political corruption of the government, though, and its concessions to the European powers in the 1800s frustrated the population and created political unrest. The Xinhai Revolution, which began on October 10, 1911, resulted in the resignation of China's last Emperor Puyi on February 12, 1912, and caused the demise of the Qing Dynasty.

The Chinese revolutionaries who overthrew the last dynasty replaced it by the *Republic of China (ROC)* (1912–1944). During this period, the Chinese economy suffered from three calamities: the internal strife of warlords, a civil war, and a Japanese invasion. By 1949, the Communist Party of China (CPC) won the civil war and established the PRC (1949 to present).

The CPC took power in 1949, elected Mao Zedong first chairman of the party, and imposed a transition into a central economic planning system. Socializing the economy began by nationalizing industries, creating large collective cultivation entities in the agricultural sector, imposing state control over the banking system, establishing government trading companies to control the distribution of commodities from producers to consumers, and introducing a Soviet type of central economic planning.

During the first three years (1949–1952) of its regime, the new government was successful in restoring the economy damaged from the war with Japan and Russia and in introducing a land reform by transferring land ownership from big landlords to peasants. During the following five years (1953–1957), the new government introduced, with Soviet help, its "First Five-Year Plan" of industrialization and socialization. This created much dissatisfaction with concentrated central planning and with the imbalanced growth between farming, which was underemphasized, and heavy industry that received massive government support for growth.

The "Second Five-Year Plan" (1958–1962) was replaced by what is known as the "Great Leap Forward" (1958–1960) policy. It was a model of Mao Zedong that emphasized decentralization of ownership and decision-making by communes while it ideologically tried to inspire higher productivity across all sectors of the economy. Unfortunately, capital shortages and bad weather reduced the output of agricultural communes and the "Great Leap Forward" experiment resulted in famine and loss of 45 million lives from starvation (Dikötter, 2010, p. 333).

The famine was partially caused by ignorance or underestimation of the economic laws that governed the behavior of the main economic decision makers at the time. As a result, China experienced a dramatic break down in its central planning system because of what is known in economics as the "agent-principal" problem.

Party representatives in the layers of the administrative hierarchy (the agents) had interests and concerns conflicting with those of the central government decision makers (the principals). The "agents" were primarily concerned about the security of their position, of not being purged because of shortages in production activities under their supervision. They were also concerned about their status within the hierarchy of the party by impressing their supervisors with the outcome of their work and thus gaining favors in the future. As a result, the "agents" had an incentive to exaggerate the production of agricultural output under their supervision, and they did so by overstating production and understating the bad harvest, even though it was a result of bad weather. In response to those inflated harvest reports, the "principals" ordered the shipment of disproportionately high amounts of agricultural products for use in urban areas and for exports leaving insufficient amounts of food for peasants to eat, thus creating one of the great famines in human history.

This famine was an "external economic cost" imposed on the country by individuals who had to use deceit for personal gain in order to survive. As Frank Dikötter (2010) explains, the circumstances were making everyone "depend on the ability to lie, charm, hide, steal, cheat, pilfer, forage, smuggle, trick, manipulate or otherwise outwit the state." Mao meant well, and his idea to inspire the whole nation to become more dedicated and productive, and thus generate a "Great Leap Forward" economic outcome, was theoretically correct, but the people in China who had to implement Mao's idea were not worthy of it. This disaster created a loss of confidence in Mao's leadership and great opposition to his ideas within the leadership of CPC.

In the years that followed (1961–1965), the government reduced investment in heavy industry and focused its investment plans on light industry and agriculture to feed the public. It replaced Mao's agricultural communes by private plots and challenged Mao's economic policy ideas. In 1964, Nikita Khrushchev was overthrown in the Soviet Union by a coup d'état from members of his own Communist party. That incident increased Mao's fears of a similar fate because his party and the whole country were dissatisfied with the catastrophic impact of his "Great Leap Forward" policy. Mao refused to give up power and, in May 1966, launched his "Great Proletarian Cultural Revolution." He proclaimed that opponents of communism in the government and all sectors of the economy were conspiring to reintroduce capitalism, and called for a violent "class struggle" to purge them before they destroy the newly established communist country.

Among the perceived enemies of the communist system were the Chinese president, Liu Shaoqi, and the general secretary of the Secretariat, Deng Xiaoping, who were officially supporting Mao Zedong. However, they became skeptical of his economic reform after the failure of the "Great Leap Forward" policy, and they began implementing less leftist-oriented economic policy reforms. Their skepticism was frequently made public on different occasions. Deng Xiaoping, for example, referring to his preference between socialism and capitalism, stated at the Guangzhou Conference in 1961, "I don't care if it's a white cat or a black cat. It's a good cat as long as it catches mice" implying that what is important for me as a political leader of China is not the color of the ideology, capitalism or communism, but its outcomes in producing the goods that satisfy the expectations of the public (Zhisui, 1994).

Buddha said, "In a controversy, the instant we feel anger we have already ceased striving for the truth and have begun striving for ourselves."[1] It appears Mao had reached that stage during this period of his life. He was angry over the failure of his "Great Leap Forward" policy and lack of support from the party. Lunging his "Cultural Revolution" was perceived as a strife for his own survival. Buddha had also said, "To walk safely through the maze of human life, one needs the light of wisdom and the guidance of virtue."[2] During that period, both wisdom and virtue were in short supply, especially among the young members of Mao's "Red Guards" and his senior decision makers. It is estimated that approximately 3 million people were killed in the Cultural Revolution (Chang and Halliday, 2005, p. 569). By 1968, the "Red Guards" had purged the majority of Mao's opponents and enabled him to consolidate his political power.

During the ten-year period between 1966 and 1976, the Chinese economy suffered dramatically from the side effects of the "Cultural Revolution." The closing of universities created a shortage of trained professionals and led to a "mentally crippled generation"; the replacement of managers and engineers by members of the Chinese People's Liberation Army created production and distribution inefficiencies; and the refusal to import foreign technology reduced the pace of economic growth.

Mao's economic ideology was dominated by two important objectives: to reduce China's dependency on foreigners, by minimizing foreign trade, and to replace market forces with central planning, by trying to abolish private ownership. During this period, China's economic interaction with the rest of the world was limited to the supervised activities of trade corporations under the jurisdiction of the central foreign trade ministry and its adherence to the principles of protectionism and balanced trade. Vital industries were protected from foreign competition by restricting foreign imports, preventing direct investment of foreign firms, and controlling foreign exchange. Imports were limited to essential industrial inputs and were financed by exporting primary goods and agricultural products that were not important for the domestic economy.

Mao Zedong died on September 9, 1976. His successor, Hua Guofeng, supported Mao and his ideology. For that reason Hua was characteristically called the "two whatevers policy" man because he was advocating that "we must resolutely uphold whatever decisions Chairman Mao made, and unswervingly follow whatever instructions Chairman Mao gave." By that time, Mao's radical economic policies had to be abandoned in order for the country to survive. As a result, more open-minded political leaders, such as Deng Xiaoping and his supporters, started introducing the "practice criterion." It was based on the notion that economic and political theories were "correct" only because they "worked" and not because Mao said so.

Hua and a small group of very close friends to Mao, who became known as the "Gang of Four," were the main supporters of Mao's reforms after his death. The Gang of Four was a group of influential radicals led by Jiang Qing, Mao's widow, and consisted of Wang Hongwen, a labor activist; Yao Wenyuan, a polemicist; and Zhang Chunqiao, a propaganda specialist. They were determined to keep China focused on Mao's idea of class struggle, public ownership, and closed to the rest of the world. On October 1976, though, Hua arrested the "Gang of Four" as a result of an internal conflict within Mao's circle. At the same time, Hua's influence in the party had been already diminished. As a result, Mao's ideology on economic policy reforms was left without significant supporters. The Mao era was replaced by the ideology of more practical leaders, such as Zhou Enlai and Deng Xiaoping, who opened the country to the rest of the world and introduced economic reforms that laid the groundwork for the new China of the future.

1.2   The Idea of the Argonauts

What most influenced the economic future of China in that period was what I call "the Argonauts' idea" that opened the country to the rest of the world. The Argonauts were a group of heroes in Greek mythology that participated in a politically motivated journey to find the "Golden Fleece" in foreign lands and bring it back to their city in order to get the legitimate ruler of their country in power. Today, there is a practical application of the Argonautic idea for countries that are searching for workable models of economic development for opening up to globalization. For many countries after WWII, their "Golden Fleece" of economic development arrived from abroad in the form of technology transfers and trade benefits that empowered their democracies with the expansion of their market economies where the public is king. That was true in East Asia for Japan, South Korea, Hong Kong, and Taiwan. The "Golden Fleece" of modern China also came from abroad. The heroism of its modern Argonauts imported political ideology, adopted foreign technology, and favored trade. Many of them traveled, worked, and studied in foreign lands to bring the "Golden" political and economic system to their country. The political leaders and economic reformers, Zhou Enlai and Deng Xiaoping, were among the first of China's modern Argonauts. Modern China benefited greatly from the experience that Zhou and Deng acquired abroad.

Zhou started his academic training at Dongguan Model Academy, a Western-style school. In 1913, he joined the famous Nankai Middle School that was using the Phillips Academy educational model of the United States. In 1917, he went to study in Japan and, in 1920, to Europe. Zhou's search for the "Golden Fleece" in Europe was "to discover the social conditions in foreign countries and their methods of resolving social issues, for the purpose of later applying these lessons to China after his return." This is what Zhou wrote on a letter to a cousin (Barnouin and Yu, 2006, p. 26).

While in France, England, and Germany, Zhou was introduced to Marxian ideas and European communism. In Paris, he met other "Argonauts," Chinese radicals who later became prominent figures in China's political system such as Cai Hesen, Li Lisan, Nie Rongzhen, and Deng Xioaping. Within that environment Zhou became one of the most senior members of the CPC in Europe. He returned from Europe to China in 1924 to support the CPC, and become the first premier of the PRC, serving his country, from this post, from 1949 until his death in 1976.

Deng Xiaoping also brought home valuable experience from abroad. He left China for France to participate in a work-study program when he was only 15 years old. The "Golden Fleece" for him was to acquire modern, Western education, and bring its benefits back to China to save his weak and poor country from the economic calamities of his time. This was exactly his charge. The night before his departure for France, Deng's father talked to him and asked him "to learn knowledge and truth from the West in order to save China" (Whitney, 2001). Deng also studied in the Soviet Union in the 1920s. When he returned to China, he served his country in different posts and became the "Paramount Leader" and reformer of the PRC from 1978 to 1992. The "Golden Fleece" that Deng Xiaoping brought to China was his radical reforms that are creating socialism with Chinese characteristics based on Western market ideas.

China's 1976 to 1985 ten-year development plan reflects the basic idea of the Argonauts. The strategy of the plan was to rely on imports of foreign high technology, on domestic education and research, and on exchanges of students and experts with foreign developed countries. The plan was presented by Hua Guofeng at the Fifth National People's Congress in February and March of 1978, the year that marks the beginning of a new era for China.

China's reform and opening-up policy (the Gaige Kaifang) along with the promotion of overseas investments by Chinese firms (the "Go Global" (Zou Chuqu) program) and China's entry into the WTO in 2001, have significantly increased China's interaction with the rest of the world for the sake of bringing the "Golden Fleece" to the country. The number of foreign trade corporations expanded from 12 firms in 1978, that were owned and controlled by the Ministry of Foreign Trade, to 800 trading firms by 1985 and 35,000 trading firms by 2001 (Lardy, 2002, pp. 40–42; Branstetter and Lardy, 2008, p. 635). China's foreign trade increased from USD 21 billion in 1978 to USD 2.56 trillion in 2008 and USD 2.97 trillion in 2010 (PRC National Bureau of Statistics).

Economic research indicates that there is empirical evidence of "golden" economic benefits associated with the implementation of the "Argonauts idea." There is a positive association between a country's interaction with the rest of the world and its economic growth (Sachs and Warner, 1995). The "Golden Fleece" that a country's Argonauts usually bring from abroad is in the form of higher productivity that creates investment opportunities and capital formation in the country, which in turn feeds back to higher productivity from capital formation and further expansion in output. In the case of China, the "Golden Fleece" also came in the form of an increasing accumulation of foreign reserves, from USD 1.37 billion in January 1979 to USD 398.68 billion in May 2011. Foreign exchange reserves represent claims of Chinese people on other countries' products.

1.3   The New China

The economic reforms after 1978 were based on elements of a free-market economy, foreign investment, and export-oriented growth. Socialism was not abandoned, but, as Deng Xiaoping said, it was rebuilt with "Chinese characteristics." The Chinese type of socialism adopted the power of the market forces in a diversified economic system in which managers and policymakers within a planned economy were given more authority on economic decisions than party officials.

The theoretical justification for allowing market forces in a planned economy was clearly presented by Deng Xiaoping as follows: "Planning and market forces are not the essential difference between socialism and capitalism. A planned economy is not the definition of socialism, because there is planning under capitalism; the market economy happens under socialism, too. Planning and market forces are both ways of controlling economic activity" (Gittings, 2005).

1.4   Understanding Capitalism

During Mao's era, capitalism in China was considered an anathema. It was understood as the economic system of unrestricted self-interest and greed that promised economic progress and benefits only to the "capitalists," the owners of productive resources, at the expense of the working class and the rest of the public. This type of capitalism, though, is undesirable even in capitalistic countries, such as the United States. Market power concentration can harm both competitors and consumers. In an effort to protect competition (not competitors) and, at the same time, exploit the benefits of self-interest, Ohio Republican senator John Sherman introduced, in 1890, the US antitrust legislation. Sherman's introductory remarks on this legislation are very descriptive and reflective of both, the American and the Maoist fears: "If the concentrated powers of a trust are entrusted to a single man, it is a kingly prerogative, inconsistent with our form of government...If we will not endure a king as a political power we should not endure a king over the production, transportation and sale of any of the necessaries of life."[3]

Self-interest can be destructive, or it can be productive and can also be irrelevant for the economic growth and prosperity of a country (Phelps, 2009). As Kay (2009) pointed out recently, unrestricted self-interest and greed "is the economic environment of Nigeria and Haiti, and it does not work: it is the commercial environment of the Ik tribe described by the anthropologist Colin Turnbull (1972) and of Lehman Brothers described by the inmate Lawrence McDonald (McDonald and Robinson, 2009), and it does not work there either."

What needs to be clarified here is the fact that self-interest and greed, unrestricted or regulated, is not the main characteristic of capitalism. China could support and rely on the self-interest of every citizen without transforming socialism into capitalism, especially when the socialist ideology facilitates the entry of other people's benefits into every citizen's individual utility function. This is what opponents of Maoism within the party had realized (Owen, Sun, and Zheng, 2008). In order to save socialism, there was no need for them to eradicate self-interest by suppressing it or declaring it illegal. As a result, they felt comfortable introducing the idea of coexistence of public and private interest to exploit the benefits of self-interest and called it socialism with Chinese characteristics (Qian and Weingast, 1996).

1.5   Special Economic Zones

The Chinese political leadership was wise enough to start the introduction of their new economic system on a small but expanding scale and on an experimental basis (Shen, 2000). The creation of Special Economic Zones (SEZs) played a very important role in this process. The process had different fronts (Jaggi, Rundle, Rosen, and Takahashi, 1996).

In December 1978, the Third Plenum of the 11th Congress of the CPC adopted the "Open Door Policy." In the new economic regime that was introduced in 1978, the Chinese government introduced capitalistic management systems in an effort to increase productivity, labor income, and personal consumption. It also adopted an export-driven policy to support economic growth.

In July 1979, the Party Central Committee decided that two provinces, Guangdong and Fujian, should start economic relationships with foreign countries under "special policies and flexible measures." The objective was to use those provinces as a controlled experiment to accelerate the infusion of foreign advanced technology, attract foreign direct investment (FDI), and increase exports. For that purpose, four cities were selected—Shenzhen, Zhuhai, and Shantou within Guangdong Province, by August 1980, and Xiamen in Fujian Province, in October 1980—and established SEZs around them (CCPR, 1987, p. 52; Su, 2001). At the same time, the SEZs invited FDI and offered special business privileges that attracted a total amount of USD 1.17 billion in FDI, or about 20 percent of the total FDI in the nation (or the country) by the year 1985 (Wong, 1987). Enterprises operating within these zones were free to make their own investment, production, and marketing decisions without government intervention. Foreign funded enterprises operating within those zones were entitled to preferential tax treatment and were exempted from import licenses and custom duties for specified imports (IMF, 1993, pp. 38–45).

The district of Hainan, within the Guangdong Province, became the fifth SEZ in 1988. These five zones were given political and administrative freedom to explore innovation, to interact with foreigners, to learn by doing, and to evolve into prototypes for the fast economic development of the country. The results exceeded everyone's expectations.

In the period 1980 to 1984, the average annual GDP growth of the nation was approximately 10 percent but the annual growth rate in Shenzhen was 58 percent, in Zhuhai 32 percent, in Shantou 9 percent, and in Xiamen 13 percent (Xu and Chen, 2008, p. 18). The SEZs in the east coast that experienced the fastest economic growth relied on FDI and government spending, and not on domestic savings to finance the expansion. Domestic savings were not sufficient to finance independent growth. As wages increase and disposable income rises, economic growth may be supported by domestic consumption and domestic investment may be financed by higher savings. Although China's savings rate today is 50 percent of disposable income it cannot, yet, sufficiently finance investment spending. High economic performance persisted in all five SEZs during the first 30 years since their establishment.

Shenzhen has been the most successful zone of all. It is located across a narrow river north of Hong Kong. It was intentionally chosen as a SEZ to enable China to learn the capitalistic methods of management and economic growth from foreigners and from the Chinese capitalists in Hong Kong. By 2008, Shenzhen evolved through brave experimentation to become a cosmopolitan city of over 14 million people out of a small fishing village of 30,000 inhabitants in 1978. By 1985, Shenzhen had attracted 123 domestic industrial projects and 286 joint ventures with foreigners (Wong, 1987, p. 37). In ten years, these numbers became 1,400 domestic manufacturers and 9,000 joint ventures (Ge, 1999, p. 113) making Shenzhen an international economic power. By 1998, Shenzhen was manufacturing 14 percent of the world supply of floppy disks, 10 percent of magnetic heads, 8 percent of hard disk drives, and 6.5 percent of PC motherboards. At the same time, Shenzhen was producing 85 percent of the domestic supply of floppy disks, 70 percent of liquid crystal displays (LCDs), 33 percent of digital wireless telephones, and 30 percent of personal computers (Wei, 2000, p. 202).

The diffusion of innovation from the SEZs to the rest of the country was expected to take place in three stages: experimentation, propagation, and harmonization. Harmonization was achieved when the growth rates in the SEZs and different parts of the country converged. By 2004, harmonization was already achieved over different time periods since 1980 (Xu and Chen, 2008, p. 24).

SEZs such as Shenzhen were also used for wage system reform, and a testing ground for merging socialist and capitalist ideologies. One such ideology was about wage compensation and profit maximization. Communism is based on the notion of income equality (each should be compensated according to his needs, and everyone's needs are approximately the same). Capitalism is based on the notion of wages being determined by the marginal productivity of the employees (each should be compensated according to his contribution in the production process; more productive workers should be paid more).

In 1983, the *Shekou wage compensation system* was introduced partially based on the capitalist notion of labor productivity. Wages in the district of Shekou, within the Shenzhen SEZ, started at a base minimum of RMB 165 per month in 1988, or approximately USD 25 per month, plus an occupational or duty pay component, plus a floating variable allowance (Sklair, 1991). The economic benefits of a compensation system based on labor productivity was clearly explained by Yuan Geng, party secretary of Shekou Industrial District and director of the Management Committee in his following statement to reporters regarding the Shekou wage reform:

> It is correct to emphasize socialist consciousness [among employees] and to strengthen their political thought; but on the other hand, socialism requires more reward for more results, and wages must accord with work performed. A wage system that treats diligence and laziness, high-level and low-level specialized knowledge, and professional and amateur skills the same cannot be called socialist. (http://ideas.repec.org/a/mes/chinec/v19y1985i2p71-72.html).

The new experiment here was also to test the ability of socialism to endure income inequality introduced through labor compensation based on the productivity of the employees.

Geng's position for the need of such an experiment was not new. Deng Xiaoping had already introduced this revolutionary idea of gradual economic change for the empowerment of socialism as follows:

> I am of the view that we should allow some regions, some enterprises, some workers and farmers, who because of hard work and good results achieved, to be better rewarded and improve on their livelihood... [T]hey will engender powerful demonstrative effects on their neighbors and lead people in other regions, work units to follow their examples. In this way, the national economy will, wave-like, surge forward, with all the people becoming relatively well off (Xu and Chen, 2008, p. 14).

These improved terms of employment attracted over 1 million workers in the SEZ by 1989 and labor productivity improved (Ip, 1995). The idea of the 1983 Shekou wage compensation system was similar to the "efficiency wage" system introduced by Henry Ford. In 1914, Ford introduced the USD 5 workday, which was twice the going wage rate at that time. As a result, both turnover and absenteeism fell in his automanufacturing firm, while labor productivity rose. Workers were so much more efficient that his firm's average production costs were lower and his profits higher even though wages were higher (Mankiw, 1998, p. 582). If China pays Chinese workers more than the market-clearing wage rate, they will have an incentive to be more efficient and productive because of the fear of losing their job. Their higher labor productivity will bring in the money to pay their higher wage. This will revolutionize the labor market in socialist China.

One serious problem with socialism is reduced productivity from workers shirking work in public-owned enterprises. Workers either work or shirk in both socialist and capitalist systems. If they are employed in a capitalist system and they shirk there is a chance of being caught and, as a result, being fired. In order for employers to reduce worker's shirking and increasing productivity, the employers can increase the worker's probabilistic loss (the opportunity cost) from shirking by increasing the wages workers stand to lose, if fired, above the market equilibrium wage (Shapiro and Stiglitz, 1984; Cappelli and Chauvin, 1991).

In socialism, if workers shirk and are caught, they do not expect to be fired from a public-owned enterprise. The political system insulates them from the risk of losing their job, or of being disciplined by being forced to take on the full consequences and responsibilities of their shirking. Instead, they share those consequences with the whole community and that makes shirking look trivial, insignificant, and not worth avoiding or preventing. This is a source of "moral hazard" that makes production processes in socialistic countries inefficient. The Shekou wage compensation system could mitigate some of these economic and social costs in a socialist China.

The government also facilitated the mobility of cheap labor from rural China to the SEZs and increased significantly the number of institutions licensed to trade. As a result, the production of labor-intensive commodities was intensified and the SEZs started to export goods at which they had competitive advantage. At the same time, mobility of labor from the agricultural sector to manufacturing in the SEZs increased the workers' income and the imports of consumer goods.

1.6   The Population Issue

Standard of living is measured as GDP on a per capita basis. It is not GDP, but GDP divided among the population that matters. One way to improve that number is to increase GDP through economic growth. The other way is to reduce the population through family planning and birth control. Under the leadership of Deng Xiaoping in 1978, China revolutionized its policy on both population fertility and output production for consumption purposes and for accumulation of wealth. In 1979, Deng Xiaoping introduced China's one-child policy to control overpopulation, reduce the depletion of natural resources, and reduce the unemployment of surplus workers (the difference between the number of workers who are needed to do the job and those available to do the job).

In 1949, when the PRC was established, the Communist Party took a pro-life position, it was against birth control and against imports of contraceptives. On April 25, 1952, the party's newspaper *People's Daily* (*Jen-min Jih-pao*) criticized birth control as being "a means of killing the Chinese people without shedding blood." Mao's support of population growth was based on his belief that people are his country's most precious assets because manpower can be used to produce wealth. What Mao was not aware of was the law of diminishing marginal productivity of labor when the capital-labor ratio and the land-labor ratio of the country are relatively low and declining. In other words, when there is not enough capital and land compared to the labor force, and the population grows faster than the country's physical capital, while the land is fixed, then labor becomes less productive and, in an agrarian economy, the farmland will produce less food per farmer.

Population in China was indeed outgrowing its resource base and the land had no meaningful use of more workers. A rising population within a fixed quantity of land was expected to generate decreasing returns in labor productivity. Adding more farmers to the fixed land could soon outstrip the land's productivity and reduce savings and capital accumulation. In order to increase labor productivity by increasing the capital per worker, family savings had to increase. The only way for China to increase savings was to reduce the number of family dependents. It was becoming obvious that the only way to accumulate capital and increase labor productivity and family wealth was to curtail population growth. A reduction in the population growth policy became, therefore, a necessary condition for China's growth in her per capita GDP.

By 1955, it became obvious that the country had already more people than needed to do the job, (overpopulation), and food was getting in short supply. As a result, China had the first official campaign supporting birth control. In 1957, the economist Dr. Ma Yin-chu, president of Beijing University with graduate degrees from Yale and Columbia Universities in the United States, took a stand with his article "New Theory of Population" arguing that China's large population and its high growth rate were the main obstacles to China's economic development (Freeberne, 1964). Dr. Ma was accused as introducing Malthusian and not Marxist ideas, and was forced to resign from the post of the Beijing University presidency on January 4, 1960. At that time, China's population was increasing by 15 million people every year. By 1962, the country experienced 45 million deaths from starvation due to food shortages, and the need to reduce population growth became intense. People were advised to practice family planning based on the slogan "Late, Long and Few." They were encouraged to get married "Late," at an older age, to wait a "Long" period of time between having children, and to only have a "Few" children. This government propaganda for voluntary population control reduced the birth rate close to 3 children per family in the late 1970s (from close to 6 in the late 1960s).

By 1979, the Chinese government was already convinced and determined to intervene because individuals were not able to make socially optimal birth decisions on their own. Hau Guofeng, the Chairman of the CPC announced in the Fifth National People's Congress, "If population growth is not controlled, there will be a dizzy peak, making it virtually impossible for the economy and all our social institutions to cope." The population issue was one of individuals being unable to align their private costs of having children with the social cost. This was a form of "market" failure that justified government intervention.

1.6.1   The One-Child Policy of 1979

The one-child policy idea was proposed by Song Jian, an engineer and a leading missile scientist who promoted it "as the only 'scientific' way out of China's demographic impasse" (Greenhalgh, 2005). People living in urban areas welcomed the one-child policy because they were working away from home for many hours, they were living in very small apartments, and those with a government job could show their support to the party by having only one child. Violators were subject to monetary fines or forced abortion before delivery. For new couples living in cities, children were already a considerable liability and they accepted easily the rule of having only one of them (Doherty, Norton, and Veney, 2001). For people living in rural areas, however, children were an asset and farmers resisted the one-child policy. Children for them were needed to assist with family work in the farm or business and to support them in their old age. As a result, rural dwellers were allowed to apply and get a permit for a second child, especially if the first one was a girl or disabled, because girls leave their parents and join their husband's families and couples with one girl have no one to take care of them in their old age. Also non-Han ethnic groups (55 of them making up 8 percent of the population) were considered minorities, and were allowed to have a second child spaced 3 to 4 years apart. The same exemption was allowed for families where both parents had no siblings. Also, urban families could have a second and a third child if they were able to pay a fine known as the "Social Maintenance Fee." The National Population and Family Planning Commission in China estimated in 2007 that 64 percent of China's population had exemptions to the one-child policy rule.

Because of these exemptions, the fertility rate in China (average number of children per family, or the expected number of children during a woman's reproductive expectancy) has been between 1.5 and 1.8, instead of 1.0 that a strict one-child policy would imply. This is below the 2.1 fertility rate required for population stability, and the 6.0 fertility rate of the past. The fertility rate is so low in China for another reason. Many families today, especially in cities such as Beijing, cannot afford the cost of rearing children. There are new families who do not even want one child. The high cost of children's education is a real concern (Greenhalgh, 2003). Nevertheless, the number of births exceeds the number of deaths in China by 1 million every 5 weeks (Taylor, 2005).

1.6.2   The Population Issue in the Future

As a result of the low fertility rate since the enforcement of the one-child policy, China will have fewer young people to pay for its old people in the near future. This is called the "4-2-1 Problem" referring to cases where one adult child is supporting his two elderly parents and four grandparents. This had a positive impact on savings since people realized that they could not depend on their one child to care for them when they get old, and since they can save more now, because they have only one child.

As China is transitioning into an industrial giant, the capital-labor ratio is rising and the importance of the population fertility rate has altered. China became engaged in the unpleasant task of controlling population growth by force in the hope of increasing wealth and preventing economic collapse and society breakdown. It seems, though, that wealth creation in the future could be enhanced by a slightly higher population growth than the current one according to the following idea by Barro and Martin (1995).

In advanced economies, human capital (educated and trained people) is the main input in research and development (R&D), which generates the new products and ideas for economic progress. A larger educated population can generate more ideas and economic growth than a smaller one. As a result, population growth could increase economic growth and wealth through more ideas and output. The condition here is that uncontrolled population in an advanced and sophisticated Chinese society of the future could grow at a slower pace that GDP, and more people such as Yuan Longping, the father of hybrid rice (see Deng and Deng, 2007, and Virmani, 1994, 1996), will make up China's future population. Yuan's hybrid rice increased the rice yield in China by 20 to 30 percent over conventional rice and that feeds today an additional population of 60 million.

Becker, Glaeser, and Murphy (1999) offer another insight to this argument. They claim that the impact of population on economic growth depends on the stage of the economy. A higher population in an agrarian economy will result in diminishing returns to labor but in a nonagrarian economy will result in increasing returns. More specifically, "under conditions that tend to prevail in poorer, mainly agricultural, economies with limited human capital and rudimentary technology, higher population usually does tend to lower per capita incomes, mainly along Malthusian lines" but "the increased density that comes with higher population and greater urbanization promotes specialization and greater investment in human capital, and also more rapid accumulation of new knowledge."

Another angle of looking at the population issue in China is Becker's (Becker and Lewis, 1973) concept of interaction between the quantity of children and the quality. Lower population through the one-child policy would increase human capital, labor productivity, and accumulation of wealth in China. This is because it is easier for families to monitor and support the education of one child than multiple ones, and more educated manpower is more productive.

Until now, surpluses in the supply of labor kept wages low giving China a comparative advantage in attracting labor-intensive, FDI. During the same time period, high economic growth kept prices low, supporting exports, and keeping domestic consumer prices at an average annual inflation rate of 1.9 percent. These realities, though, are not expected to continue in the future. Approximately half of the employers in mainland China raised salaries by between 6 percent and 10 percent in 2010.[4] This was a result of the fact that China's economic progress increased the demand for labor, and the one-child policy created shortages in the labor supply. This resulted in higher wages and rising commodity prices, which gradually could eliminate China's low labor-cost advantage. Also, the inflation rate in China rose to 5 percent in 2011. Among the main challenges that would be crucial for China's future, are agriculture (food) challenge, the employment challenge, and the urbanization challenge (Shen, 1998).

1.7   Consumer Revolution in China

During the Mao era, everything that was foreign was denounced as "capitalist" and a symbol of "imperialism" (Hooper, 1986), while in the post–Mao era, it is evidence of success (Chao and Myers, 1998; Conghua and Deloitte & Touche Consulting Group, 1998; Davis, 2000).

In the centrally planned economy of the pre-1978 China, consumption activity was characterized by patterns of homogeneity and equality. In such a system, the state controls all factors of production and decides what commodities will be produced and how they will be allocated for consumption throughout the state-controlled redistribution system. As a result, many commodities found in free-enterprise societies will never be produced in centrally planned societies, and will never become available for consumption. Decisions on consumption are dominated by the choice of the state planners, and personal consumer preferences are ignored. As a result, consumption is a private activity of public choice. Large numbers of people wear the same type of clothes (the characteristic Mao type of a uniform), eat the same type of food, and even enjoy the same leisure activities. Personal consumption and enjoyment is controlled by the state. Individuals are not allowed to have productive substances, and the main form of personal wealth is to hoard goods for consumption (Lu, 2000, p. 130). This is what dominated consumption behavior during the Mao era.

China's 1978 reforms gave birth to people's personal space in the economy. The state monopoly power on the allocation of resources was gradually shared with market representatives. Centrally planned state decisions have been gradually replaced by individual choices and public uniformity with private taste. The outcome is a silent consumer revolution. Personal preferences can now be publicly expressed, especially in cities, and individual choices are valued and honored. "Chinese consumers are spending a higher disposable income on pursuing those products or services that satisfy their emotional and aesthetic needs, rather than consuming practical, reliable, durable products or services...It's not enough to only buy the best or most popular, most fashionable goods, buying a good that is known to others is also very important" (Conghua and Deloitte & Touche Consulting Group, 1998).

This gradual transformation in the process of production and distribution of commodities allows for product differentiation to satisfy different consumer preferences. It also creates consumption inequality that inspires labor efficiency in production, and incentives for workers to qualify for higher market wages that will enable them to afford more expensive consumption. The government plays a very crucial role in this consumer revolution. The central government still has a great deal of power and control but it willingly shares it with others. This allows for differentiation and diversity within the economy, and quietly transfers choice powers to "those on the spot" (Hayek, 1944; Sen, 2004) who make up the public. This is not a form of public protest and opposition to government oppression.

The purpose, now, for accelerating economic growth is to improve material life and prosperity by increasing and improving personal consumption. To increase personal consumption, China is slowly increasing consumer income and the availability of consumer goods such as washing machines and refrigerators imported from foreign countries that were not available before (Davis, 2000). Consumer income has been rising but, initially, the income increase was a result of labor mobility from agriculture to manufacturing. Wages in manufacturing, though, remained low because of ample labor supply and that kept down consumer spending and the availability of consumer goods. Rising wages in SEZs have only recently reached a 6 percent growth rate in 2010. Increasing wages in response to anticipated labor supply shortages, along with a broader monetization of economic transactions and marketing campaigns by distribution firms is expected to increase the demand of consumer goods and their supply in China's consumer markets.

Consumer demand is also expected to rise as a result of reduction in private savings because of the increase in the availability of consumer products in the future. China and India rank first and second in savings rate per household although they rank 154th and 165th in per capita GDP. China saves half of its GDP and its marginal propensity to save (MPS) approached 60 percent during the 2000s (Ma and Yi, 2010). The Chinese economy is growing at double-digit rates but most of excess GDP is exported. In the process, disposable income is rising but the majority of the Chinese consumers are still poor, with annual 2008 per capita GDP estimated by the World Bank at USD 3,263, while the US per capita GDP was USD 46,716. The United States is better able to afford saving, yet, Americans are saving only 4 percent of their disposable income. What makes the Chinese save 50 percent of their meager income could be the lack of a social safety net (health care and old-age pension benefits) along with insufficient supply of consumer goods. This is like the United States in WWII. Income in the United States during WWII was growing, but there were insufficient consumer goods in the market. As a result, the growing income instead of increasing consumption was increasing savings.

One reason for insufficient consumer goods in China has been the existence of institutional barriers. The distribution of consumer goods, especially in the rural areas of the country, has been constrained by the control of local governments over distribution channels. Another barrier has been the lack of an adequate transportation system (Rosen, 1999, pp. 159–196). Both these barriers made distribution adventures unprofitable and curtailed the availability of consumer goods in the country. These barriers have been gradually removed.

In addition, the incentives of many small and medium-size state-owned manufacturing enterprises that were producing consumer durables have been altered. Between 1998 and 2002, most of these firms were sold to their managers or to manager and employee investment groups and their profit incentive is bringing more commodities in China's consumer markets. By 2003, China also experienced an increase in the availability of consumer credit. As a response, the domestic demand for consumer durables such as apartments and automobiles significantly increased.

As income in China continues to grow and consumer goods become more readily available, consumer demand is expected to rise. The personalized consumption patterns will transform the Chinese society with large differences exhibited among rural and urban areas, as well as affluent and poor regions. Increased consumer spending will also become an important driving force for the country's economic growth in the future, as is the case in the United States where 70 percent of the country's GDP is supported by domestic consumption. In China, consumption has been only around 35 percent of GDP.

1.8   The Growth Experience

The average annual growth rate during the 1950–1978 period was 2.5 percent, and the total factor productivity (TFP) during the same period grew at an average rate of only 0.5 percent per year. During the postreform period of 1978–2011, the annual growth rate became 10 percent and the TFP during the same period grew at an average rate of 3.8 percent per year (Islam, Dai, and Sakamoto, 2006; Perkins and Rawski, 2008; Dekle and Vandenbroucke, 2011). These growth rates have been export driven and are unsustainable by foreign trade in the long run. World demand cannot continue growing at this rate any longer, but domestic demand can. This requires a more balanced distribution of the generated income among profits and wages, among urban and rural areas, and among coastal regions and the rest of the country. A gradual increase in labor income can support growing rates of domestic consumption. Also, domestic innovations by growing domestic firms can replace China's dependency on investment by foreign firms. China's economy in the future will be fueled more by domestic demand from consumers and investors and less from exports to the rest of the world. This is expected to benefit the FDI of American, European, and Japanese firms whose investment has been focused on the domestic market, while the FDI by Hong Kong and Taiwan has been initially focused on processing inputs for export purposes.

1.9   Foreign Exchange Policy

China's growth has been also affected by its foreign exchange policy. Prior to 1978, China maintained an overvalued currency that enabled the country to import high-technology investment goods from abroad at a lower cost. After the introduction of the reforms, China devalued its currency gradually over time from RMB 1.5 to the US dollar in 1981 to RMB 8.7 in 1994, to RMB 7.8 in 2007, and to RMB 6.5 in the first half of 2011. This devaluation increased the international competitiveness of Chinese exports and China's aggregate demand and economic growth. Chinese exports kept increasing from USD 266.1 billion in 2001 to USD 1,577.9 billion in 2010. Also China's holdings of foreign exchange reserves increased from USD 108.1 billion in January 2001 to USD 387.1 billion in January 2011.

1.10   World Implications

There are only a few countries as important for the global economy as China. China's expanding interaction with the rest of the world enabled the country to conform its production to its "comparative advantage." This raised the productivity of its inputs and reduced the production cost of its products. Productivity gains enhanced household incomes and consumer welfare in China by reducing the price of consumer goods and increasing the goods availability to the public. At the same time, by supplying foreign consumers with commodities at low prices, China created an income effect that enabled foreigners to buy more commodities with the same income. China also created demand for natural resources and high-technology intermediate inputs exported by other countries. This created income and supported the economic growth in other parts of the world. China's demand for imports from other countries is expected to grow in the future as workers' disposable income expands and the market for consumer goods in China develops. Foreigners also benefit from returns they receive from their investment in the Chinese business.

China's cheap labor (USD 7 a week) and the country's export-oriented growth have benefited underemployed Chinese farmers, who moved to SEZs and got full-time jobs. It also benefited neighboring countries that exported inputs and high tech products to China, along with worldwide consumers who got cheap goods. China's expansion in international trade had an impact on international relative prices and the composition of production in other expanding economies (Coleman, 2007). The increase in China's capital-labor ratio is also beneficial for both China and the rest of the world. The resulting higher productivity will keep Chinese products cheap for the world consumers and increase wages for domestic workers. The opening up of China and the resulting productivity growth is thus welfare improvement for both China and the rest of the world (Fujiwara, Otsu, and Saito, 2008).

Persistent trade surpluses finance further investment and increase imports of investment goods from other countries. If the imports embody high technology, they contribute to further productivity growth with domestic and global benefits.

1.11   Lessons of the Recent Past for the Future

China today is economically better off than what it was thirty years ago. It has been increasing its GDP at close to an annual rate of 10 percent. Its capital accumulation is higher than before and its labor force is more productive. Its relationship with the rest of the world has significantly improved and the efficiency of using natural resources has been significantly improved. However, China is still a poor country with an average 2011 income close to USD 10 a day, or USD 3,600 annually in per capita GDP.

Will the recent economic trend persist? Will it be modified and improved? Are there more reforms anticipated in the future and what they would look like? Is socialism going to resist or acquire new strength altogether? Is income distribution going to improve and are welfare benefits expected to rise? After all, if universal health care and retirement plans are good for a capitalist America they should definitely be good for a socialist China! (Zhu, 2002). Is education in the socialist China going to be 100 percent government subsidized? If the reduction in the size and the intervention of the government is desirable in a capitalist country, such as the United States and Japan, where do you stop with reducing the government interference in China? (Holz, 2008). Why should we care? We care because what happens in China affects the rest of the world since globalization has made all countries in the world interdependable.

The aspiration of each country is to improve its economic performance, and China is not an exception. This can be achieved by an improvement in TFP within a global environment of limited natural resources, or by an increase in the quantity of output produced given the quantity of input utilization, the availability of physical capital, and the magnitude of the labor force. This can happen when there is more R&D, and there is enough capital in the country to adopt the new discoveries and turn them into new products, along with enough labor to do the job. The amount of domestic R&D expenditures can increase and the R&D transferred by FDI can be intensified. There is also beneficial interaction between productivity and capital accumulation.

An increase in the capital labor ratio of a country makes its labor force more productive. That feeds back to capital accumulation because higher TFP creates incentives for more investment and capital accumulation. This was part of the story of China's recent experience of economic growth. During the first decade after 1978, the rate of capital accumulation, as a percentage of GDP, was stable, and twice it dropped, but TFP increased during the 1980s as a result of the economic reforms. Growth in TFP increased GDP, and raised the rate of capital formation. This pattern of economic growth which starts with economic reforms that increases TFP and leads to higher GDP and capital accumulation that feeds back to TFP has been experienced by Japan, South Korea, and Taiwan earlier (Perkins and Rawski, 2008). China's main economic reforms are summarized in table 1.1.

Table 1.1   China's chronology of main economic reforms

Period	Institutional and Policy Reforms
1979–1984	Replacement of agricultural communes with household owned of farm land Experimentation on SEZs with market-oriented preferential policies Opening up of foreign trade, based on comparative advantage Reduction of government control over consumer markets Corporate taxes replace transfer of all corporate profits to the government budget
1985–1988	A "Contract Responsibility System" replaces a quota mandatory purchase system Industrial inputs sold in open markets, and labor contracts enter in SOEs Unemployment insurance is introduce as a safety net for the labor market An Enterprise Law is enacted to "privatize" SOEs Foreign banks are allowed to operate branches in the SEZs
1989–1994	Two securities exchange are established, one in Shanghai and another in Shenzhen Fiscal & monetary policy are used to control inflation and manage recovery The market system is accepted as compatible with socialism Deng Xiaoping calls for more economic reforms and opening up A Bankruptcy Law is introduced and unprofitable enterprises declared bankrupt
1995–2000	Acceleration of FDI Commercial banks are liberated from mandated lending obligations Reforms to meet free trade conditions by the WTO Reduction of government ownership and control of the industrial sector

Source: IMF (1993), Jaggi (1996), Shen (2000), and Owen (2008)

These reforms increased TFP and created a large number of profitable investment opportunities that kept investors willing to invest. Higher TFP is associated with higher GDP that is needed to create the necessary savings to finance capital formation. Higher TFP also creates an attraction for FDI. Capital formation in China can further grow as a result of growing domestic investment financed by domestic savings of growing GDP. Even in the past, the contribution of FDI to China's capital formation, although important, was relatively small in comparison to the total capital (Jiang, 2006).

The China of the future is expected to support the policies of reform and opening up. This is part of China's commitment for its membership to the WTO (Chow, 2003). It is also a conviction of its present political leadership. On December 18, 2008, China's President Hu Jintao addressed an audience of over 6,000 people at Beijing's Great Hall of the People for the thirtieth anniversary of China's decision to open its economy to the rest of the world and declared, "Standing still and regressing will lead only to a dead end." He also said, "Reform and opening up are the fundamental causes of all the achievements and progress we have made." Deng's vision three decades ago was "completely correct" (CNN World News). China's opening up in the future will have another important characteristic, China's outward FDI to exploit foreign natural resources (Liu, Buck, and Shu, 2005; Zhang and Daly, 2011).

The China of the future is also expected to domestically generate the necessary savings for its economic growth. Household savings are still expected to play an important role. Household savings in the past accounted for 50 percent of total savings, enterprise savings accounted for 35 percent, and government savings for 15 percent of the total savings since the 1990s (Perkins and Rawski, 2008, p. 846). Both, rural and urban households save approximately 25 percent of their disposable income in recent years (Kuijs, 2006). The simple mobility of farmers to urban occupations made them twice as much productive as reflected by their wages. The wages in a competitive economy should be equal to the marginal revenue product of the workers. Zhang, Zhao, Park, and Song (2005) have found that wages of primary school graduates in urban areas were more than twice as much the wages of rural workers with similar education.

An increasing capital stock needs the support of a high savings rate and a labor force skillful enough to make the capital productive. It is expected that the relatively low dependency rate in China will perpetuate the high rate of household savings to finance capital formation. However, this is not enough. Unless there is an effective demand to purchase the produced output, the economy will not grow. If the global demand for China's products cannot grow further to increase China's exports, then current growth trend in China's GDP can be sustained only by the support of domestic demand. Domestic demand is made up by consumer spending, business investment, and government spending. Will rising education in China increase consumer spending or household savings, as suggested by chapter 7 in this volume? How much the China of the future will depend on government spending to support aggregate demand?

During the central planning period of the Mao era household savings were impossible because of the lack of private ownership. Surpluses, though, were saved and dispersed by collective units. Work units in urban areas were expected to accumulate savings and use them to provide generous pensions to city dwellers upon their retirement. Collective farms in rural areas were also expected to accumulate reserves and use them to provide retirement income to farmers. The retirement income for farmers was relatively small, and upon retirement farmers had to rely on their children for their support. Medical care and child education were determined by nonmonetary considerations (Perkins and Rawski, 2008, p. 846). All investment during this period was financed by surpluses in rural communes and profits by government enterprises.

With the 1978 reforms, which introduced the privatization of collective production units, China lost the social safety net for households. As a result, people now in China have to accumulate household savings for a better education of their children, for most of their medical care, and for their needs in their old age. This is a serious handicap for the socialist regime of the country that is expected to be addressed in the future. China's government resources, though, are not adequate enough to finance a meaningful social security system for the whole population in the near future.

This necessitates the accumulation of family savings during the prime working ages to pay for their children's needs and for their retirement years, according to the life cycle model of savings (Kraay, 2000; Modigliani and Cao, 2004). The number of dependents influences the amount of savings. The smaller the number of children in the family, the larger is the amount of savings out of a given level of income. The one-child policy of the early 1970s reduced the dependency rate and increased domestic savings that were needed to finance investment and capital accumulation for China's economic growth boom.

The profits of state-owned enterprises (SOEs), as a percent of GDP, kept declining from 1978 up to 1996, but they kept rising after 1997 when mass SOE layoffs began and managers became more independent (Naughton, 2008, p. 108). The main government expenditures in the future are expected to be on public education, rural infrastructure, and welfare programs to alleviate poverty. Rising profits from SOEs are expected to generate savings to be used for capital formation.

In order to remain faithful to its socialistic ideology, China must promote equality and fairness and to take more effective measures to fight corruption. The country should try to create a favorable environment discouraging any collaboration between power and money.

As a big success story in the empirical evidence of economic development, China has shown in the recent past that reforming and opening up is the only road to prosperity and the happiness of its citizens. It would not be an overstatement to claim that China's success should be attributed to the country's ability to break through ideological barriers and the courage of its "Argonauts" to seek and bring home the "Golden Fleece" from abroad.

Notes

1. Buddha. BrainyQuote.com, Xplore Inc, 2011. http://www.brainyquote.com/quotes/authors/b/buddha.html, accessed June 24, 2011.
2. Buddha. BrainyQuote.com, Xplore Inc, 2011. http://www.brainyquote.com/quotes/authors/b/buddha.html, accessed June 24, 2011.
3. Federalist Paper 10. Congressional Record, vol. 21, 1890, p. 2457.
4. http://www.foxnews.com/world/2011/04/28/chinas-child-policy-aging-population/#ixzz1QSMLjZpD.

References

Barnouin, Barbara and Yu Changgen (2006), *Zhou Enlai: A Political Life*, Hong Kong: Chinese University of Hong Kong, ISBN: 962-996-280-2.

Barro, Robert J and Sala-i-Martin (1995), *Economic Growth*, New York: McGraw-Hill, Inc. ISBN: 13: 978-0262025539.

Becker, Gary S., Edward L. Glaeser, and Kevin M. Murphy (1999), "Population and Economic Growth," *The American Economic Review* 89(2), pp. 145–149.

Becker, Gary and H. Gregg Lewis (1973), "On the Interaction Between the Quantity and Quality of Children," *The Journal of Political Economy* (81)2, Part 2: New Economic Approaches to Fertility, pp. S279–S288.

Branstetter, Lee and Nicholas Lardy (2008), "China's Embrace of Globalization," in Loren Brandt and Thomas G. Rawski, eds., *China's Great Economic Transformation*, New York: Cambridge University Press, pp. 633–682.

Cappelli, Peter and Keith Chauvin (1991), "An Interplant Test of the Efficiency Wage Hypothesis" *The Quarterly Journal of Economics* 106(3), pp. 769–787.

Chang, Jung and Jon Halliday (2005), *Mao: The Unknown Story*, London: Jonathan Cape.

Chao Linda and Ramon H. Myers (1998), "China's Consumer Revolution: The 1990's and Beyond," *Journal of Contemporary China* 7, pp. 351–368.

Chow Gregory, C. (2003), "Impact of Joining the WTO on China's Economic, Legal and Political Institutions," *Pacific Economic Review* 8(2), pp. 105–115.

CCPR (China City Planning Review) (1987), "Shenzhen," *China City Planning Review* Special Double Issue (nos. 1–2), p. 3.

Conghua, Li and Deloitte & Touche Consulting Group (1998), *China: The Consumer Revolution*, New York: John Wiley & Sons.

Coleman, W. J. II (2007), "Accommodating Emerging Giants," mimeo, Duke University.

Davis, Deborah S. ed. (2000), *The Consumer Revolution in Urban China*, Berkley: University of California Press.

Dekle, R. and G. Vandenbroucke (2011), "A Quantitative Analysis of China's Structural Transformation," mimeo, University of Southern California.

Deng Xiangzi and Deng Yingru (2007), *The Man Who Puts an End to Hunger: Yuan Longping, "Father of Hybrid Rice,"* Beijing: Foreign Languages Press, ISBN: 9787119051093.

Dikötter, Frank (2010), *Mao's Great Famine: The History of China's Most Devastating Catastrophe, 1958–62,* New York: Walker & Company, ISBN: 0802777686.

Doherty, Jim P., Edward C. Norton, and James E. Veney (2001), "China's One-Child Policy: The Economic Choices and Consequences Faced by Pregnant Women," *Social Science and Medicine* 52(5), pp. 745–761.

Freeberne, Michael (1964), "Birth Control in China," *Population Studies* 18(1) (July), pp. 5–16.

Fujiwara, Ippei, Keisuke Otsu, and Masashi Saito (2008), "The Global Impact of Chinese Growth," Institute For Monetary and Economic Studies, Bank of Japan, Discussion Paper No. 2008-E-22.

Ge, Wei (1999), "Special Economic Zones and the Opening of the Chinese Economy: Some Lessons for Economic Liberalization," *World Development* 27(7), pp. 1267–1285.

Gittings, John (2005), *The Changing Face of China*, Oxford: Oxford University Press.

Greenhalgh, Susan (2003), "Science, Modernity, and the Making of China's One-Child Policy," *Population and Development Review* 29(June), pp. 163–196.

Greenhalgh, Susan (2005), "Missile Science, Population Science: The Origins of China's One-Child Policy," *The China Quarterly* 182(June), pp. 253–276.

Hayek, Friedrich (1944), *The Road to Serfdom*, London: Routledge.

Holz, Carsten (2008), "China's Economic Growth 1978–2025: What We Know Today About China's Economic Growth Tomorrow," *World Development* 36(10), pp. 1665–1691.

Hooper, Beverley (1986), *China Stands UP: Ending the Western Presence, 1948–1950*, London: Allen & Unwin.

IMF (1993), "China at the Threshold of a Market Economy," Occasional Paper No. 107, Washington: IMF.

Ip, Olivia K. M. (1995), "Changing Employment Systems in China: Some Evidence from the Shenzhen Special Economic Zone," *Work, Employment, Society* 9(2), pp. 269–285.

Islam, N., E. Dai, and H. Sakamoto (2006), "Role of TFP in China's Growth," *Asian Economic Journal* 20(2), pp. 127–159.

Jaggi, Gautam, Mary Rundle, Daniel Rosen, and Yuichi Takahashi (1996), "China's Economic Reforms: Chronology and Statistics," *Working Paper* 96(5), Institute for International Economics.

Jiang, Wei (2006), "M&As Emerge as Key Drawcard for Foreign Investment," *China Daily* September 9–10, p. 5.

Kay, John (2009), "The Rationale of the Market Economy: A European Perspective," *Capitalism and Society* 4(3), pp. 1–10, in http://www.bepress.com/cas/vol4/iss3/art1.

Kraay, Aart (2000), "Household Savings in China," *World Bank Economic Review* 14(3), pp. 545–570.

Kuijs, Louis (2006), "How Will China's Saving-Investment Balance Evolve?" World Bank China Office Research Working Paper 5. Washington, DC, World Bank.

Lardy, Nicholas (2002), *Integrating China into the Global Economy*, Washington, DC: Brookings Institution.

Liu, Xiaohui, Trevor Buck, and Chang Shu (2005), "Chinese Economic Development, the Next Stage: Outward FDI?" *International Business Review* 14(1), pp. 97–115.

Lu, Hanlong (2000), "To be Relative Comfortable in an Egalitarian Society" in Deborah S. Davis, ed., *The Consumer Revolution in Urban China*, Berkeley: University of California press.

Ma, Guonan and Wang Yi (2010), "China's High Saving Rate: Myth and Reality" BIS Working Papers No. 312, June.

McDonald, Lawrence G. and Patrick Robinson (2009), *A Colossal Failure of Common Sense: The Inside Story of the Collapse of Lehman Brothers*, New York: Crown Books.

Mankiw, Gregory N. (1998), *Principles of Economics*, Fort Worth: The Dryden Press.

Modigliani, Franco and Shi Larry Cao (2004), "The Chinese Saving Puzzle and the Life-Cycle Hypothesis," *Journal of Economic Literature* XLII(March), pp. 145–170.

Naughton, Barry (2008), "A Political Economy of China's Economic Transition," in Loren Brandt and Thomas G. Rawski, eds., *China's Great Economic Transformation*, NewYork: Cambridge University Press, pp. 91–135.

Owen Bruce M., Su Sun, and Wentong Zheng (2008), "China's Competition Policy Reforms: The Anti-Monopoly Law and Beyond," *Antitrust Law Journal* 75(1), pp. 231–265.

Perkins, Dwight H. and Thomas G. Rawski (2088), "Forecasting China's Economic Growth to 2025," in Loren Brandt and Thomas G. Rawski, eds., *China's Great Economic Transformation*, NewYork: Cambridge University Press, pp. 829–886.

Phelps, Edmund S. (2009), "Refounding Capitalism," *Capitalism and Society* 4(3), pp. 1–11, http://www.bepress.com/cas/vol4/iss3/art2.

Qian Yingyi and Barry R. Weingast (1996), "China's Transition to Markets: Market-Preserving Federalism, Chinese Style," *The Journal of Policy Reform* 1(2), pp. 149–185.

Rosen, Daniel (1999), *Behind the Open Door: Foreign Enterprises in the Chinese Marketplace*, Washington, DC: Institute for International Economics.

Sachs, Jeffrey D. and Andrew Warner (1995), "Economic Reform and the Process of Global Integration," *Brookings Papers on Economic Activity*, 1, pp. 1–118.

Sen, Amartya (2004), "An Insight into the Purpose of Prosperity," *Financial Times*, September 20.

Shapiro, C. and J. Stiglitz (1984), "Equilibrium Unemployment as a Worker Discipline Device," *American Economic Review* 74(3), pp. 433–444.

Shen, Jianfi (1998), "China's Future Population and Development Challenges," *The Geographical Journal* 164(1), pp. 32–40.

Shen, Raphael (2000), *China's Economic Reforms: An Experiment in Pragmatic Socialism*, Westport: Praeger Publishers.

Sklair, Leslie (1991), "Problems of Socialist Development—the Significance of Shenzhen Special Economic Zone for China Open-Door Development Strategy," *International Journal of Urban and Regional Research* 15(2), pp. 197–215.

Su, Dongbin (2001), *A Brief History of Chinese Economic Special Zone*. Guangzhou, China: Guangdong Economic Press, (in Chinese).

Taylor, John (2005), "China-One Child Policy," Australian Broadcasting Corporation, February 8, 2005. Accessed June 27, 2011, http://www.abc.net.au/foreign/content/2005/s1432717.htm.

Turnbull, C. M. (1972), *The Mountain People*, New York: Simon & Schuster.

Virmani, Sant S. (1994), *Heterosis and Hybrid Rice Breeding: Monographs on Theoretical and Applied Genetics*, No 22, Berlin: Springer-Verlag.

Virmani, Sant S. (1996), "Hybrid Rice," *Advances in Agronomy* 57, pp. 377–462.

Wei, Xie (2000), "Acquisition of Technological Capability through Special Economic Zones (SEZs): The Case of Shenzhen SEZ," *Industry and Innovation* 7(2), pp. 199–221.

Whitney, Stewart (2001), *Deng Xiaoping: Leader in a Changing China*, Minneapolis: Lerner Pub Group, ISBN: 978-0822549628.

Wong, Kwan-yiu (1987), "China's Special Economic Zone Experiment: An Appraisal," *Geografiska Annaler Series B, Human Geography* 69(1), pp. 27–40.

Xu, Xianxiang and Xiaofei Chen (2008), "SEZs: The Starting Point of Progressive Revolution and Opening of China," *World Economic Papers* 1, pp. 14–26, (in Chinese).

Yeung Yue-man, Joanna Lee, and Gordon Kee (2009), "China's Special Economic Zones at 30" *Eurasian Geography and Economics* 50(2), pp. 222–240.

Zhang, Junsen, Yaohui Zhao, Albert Park, and Xiaoqing Song (2005), "Economic Returns to Schooling in Urban China, 1988 to 2001," *Journal of Comparative Economics* 33, pp. 688–709.

Zhang, Xiaoxi and Kevin Daly (2011), "The Determinants of China's Outward Foreign Direct Investment," *Emerging Markets Review* 12(4), December, pp. 389–398.

Zhisui, Li (1994), *The Private Life of Chairman Mao*, New York: Random House.

Zhu, Yukun (2002), "Recent Developments in China's Social Security Reforms," *International Social Security Review* 55(4), pp. 39–54.

2

The Role of Governments in China's Developing Economy: A Public Economic Analysis of the Chinese Model

Bingtao Song

In traditional development economics, which is based on neoclassic economic growth theory, the role of governments in the economy has long been believed to be negative. However, the role of governments is still often mentioned in development economics, especially in the recent discussion on the Chinese model or the East Asian model, which is quite different from the Western one. In this chapter, by establishing a new economic development model, which not only includes the technical progress, capital, labor, and the entrepreneurs' contributions, but also includes the institutional change of state, we show that governments play an important role in economic development. We will also try to analyze the catching-up strategy employed by China, from the perspective of public economics. That is, by copying the structure of public goods in the West, the governments of China and East Asian economies provided a suitable condition to the market economic development, even if there is no negotiation mechanism between the government and economic entities.

2.1 Introduction

The industrialization transformation in underdeveloped areas has been a hot topic not only since the 1950s, but was even a focus of Classical Economics in Smith's, Ricardo's, and Marx's works (Meier and Stiglitz, 2001). Therefore, some economists (Jomo, 2005) stressed that economic development is a major factor concerning economics in the introductory stage. Our society's choice to focus on the economic equilibrium and the stability of economic growth is just a new trend in the recent decades.

However, the people in most underdeveloped areas did not find success in improving their everyday life; and development economics has also failed to supply a convincible model, and to cast a light in the black box of economic development. The prevailing development economics neither poses as an interpretation to the original industrial revolution in the West, nor as an explanation of the success of the East Asia, especially China, in catching-up to developed countries, and interpreting the failed cases amongst them.

Even though there is no satisfactory explanation, the completion of the transformation to a market economy in developed economies after the WWII still made the mainstream economics in the West, especially in the United States, turn the other way. The topic of development economics, which focuses on the underdeveloped economies, has been disappearing from the study of economics since that time.

The analysis of the process of development is now being replaced by the description of the result of development. In addition, the long and difficult process of development in its early stages has disappeared from most of the influential works. Therefore, the so-called discussions on economic development are just an application of the framework of the mainstream economics (North, 1981; Ray, 1998) in underdeveloped areas, which is derived or generalized from the Kaldor typical facts, and only exists in developed countries after WWII (Barro and Sala-i-Martin, 2004), especially in the United States. Development economics has no system by itself; therefore, it is being marginalized in economics step-by-step. This kind of economic theory naturally leads to the failure of most developing countries, whose interest is to copy the existing political institutions and economic structure from rich economies.

2.2   The Sway of the Role of Governments in Development Economics

The evolving history of economic development theory after WWII epitomizes the history of the main economic growth theory. Due to the lack of the positive role of governments and entrepreneurs, the variables in development economics, including capital, investment, and technology, are very similar to those in the economic growth theory.

In the 1950s, based upon the impact of the Great Depression and Keynesian economic theory, development economists coming from developed countries began to doubt the function of the market, and tried to replace the market with governments in distributing resources. Considering the capital accumulation as the critical base, both development economists and politicians in socialist countries posed a similar prescription to the industrialization of less developed areas. Distributing resources or accumulating capital, according to the centralized plan controlled by government, was seen as the only, or at least the optimum, strategy to speed up the economic development, and catching-up to the rest of the world. Ignoring the role of entrepreneurs and market activities, the specialization and labor division was unattainable and overlooked the institutional change of state, which was a very slow and painful process (Bardhan, 2001), wherein the efficiency of governments could not be improved. Depending upon the central plan, the final failure of the development strategy was either way unavoidable.

The failure of the development strategy in the 1950s–1960s made people doubt the function of governments again. In the view of the second generation of development economists, returning to neoclassical economics was the only way to correct the development strategy. They ignored the differences between the different stages of economic development, and they tried to copy the existing political structures and market systems of developed countries. Not only were the structural improvements of the governments not yet recalculated in economic development, but the cause of the efficiency of the market system was also not analyzed in detail. So naturally, a new failure occurred again.

Fortunately, the ability of Eastern Asia to catch up quickly and the prevailing role of new institution economics changed the view of scholars about the role of governments (Taylor, 1998; Meier, 2001a). When discussing the task of development economists, Meier (2001a) pointed out that appropriate institutions, historical experiences, the context of social capital, and the relation between state and market in the process of development should be the key variables in the model of development economics. When discussing the contribution of the Neo-institutional School, Bardhan (2001) suggested correctly that the absence of government functionality in underdeveloped countries, the inefficiency of collective actions, and the ability of government to coordinate conflicts among different interest groups comprise the crux of the issue, but are not dealt with enough in development economics. Besides voicing his concerns over the political institutions and social structure, Meier (2001b) also told the new generation of development economists that the causes of economic growth still remain an unsolved puzzle. After half a century, the growth surplus mentioned by Abramovitz (1956) still remained a black box. However, even the role of the institution has attracted lots of attentions from many scholars, and there is no foolproof answer to the question of what is the right institution. Therefore, he concluded that in the future the role of the state, the inner mechanism of the government, and the process of game in negotiation would be the hot topics of development economics.

However, even if the political institutions and the social structures were integrated into the scope of development economics, it would remain very hard to get some innovations in the knowledge of the origins of economic growth if the economic growth continued in the domain of the production function. Therefore, it is necessary to combine the role and function of the entrepreneur and the government into the model of economic growth or development, and not just to place an emphasis on the function of culture (Meier, 2001a) and the role of institutions in protecting property rights and stimulating investment (Rosenberg and Birdzell, 1986).

Just as Hoff and Stiglitz had said (2001), the model of institutional changes has replaced the neoclassical model as an important tool of analysis in development economics. In fact, the earlier development economist Hirschman, pointed out that even in the 1950s, the traditional production function could not explain economic developments. He realized correctly that the modern economic development is a transformation of an economic system in which not only the production functions but also the utilization functions change; even though it is a very hard process.

It is clear that the problems, which development economics try to solve, do not just exist in economic growth, but exist also in the process of institutional change or in the process of establishing conditions and supplying the modern public goods, which drive the success of the market economy and serve the success of modern market economic development. Therefore, it is necessary to combine the institutional change of governments into the model of economic development.

2.3   A New Explanation of the Role of Governments in Economic Development

Even while new and endogenous economic growth theory has achieved great success, the development economists cannot enjoy the same pleasure. The discussion on the topics of complementary problems and multiequilibrium by development economists, led them to have a reasonable doubt on the effectiveness of those economic growth theories. They were especially cautious on the effectiveness of the equilibrium theory and the convergence theory, of which the mainstream economists take much pride in. It is common knowledge that the model of economic growth based on the production function cannot make the development economists satisfied when they are mainly concerned with the transformation of the economic system (Bardhan, 1998, 2001).

As is generally known, in typical microeconomies without entrepreneurs, perfectly competitive markets are defined by two primary characteristics (Mankiw, 2004): (1) the goods being offered for sale are all the same, and (2) the buyers and sellers are so numerous that no single buyer or seller can influence the market price. Since buyers and sellers in perfectly competitive markets must accept the price that the market determines, they are said to be price takers. Here, the price is an exogenous variable in the model of economic growth, and a prerequisite for which economic entities make their decisions. Therefore, not only is the role of entrepreneurs excluded, but the economic bargaining in markets also is thrown out of mainstream economics. What is left is solely the decision-making of the economic entities and the activities in production.

The discussion on the improvement of the market gives way to the analysis of capital accumulation and technological innovation in the process of production (Aoki, 2001). The study on the necessity of institutional change and the analysis of the evolving path disappeared in the mainstream economics step-by-step (Arrow, 1998).

In the real world, however, any price in markets is determined by the people, and not by a market without people. The factors of whether or not to enter a market as well as the price of the goods are the outcome of the first decision made by entrepreneurs. Whether or not to buy some goods after factoring the asking price is the first decision made by the purchasers. The negotiation between sellers and buyers after the first bidding, based upon the bidding price and the information provided by an economic entity (Stiglitz, 2004), is the typical process of a business. In a real market though, the price is the result of bargaining and decisions, and not exogenous information before the decision. Similarly, Knight stressed very early (1921) that the function of entrepreneurs is irreplaceable; it is the entrepreneur who makes the market economy an efficient economic system, but which is overlooked by information economists, who focus their attentions on the imperfect information.

Since the new economic growth theory is still production based, in which the price is exogenous and the entrepreneurs cannot find their position (Leibenstein, 1968), the failure of the new economic growth theory in explaining economic development makes sense.

Moreover, confusing the term capitalist with entrepreneur will enlarge the problem with mainstream economics. The terms for capitalism and capitalist, which originated from the classical writers and prevailed in the ideological counteraction, have been holding the focal position of the economic growth theory for quite some time. It seems that the capitalists control the major role of market economy, and that the economic growth is derived naturally from capital. Based upon this, it seems, the most important thing in economic growth is just to accumulate capital (McDaniel, 2003). However, this point has been proven wrong by many developing strategists.

In fact, in a market economy the real drivers of economic development are entrepreneurs who run the business, and not capitalists who just seek rent. From the Republic of Holland to the Great Britain, the negative relationship between the capital accumulation and the economic growth consistently showed the negative nature of capital gains, however, the active role of entrepreneurs never changes. Therefore, scholars outside of mainstream economics never cease their efforts in discussing the function of entrepreneurs and their relationships with the economic growth (Kirzner, 1985, 1989).

As a matter of fact, it is the process of negotiation, not the process of benefiting the maximum amount of people, that may be the real origin of the efficiency of the market economy. Therefore, the lack of information about prices is not a problem in a market economy, but has become the expected norm. Perhaps, Buchanan (1989) is right that the base of economics is not a form of mathematics but the theory of price is, because the real market economic activity is not making decisions that benefit the maximum, but rather making decisions on the price negotiations. Therefore, to establish a new model of economic development, we have to include the function of entrepreneurs in bidding prices and bargaining with consumers into the economic analysis.

Indeed, most of the criticisms on mainstream economics focus on the fact that it considers the problem faced by economists as a simple problem of distribution of resources (Woo-Cumings, 1997). The economic models of resource distribution share two problems about market economic activities. One is the big gap between the model and the real economic facts. The impossible variables of information before decision-making, such as prices, are assumed as a precondition for decision-making, in which the function of entrepreneurs and the role of the government is neglected. The other is the difference between the information and market structures as seen by agents within models versus those seen by observers outside models (Matsuyama, 1997). Indeed, it is a very simple process to present a mathematical solution to the designers, readers, learners, and users of models or anyone outside of the model. However, it is very hard work with a huge risk to the agents inside of the model or in the markets, who are not allowed to know all of the market information, and cannot know the results of every choice before the decision is made. In fact, what they can do in a market is to guess the outcome, and not to compare the results of different choices. In most situations, they have to face the risk of bankruptcy, which means the end of an income flow for life. In a real market, if an economic agent gets the outcome of one choice, that means he cannot try any other choice. So, a real economic entity is never granted the chance to make comparisons between the different choices, and then make the best decision. What they can do is, though, just guess the outcome before making a decision and to obtain more benefit by bargaining. Therefore, to the agents in the real world the process of seeking the best solution is just a guess rather than a comparison. Since the process of trial and error can never be repeated and is irreversible, it is impossible for one economic agent to try different choices repeatedly. It is an economic fact that different agents try different ways, and eventually only one tries the right way and can survive in the market. That one is the successful one, while the others will be phased out. This is a typical process of the so-called market choice as presented by Alchian (1950).

These criticisms have made the efficiency of the market economy and the relationship between markets and governments hot topics in politics and economics (Stiglitz, 2004). However, because of the absence of the theory of public economy and the misunderstanding of the role of governments in the process of economic development, development economists use their efforts to discuss the difference between this vicious cycle and the normal development cycle. They overlook the transformation from the vicious cycle to a good one, which is a process of institutional changes of governments. In fact, the motivation to get to the surplus of profits derived from the improvement in governments' efficiency is the real driving force of the transformation of the economic system. However, without the comprehensive model of economic development including the bargaining activities of entrepreneurs and the public economic activities of governments, not only are the mainstream growth theorists unable to explain the role of entrepreneurs and the endogenous prices in markets, but the interpretation posed by North (1987) in terms of transaction cost and institutional change is also unable to recognize the positive role of the government in economic development. This leaves the question of whether the state or government is a problem or a solution in the economic development, and whether it is open to discussion in an economic theory debate (Evans, 1992).

In fact, in the history of economic development, the institutional change of state is much earlier than the success of the market system. It is unavoidable to analyze the transformation from the traditional economic system to the new system without the neoclassical economic model, which is derived from the market economy. Just as North stressed, the theory of the state is the essential base of economic development, because the state defines the structure of property rights. It is the state that should be responsible for the efficiency of the property rights system resulting in either the economic growth, or stagnation and depression. Therefore, the theory of state should be able to explain the inefficiency of political and economic institutions, prevailing in history as protecting property rights, and the change of those institutions. Unfortunately, the fundamental base has been neglected in discussing the institutional changes in the long run in economic history (North, 1994), with the only exception being Marxian economics. Marxian economics contributed the best explanation to long-run institutional changes in history. This is because its model includes all factors such as institutions, property right, state, and ideology. In the following sections of this chapter, we will combine the public economic activities of governments into the economic models.

In fact, many people have placed their effort in establishing a new model. When discussing the role of governments of East Asia in its economic miracle, Wade (1990) once provided a comprehensive analysis model that combines the public economic system and the private market economic system. It emphasized the function of public economic institutions in economic development. Similarly, Nelson (2002) tried to include the contribution of the neo-institution economics into the framework of the mainstream economics. Becker (Becker, 1985; Becker and Mulligan, 2003) not only makes his effort to include governments into the framework of analysis, but also discusses the negotiation and bidding activities of interest groups. Based upon the contributions of Buchanan and Tullock, governments and markets were included in one framework by Dye (1987). Furthermore, Gabe (2004) discussed public economy and market economy in one model in a way similar to the market economic analysis. In these models, the roles of the entrepreneurs and the governments were not yet inquired upon, and the institutional changes and the transformation of economic systems could not be explained convincingly.

Based upon these works, a framework of analysis is constructed here to discuss the causes of economic development, the transformation of an economic system, and the comparison between benefits and costs from the process of economic activities. More factors will be included in this model, especially from the process of production and trade, from the institutional factors (including market institutions and public finance system), and technological factors. This will allow all transformations, and all growths from trades, and production and institutional changes to be explained in this model.

If we let U represent the total utility of all consumers, let C represent the total costs in all processes of economic activities, and let Y represent the gap between U and C, then Y is the result of economic development.

Then, we have,

$$Y = \Sigma Yi, \; Yi = Ui - Ci$$
$$Ui = Pi(fi, \, di, \, 1/qi, \, ni) * qi(li, \, ri, \, ti, \, ki)$$
$$Ci = Cmi(li, \, ri, \, 1/tmi, \, ki) + Csi(1/g1, \, 1/g2) + Cci(li, \, ri, \, 1/tci, \, ki)$$

Here, i is the index number for each one of some goods, P is the price for each one of these goods, f is the preference of consumers for each one of these goods, d is the measure of labor division and the depth and breadth of exchanging goods in markets for each one of these goods, q is the quantity of each one of these good, n is the number of consumers for these good, l is the labor used in the production of these goods, r is the resources used in the production of these goods, t is the technology used in these goods, and k is the capital used in the production of these goods. Cm is the cost of the process of manufacturing these goods, tm is the technology used in manufacturing these goods. Similarly, Cs is the cost in the process of institutional changes and politics, which is the cost of public goods. ($g1$ is the cost to change ideology, $g2$ is the cost to change laws and institutions). Cc is the cost in trades and tc is the technology used in trades.

Therefore, even if technology brings users less and less interests or profits because of running businesses in a market, it can still result in the increase of wealth per capita.

Usually, the price of some goods is based upon the increasing function of preference of consumers, the number of consumers, and the depth and breadth of the market, as well as the decreasing function of the quantity of these goods. The quantity of goods is based upon the increase in the function of labor, technology, resources, and capital. The cost of production is based upon the increase in the function of the labor, resources, and capital used in production, and a decrease in the function of technology. In economic development, productions can increase the quantity of goods, trades can raise the price of goods, technology can decrease the cost per goods, and innovation can increase the kinds of goods, and there is no limitation on the variation of increases. Aside from labor, all changes can result in the growth of income per capita.

This model shows us a characteristic of multifactored determinism in economic development and the transformation of the economic system. The increase of profits, in economic development, is the outcome of all kinds of factors interacting together, in a complex comprehensive process. There are many relationships between these factors, which are changing every day. Not only can capital not exist independently from technology, but also institutions heavily rely upon technology. As Wright pointed out (1990), the abundance of natural resources in the United States in its early stage of economic development was not a gift from God or droppings from the winds, but the consequence of some technological development.

The transformation during industrialization is a process of modern economic development, in which most people get rid of the constraints of poverty trap, start to pursue a new objective, and enjoy a different life (Hayami and Godo, 2005). In this model, the economic development is derived either from the decrease of cost resulting from the institutional changes, or from the increase of utility resulting from the increase of kinds of goods and the enlargement of the scope of markets. Similarly, it is also due to the change in production mode that the labor is being replaced with technology and resources. In any case, all kinds of economic growth or development, which can or cannot be explained by the mainstream models (Cameron, 1985; Mokyr, 2000, 2001, 2002,), will be included in this model of economic development.

In this model of modern economic development, the improvement of economic efficiency that brings us the economic growth and development is derived from progress in six areas. The first area is trade in which entrepreneurs calculate the preferences exactly of each and every consumer. The ability to move the good from someone who has a low preference for this good, to another potential customer who has a high preference for this good is an important focus. Through this, the marginal utility of goods increases and the price of those goods (whose marginal utility has increased) rise in the markets. Then, the profits will increase and reflect in GDP as income. The second area is the improvement of transaction technology, such as the appearance of money and transportation tools, which results in the decrease of transaction costs and the increase in profits. This will then translate back into the market as lower prices and provide the consumer with cheaper goods. The third area is the institutional changes in protecting property rights. This also results in the decrease of transaction costs and the extension of the scope of market, embodied in the increase of consumers and the deepening of labor division and specialization. The fourth area is the area of production, in which the progress of technology results in the improvement of production technology and production structure, which then reformulates as a decrease in production costs. The fifth area is the efficiency of public economy, in which the improvement in efficiency comes from the institutional changes of public finance, and provides a decrease in transaction costs. Last is the utilization of resources and capital, which will not directly result in the improvement of economic efficiency, but can provide some economic growth per capita, and is represented in the replacement of labor work with the work of machinery, which has become the symbol of the second economic revolution. Finally, though, the labor work or employments will result in neither the improvement of efficiency, nor the economic growth per capita. The development economist's main concern is the improvement of economic efficiency. However, the utilization of machinery as well as energy will not lead to progress for the society. It is accepted as a tool of economic development in the short run only because it can benefit most of the poor people in developing countries.

Since the contributions of labor, capital, resources, and technology in the modern economic development have been discussed perfectly in the neoclassical model, and the neo-institutional school has analyzed the effect of market institutional changes, the role of entrepreneurs and institutional changes of public finance are the only two keys in the economic development theory that are left to be analyzed.

In the following section, we will discuss the theory developed by North and Thomas (1973). We will discuss the influence of institutional changes of state, as a public economic institution, on the modern economic development. We will leave out the role of entrepreneurs to be discussed in the future.

2.4   The Causes of the Inefficiency of a Public Economy

Is the state or government a trouble maker, or a solution? The reason why the question posed by Evans (1992) is hard to answer is that the concept of government itself, cannot determine the role of the government in the economic development, just as we cannot judge whether an enterprise will earn profits, or if it will be faced with losses until after the fact has already happened. Some governments are solutions to the economic development, while others are probably troublemakers. The model of economic development above tells us that the role of governments in economic development is determined by the efficiency of public economic institutions, which determine the transaction costs of business. However, the answers to what type of public economic institution is efficient and why it is efficient lie in public economics.

Indeed, the success of the governments in East Asia itself cannot guarantee that all governments are the drivers of economic development. Similarly, the failure of some governments in South America also cannot prove that all governments are an obstruction to economic development. What we can learn is that the role of the government should not be overlooked in discussing the causes of economic development, and the efficiency of government, as public economic institution, is a key determinant in economic development.

The ability of a government or its efficiency to promote market economic development, however, does not depend upon the brains of politicians, but on what kinds of public goods are supplied and how they are supplied. Therefore, the first step when inquiring about the causes of economic development is to discuss what kinds of public goods should be provided and who should make the decision of public economic problems.

As O'Brien (2003) cited, Menard and Shirley (2005) insisted that the new institutional economics redraw the attention of economists to the significance of state sponsored and regulated institutions for the promotion of long-term economic development. Their main focus was placed on the protection of property rights. However, a theory of the efficiency of public economy, which is similar to the theory of market system efficiency, that dealt with the activities of states as endogenous economic variables and predict the evolution of political organizations in human history, did not yet appear.

In fact, 40 years ago, Buchanan (1968) once enjoyed an exciting feeling for a similar expectation of the revival of a positive theory of public goods, to explain the efficiency of governments. Having realized the benefits of individuals securing themselves from exchange of public goods, and the difference between the bargaining model in small group and that in the large group, he reasonably hoped that economists' attention would be drawn to the processes and mechanisms in which the decisions about public goods were made and how efficiency could be attained. However, some decades later, unavoidable disappointment encompassed him when the public economy still "remained obscure" in the 1980s and the statement that "the theory of public goods remains in a pre-paradigm stage of development" was still effective (Buchanan, 1968, 1986; Brennan and Buchanan, 1980, 1985). Compared to the development of the theory of private finance and the booming of normal or "standard" public finance on the base of welfare economics aiming at income redistribution, he felt that more knowledge of the public economics should have been accessible.

In addition to the intervention of Keynesian Economics and socialism in the mid-twentieth century, which focused on the collective management of private activities in providing a guarantee for public goods, the coordination dilemma and free riding from the extension of suffrage or political democracy into a large group also restrained the development of public economics. In particular, the investigation on the efficiency of public goods provision was restrained.

Few scholars pursued the path of researching public economics, and instead focused on the bargaining process of public goods and the process of fiscal decision-making. This was true until the contribution of game theory in cooperation equilibrium in recent decades started to become recognized. A lot of this was due to the advantages of Musgravian theory of public finance in mathematical mode and optimal availability of social benefits, as well as the influence of Samuelson in neoclassical economics. Also, the efforts made by Wicksell and Lindahl in analyzing the political process had been ignored by most economists. Therefore, it is legitimate to worry about "scientific" features of public choices being magnified and to highlight its political characteristics of negotiating process in the public economy (Brennan and Buchanan, 1980, 1985). This concern likely took their attention away from the discussions on the economic efficiency in trading public goods, and turned it onto the political limitations on governments' powers.

Of course, there is a consensus among economists that we absolutely need a theory of public economy different from that of market economy. O'Brien pointed out (2003) that most historians have realized that the public economy with government intervention as an avenue is different from standard market places (Aron, 2002). However, there has been no attempt to model the rulers' activities with reference to "trade-offs," "rent seeking," and "revenue maximizing" in the mathematical form (North, 1981), and no attempt to discuss it in the context of an economic analysis as the suppliers of public goods. North mentioned to us that a possible reason is the complexity of interest relationship between leaders and taxpayers in the formation of state. Due to this theory, the lack of public economic efficiency seems to be plausible. In fact, O'Brien had correctly stressed that the "bad public" is the cost of state formation. In other words, there are either benefits or costs, or both, in a public economy similar to that in market economy. However, without linking the returns to the costs, the development of public economy and the formation of state meet many challenges from the vested interests of the business people.

It is well known that in the study of economics, efficiency always means an efficient allocation of resources through the market system. The improvement of efficiency always means more share of the market economy against the share of public economy, which often is inaccurately called governance economy. Most economists agree that a market reaches its stage of efficiency when its resources are at a stage of optimal distribution. It is very well documented theory in micro-economics that three mechanisms support the efficiency of distribution. They are competitions, decentralized decisions, and negotiations between buyers and sellers. On the assumption that the activities of governments are negative, they always insist on constraining governments to the only area where the market failed. No effort is made to inquire about the causes of inefficiency in the public economy. It seems that the inefficiency in a public economy, which is considered an extension of the government, never will exist.

However, if efficiency means to obtain more benefits from an economic action than its cost, it is possible to attain efficiency in a public economy, according to this definition. In fact, in the endogenous-growth theory, there are some scholars who have investigated the contribution and efficiency of infrastructure invest-ment or public investment in public economy. Although they have written on the topic, most of them focus on the empirical relation between public spending and economic growth.

The ignorance of economists on the efficiency of public economy may seem legitimate at first glance, but implausible after a detailed investigation. Indeed, on comparing to market efficiency in the three above mentioned areas, the puzzle of public economy from the externalities to the free riders seems to have no solution in economics. However, the trap of assuming constant inefficiency in public finance has been unleashed in practice by the British 200 years ago. The comparison between the success of Britain and the failure of others in Europe, especially Holland, in the efficiency of the public economy may suggest some helpful hints to us.

To find the origins of the efficiency of a public economy, it is necessary to inquire the causes of the inefficiency of a traditional public economy first. On the bases of Olson and Buchanan, we discuss the features of public economics and the causes of inefficiency of a traditional public economy in three different aspects.

First, the inefficiency of public economy comes from the separation of demand from supply of public goods in time and space.[1] As we know, the separation of demand and supply of private goods resolves itself in the market, in accordance with both time and space. The efficiency of resources allocation in a market depends heavily upon the bargaining, quantity of goods available, checking the quality of goods, and payments in a market—in the same time and in the same place. If the supply and demand (payment) cannot be combined together and enforced simultaneously for goods and services, such as estates and construction, the possibility and efficiency of trade will rely strictly upon the credit between demanders and suppliers with the help of transaction tools, such as payment on a lending bank, business drafts, and checks. Even so, this kind of trade induces more conflicts than the trade by bargaining in the market, and likely lowers the efficiency of the transaction. The exchange of public goods is precisely this kind of trade, in which supply is separated from payment in time and space, and there is a good credit record between the governments as suppliers and the taxpayers as demanders because of the lack of necessary credit tools and the existence of the possibility of people free riding. Therefore, the inefficiency of a public economy is naturally a popular scenario in human history.

Second, the indivisibility of public goods makes it impossible for purchasers or taxpayers to bargain individually with suppliers and consume public goods individually after trade. The fact that purchasers have to conduct the process of negotiation with suppliers as a group and share public goods together, leads to two dilemmas of collective actions. The first is the coordination dilemma of different preferences among them, or the decision-making of public demand—which is a hard task for any group, especially for such a large numbered one. The key factor in determining the efficiency of coordination is the number of people in a group and the structure of income or power distribution among them. Second, who will be the agent of the group to conduct the negotiations with the suppliers of public goods, despite the credibility of the agent being extremely suspect? The status of the agent, who makes the decision of public choice or represents the preferences of public goods, is a key determinant to push the transformation of public goods structure from survival mode to a developmental one—the conditions of market economic development. These two problems pose an important curb on the efficiency of public economy.

Third, as a natural development of the two problems above, the last one is how to prevent the people from outside of a payment group from consuming these public goods. That is, how to solve the problem of free riders, and enforcing people not to use public property without tax payment. To assure the collection of tax before trade, it is not only necessary to authorize coercion to suppliers, but it is also imperative to control the power of suppliers to guarantee the exact acquisition of goods purchased by taxpayers. These two requirements contradict one another. In the real world, most of the society chooses to provide unlimited coercion to the suppliers in order to ensure there is an enforcement of the supply of public goods. Only a few countries, such as Poland and Holland, tried the opposite way, but unfortunately, they could not survive a long time in a world, which urgently needed the basic public goods, such as defense.

However, the prevailing solution results in another problem of contract breach. That is the suppliers with coercion possibly provide few or bad public goods after the payment is done under coercion. Even more, the suppliers could cancel the negotiation itself if they have enough power, and in fact, this has been done over most of human history. This paradox contributes to the main cause of the inefficiency of public economy in human history and becomes the main obstacle in the way of economic development.

By virtue of these three causes, the ability of the state to provide public goods or the efficiency of public economy is not just depending upon the extent to which the constitution or democracy is enforced, but also on the mechanism of making decisions about budget or the structure of public goods.

2.5   The Efficiency of the Britain Model: The Mechanism of Constitution and the Market Condition

Additionally, if our objective is the market economic development, or like many Chinese people think, the GDP per capita, the major public goods supplied by governments will be those which serve and encourage market economic activities. That is, they serve and encourage the business of entrepreneurs and their innovation in market. The problem is identifying which kinds of public goods will benefit in the creative activities of entrepreneurs, and how do we know them to be true?

Differing from the constant need of the populace on public goods in traditional society, whose major objective is just the survival and extension of people group, no elite government could know exactly what kind of public goods would help promote market economic development before the success of Britain in the eighteenth century. The success of market economic development carried a small probability of success until that point.

Fortunately, because of the conflicts between the Kings and the Nobles and the dependence of wars on the public finance, the traditional parliaments became a mechanism of negotiation and budget, which provided more and more opportunities to the businesspersons or merchants to exert some impact on the budgets. Eventually, it came to a point that the businesspersons or entrepreneurs completely controlled the decisions of budget on which kinds of public goods would be supplied by governments.

Factually, we once concluded in other works (Song, 2007; Song and Zhang, 2007) that the real major cause that drove the British away from the usual traditional path and to enter a new system—the modern market economy—was the mechanisms of budget in governments and its efficiency. In those works, we suggested that most of the efficiency of the British public economy depended upon the ability of the government to supply necessary public goods and the mechanism of the levels of communication between economic entities in a market economy and those in the public economy. That is, the communication between the suppliers of public goods and the entrepreneurs. The following three mechanisms guaranteed the efficiency of the British government in supplying the necessary public goods to encourage market economic development: the absolute state sovereignty to enforce laws and contracts, the mechanism to make decisions and supervise the actions of governments by taxpayers, and the mechanism to show and coordinate the preferences of taxpayers on public goods and to set negotiations between taxpayers and governments. Being similar to the system of negotiation in markets, the motivation and drive of the quasi-market system of negotiation between taxpayers and governments is the basis for the improvement of the efficiency of a public economy.

Indeed, the inefficiency of the public economy once played a critical influence on the economic development and the thoughts of economists. As a result, economic historians have observed (O'Brien, 2003) that, in a typical model of Smithian economics, the increase in the burden of taxation operated absolutely to restrain the capacities of a competitive market economy to achieve optimal levels of efficiency and output. However, since the rise of Britain over that final "long century" (1689–1815) mercantilism, the concentration of liberal political economy on the cost of higher taxes is not a correct direction of analysis. In particular, it neglected the significance of state formation and the effect of benefits from the public economy. Liberal historians, who heavily influenced the development of Classical Economics, had been condemning the adverse affect of public economics on economic growth, but they could not explain the fact that the success of Britain was based on higher taxes. Only a few scholars realized that the real foundation and potential for industrialization attained by Britain lay in the efficiency and mechanism of its public economy. In another perspective, O'Brien contributed a similar view that public economy is a good index to discuss the social developments.

Most historians understood that states attained an efficient form to raise revenue by the shift from domain state to tax state. However, the British government, as O'Brien noticed (2003), was factually an exception. In effect, almost all of ancient states, such as China, India, and even the seventeenth-century France, developed a tax state very early, but they failed to attain the efficiency of public economy and the success of industrialization because the capacity to raise taxation is not a sufficient condition to the efficiency of a public economy, even though it is a necessary one. Similarly, some European states, such as Holland and other city-states and republics in the Continent of Europe, exerted the limitation of constitutions on the government's ability to raise revenue much earlier than the Britain, but they failed in improving the efficiency of public economy and attaining industrialization as well. Therefore, neither tax state itself nor constitutional state itself is a sufficient condition to ensure the efficiency of public economy and the success of industrialization. The experience of the British and the lessons of other societies lead us to the theory of the efficiency of public economy along an alternative or different path.

Maybe, the most striking feature of the British public economy as a unique exception, is that its parliament as the representative of taxpayers never changed the principle of tax. "No vote, no tax" held them back from shifting the burden of tax to a weak group in society. Such a principle not only means that all taxes have to be approved by vote, just like its traditional context, but also means that those people without representatives in parliament, especially the poor, should not be levied tax. This principle connects the public economy with private economy as a normal economic cycle or transaction on the base of mercantilism, and lays a foundation for the exchange and negotiation between business people as demanders of public goods and rulers as suppliers. Congleton (2007) caught the striking characteristic of exchange of public goods between William III and the parliament, which benefit both of them and led to a positive reciprocity in the expansive cycle of a public economy.

It was the first time in human history that the objectives of public economy included serving market economic activities, according to the willingness of tax-payers, and not just for the survival of subjects and the security of territory. This implication opens a new area for the development of public economy. To provide protection and order as cheap as possible is not the only goal of governments. At this point, the development of public economy can play a similar role and can lead in a similar way to a market economy in improving its efficiency in the modern economic development.

Thus, as a negotiation process similar to that in market economy, the efficiency of public economy derives from the improvements in the following three kinds of mechanisms: (1) the revelation mechanism of demand preference participation by taxpayers and the negotiation mechanism between taxpayers as demanders and governments as suppliers; (2) the coordination mechanism among taxpayers or demanders and the qualification to control the number of people participating in bargaining; and (3) the coercion mechanism of governments as suppliers to ensure enforcement and the supervision mechanism of demanders on the powers owned by suppliers to make sure the provision of public goods is consistent with the requirement of taxpayers.

In fact, the success of the British in the Industrial Revolution did originate from the efficiency of the British public-economic activities to provide those public goods, such as the security of trade and transportation, the enforcement of economic contracts, and some new markets that was necessary to the market economic development. It did not come from the lower tax burden—nonaction of government (its tax burden stands as the most heavy one in the eighteenth- and nineteenth-centuries Europe) or from the equality or fairness (only a few nobles owned most of the lands and assets in Britain, and only they could make all decisions of public economy). However, the reason that the British businesspersons or entrepreneurs could enjoy the public goods that exactly met their needs lay in the mechanism of a government budget. As the decision makers of the budget, the major taxpayers, that is, the businesspersons or entrepreneurs in the eighteenth-century Britain certainly knew what they needed in public goods, and pushed for the transformation of public goods structure from a survival one to a developmental mode. Therefore, the governments of the eighteenth-century Britain were the earliest developmental governments in the world, and reasonably promoted the first Industrial Revolution. However, the experience of the Great Britain does not mean that the mechanism of budget, like the parliaments in UK, is a necessary condition to the modern market economic development, but means that the right public goods or the right structure of public goods provided by governments is a necessary condition to the market economic development. This is the real reason why some countries are called developmental states. As a consequence, not only a country like the United States that established a similar mechanism of budget to the British one can be a developmental state, but a country like Japan that copies the structure of public goods and supplies the same public goods, which is the necessary condition of market economy, can also be a developmental state—even if it does not have a system of budget or has a different system of budget. China is an example of the latter case.

2.6   The Nature of China's Model: The Developmental Governments and the Copy of Public Goods Structure

Indeed, we mentioned in the section 2.4 that no elite figure in governments could have known exactly what kind of public goods will promote market economic development before the success of Britain in the eighteenth century. However, it is not the case 200 years later. In fact, in the eighteenth and the nineteenth century, besides some nation states copying the British budget system or the political system in Europe, there were some countries, such as Germany, Russia, and Japan, that tried to copy the structure of public goods provision in a traditional system, basing it on the modern idea their elite leaders learned from the West. Even as a late arrival, China got on the exact same way, as the following case shows. We will discuss the Chinese case briefly.

According to the model above, the transformation of industrialization is a process of modern economic development, in which most of the people get rid of the constraints of poverty and start to pursue a new objective (Hayami and Godo, 2005). In this process, the economic development derived either from the decrease of cost resulting from the institutional changes, or from the increase of utility resulting from the increase of kinds of goods and the enlarging of the scope of markets. Similarly, it is from the change of production mode that replaces labor with technology and resources in machines. All in all, all kinds of economic development come from some new economic activities, that is, market economic activities.

However, the market economy is never an outcome of natural evolution, but the result of governments' provision of necessary public goods to permit, protect, and encourage the market economic activities. Even though there has not yet been a mechanism in China to let entrepreneurs make the public choice on the structure of public goods, the condition of market economic development has still been supplied by the developmental governments based on the learning and copying of the experiences of successful countries in the past. The success of China over the last 30 years is just the result of the structural change of public goods, which brings us to the improvement of their market economic efficiency in six areas.

The first area to start economic development in China is also trades in which entrepreneurs can learn the exact preference of consumers, and move the goods from ones who have a low preference on these goods to other ones who have a high preference for this good. Consequently, the marginal utility of this good increases and the price of the good rises in the markets. In the 1980s, the reform of the economic system in rural areas and state-owned enterprises first announced an approval of governments to private individuals to sell products in the markets, and at the same time, changed the decision makers of business from collective organization leaders or planners, to private individuals who were the leaders of a family or a state-owned and collective enterprise. Then, the boom of commercial business rapidly appeared and arrived at the first summit of the Chinese economy in 1984 and 1985. The first wave of economic growth mainly came from the move of existing products in state-owned enterprises and the encouragement of the efforts of the producers in production. Although the public goods supplied by governments is a rather passive action to permit private individuals to do business, and not an active action to do something for themselves, it was significant to the transformation of traditional economic system in a conservative economy where commercial businesses had been suppressed for more than 2000 years of long-term history. The commercial businesses had been always suppressed aside from the Song China in 1000–1200 and the Republic of China in the 1930s. However, the radical change of the governments and the public goods structure was not the outcome of negotiation between taxpayers and governments in a mechanism of constitutional parliaments, but the consequence of the decision made by the elite in the governments, led by Deng, to copy the structure of public goods in developed countries by learning and investigating their experiences.

The second origin of the economic development in China is the improvement of transaction technology too, but mostly focuses on transportation improvements. This resulted in the decrease of transaction costs and the increase of profits, and the deepening and expanding of market into cheap consumers' goods and the remote rural areas. In 2009, the total length of highways in China was 75,000 km, which just stands shy of 80,000 km total highway length in the United States. The total length of railways in China is 86,000 km, which is also the second largest in the world. However, the improvements in transportation are not exactly the consequence of the government's investment or provision, but a result of copying of the old policy used by the British in the eighteenth-century Transportation Revolution (Bogart, 2005).

The third origin of the economic development in China is, a real exception in China, the institutional changes in protecting property rights, which have been considered by the neo-institutional economists as the major origin of economic growth, and maybe even an economic revolution on analyzing the success in the west. There has been some progress in the governments' policy and enforcement of economic contracts, but only a few improvements in the areas of law system. This will provide a huge space in the future economic development in China, based upon the copy of public goods structure in the West, or the negotiation between new entrepreneurs and governments.

The fourth origin of the economic development in China is the progress of production technology, which results in the decrease of production costs. Even the encouragement of governments on innovation has not been successful because of the education system, and the investment of the government in technological innovation is far from meeting the needs of economic development. China's government did a major job by introducing and copying the manufacturing technology through foreign direct investments. To advance the production technology with learning by doing, all governments of China, especially those local governments who are encouraged by the promotion policy of central government, listed out many favorable conditions and concessions to outside investors, ranging from the tax deduction to free land. However, now there are many complaints about the profits moving out through the foreign investors, but the manufacturing technology learned by Chinese people is still kept in China, and these technologies have constructed the base of the domestic companies in recent decades, which is becoming the major origin of the economic development in the inland China. Of course, the reform of the education system appears on the agenda of governments and the structure of the public, and the technological innovation will also provide a huge lift to the economic development in China in the future.

The fifth origin of market economic development is the efficiency of governments in providing public economy, and is represented in the decrease of transaction cost. Even though there are too many regulations and centralized controls by governments in China that obstruct the private businesses and discourage the efforts of local governments to develop their regional economy, with the power and the ability of the central government to exert unified sovereignty and to implement unified policies in entire China it does a good job making sure the unification of market and the efficiency of public goods is provided. Whether it be Smithian growth or market economic development, the ability of central government to exert unified sovereignty is emphasized respectively by Acemoglu (Acemoglu, 2005; Acemoglu and Robinson, 2008) with the case of the world today and Africa, and Epstein (2000) with the case of Europe in the late middle ages. At the same time, beside the unification of domestic market, the more important public goods provided by the central government is to open and expand the overseas market. This has been proven as the key determinant of the industrialized transformation in the first stage by the export-oriented case of Japan in the 1950s and 1960s, as well as the case of Britain in eighteenth century, whose exports increased more than 444 percent when the total sale in domestic market just increased 52 percent in 100 years (Wilson and Parker, 1977). From 1993, we observed a trend of policy pushed by the central government of China to establish market economic systems and to expand the market space for Chinese companies all over the world. A striking example is the entry of China into World Trade Organization (WTO), and then, we also observed many efforts of the central government to supply public goods for Chinese businesspeople, from the navy cruise in Gulf of Aden to the establishment of close relationship with the Africa and the Europe. However, there is a huge opportunity in the improvement of the efficiency of the government to supply appropriate public goods to advance the market economic development of China in the future.

The last origin of economic development, as a by-product of technological progress, is the utilization of resources and capital, which cannot result in the improvement of economic efficiency, but can create great growth in GDP per capita, and is highlighted with the replacement of labor work with the consumption of energy, which was once the symbol of the second economic revolution. Even if it is not the objective of governments in public goods provision, and is the target of attack of environment protectionists, the utilization of energy is still the first and most important way used by local governments and manufacturing enterprises, in the short run, because of its effectiveness in GDP growth.

Of course, there are still other factors making their contributions to the economic development in China, such as the improvement of education and health of populations, the influence of new technology in Information Technology (IT) or internet area, and so on, but not yet mentioned in our model. The explanation here about the model of China from the perspective of public economics is just a very rough idea; there is lots of work to be done to confirm it in the future.

Note

1. Wolf has realized the impact of this kind of separation on the efficiency of nonmarket economic activities (1993).

References

Abramovitz, Moses (1956), "Resource and Output Trends in the United States Since 1870," *American Economic Review* Vol. 46, No. 2, AEA Papers and Proceedings, May, pp. 5–23.

Acemoglu, Daron (2005), "Politics and Economics in Weak and Strong States," *Journal of Monetary Economics* Vol. 52, pp. 1199–1226.

Acemoglu, Daron and James A. Robinson (2008). "Persistence of Power, Elites, and Institutions," *American Economic Review* 98(1), pp. 267–293.

Alchian, Armen A. (1950), "Uncertainty, Evolution and Economic Theory," *Journal of Political Economy* Vol. 58, pp. 211–221.

Aoki, Masahiko (2001), *Toward a Comparative Institutional Analysis*, MIT Press, p. 95.

Aron, J. (2002), *Building Institution in Post-Conflict African Economies*, Oxford, UK: United Nations University, World Institute for Development Economic Research, pp. 321–452.

Arrow, Kenneth J. (1998), "The Place of Institutions in the Economy: A Theoretical Perspective," in *The Institutional Foundations of East Asia Economic Development,* edited by Yujiro Hayami and Masahiko Aoki, Tokyo, Japan: Macmillan Press, pp. 36–78.

Bardhan, Pranab (1998), "The Contributions of Endogenous Growth Theory to the Analysis of Development Problems: An Assessment," in *Theories in Growth and Development,* edited by Fabrizio Coricelli, Massimo di Matteo, and Frank Hahn, London: MaCmillan Press Ltd, pp. 97–110.

Bardhan, Pranab (2001), "Distributive Conflicts, Collective Action, and Institutional Economics," in *Frontiers of Development Economics,* edited by Gerald M. Meier and Joseph E. Stiglitz, Oxford: Oxford University Press, pp. 269–290.

Barro, Robert J. and Xavier Sala-i-Martin (2004), *Economic Growth,* 2nd ed., Cambridge, MA: MIT Press, ISBN: 978-0262025539.

Becker, Gary S. (1985), "Public Policies, Pressure Groups, and Dead Weight Costs," *Journal of Public Economics* Vol. 28, pp. 329–347.

Becker, Gary S. and Casey B. Mulligan (2003), "Deadweight Costs and the Size of Government," *Journal of Law and Economics* vol. XLVI (October), pp. 293–340.

Bogart, Dan (2005), "Turnpike Trusts and the Transportation Revolution in 18th Century England," *Explorations in Economic History,* Vol. 42, pp. 479–508.

Brennan, Geoffrey and James M. Buchanan (1980), *The Power to Tax: Analytical Foundations of Fiscal Constitution,* New York: Cambridge University Press.

Brennan, Geoffrey and James M. Buchanan (1985), *The Reason of Rules: Constitutional Political Economy,* Cambridge: Cambridge University Press.

Buchanan, James M. (1968), *The Demand and Supply of Public Goods,* Chicago: Rand McNally & Company.

Buchanan, James M. (1986), *Liberty, Market and State : Political Economy in the 1980s,* Brighton: Wheatsheaf.

Buchanan, James M. (1989), *Freedom, Market and States,* Shanghai: Shanghai Sanlian Bookshop, p. 17.

Cameron, Rondo (1985), "A New View of European Industrialization," *Economic History Review* New Series, Vol. 38, No. 1, pp. 1–23.

Congleton Roger D. (2007), "From Royal to Parliamentary Rule without Revolution, the Economics of Constitutional Exchange within Divided Governments," *European Journal of Political Economy,* Vol. 23, No. 2, pp. 261–284.

Dye, Thomas R. (1987), "The Politics of Constitutional Choice," *Cato Journal* Vol. 7, No. 2, Fall, pp. 337–344.

Epstein, S. R. (2000), *Freedom and Growth: The Rise of States and Markets in Europe, 1300–1750,* London: Routledge.

Evans, Peter (1992), "The State as Problem and Solution: Predation, Embedded Autonomy, and Structural Change," in *The Politics of Economic Adjustment: International Constraints, Distributive Conflicts, and the State,* edited by Stephan Haggard and Robert R. Kaufman, Princeton, NJ: Princeton University Press, pp. 39–81.

Gabe, Todd M. (2004), "Tradeoffs Between Local Taxes and Government Spending as Determinants of Business Location," *Journal of Regional Science* Vol. 44, No. 1, pp. 21–41.

Hayami, Yujiro and Yoshihisa Godo (2005), *Development Economics: From the Poverty to the Wealth of Nations,* 3rd. ed., Oxford: Oxford University Press, pp. 3–4.

Hoff, Karla and Joseph Stiglitz (2001), "Modern Economic Theory and Development," in *Frontiers of Development Economics,* edited by Gerald M. Meier and Joseph E. Stiglitz, Oxford University Press, pp. 389–445.

Jomo, K. S. (2005), "Introduction," in *The Pioneers of Development Economics*, edited by Jomo K. S., London, UK: Zed Books.

Kirzner, Israel M. (1985), *Discovery and the Capitalist Process*, Chicago, IL: University of Chicago Press.

Kirzner, Israel M. (1989), *Discovery, Capitalism, and Distributive Justice*, Oxford: Basil Blackwell.

Knight, F. K. (1921), *Risk, Uncertainty and Profit*, Boston: Houghton Mifflin, pp. 22–32.

Leibenstein, Harvey (1968), "Entrepreneurship and Development," *American Economic Review* Vol. 58, No. 2, AEA Papers and Proceedings, May, pp. 72–83.

Mankiw, N. Gregory (2004), *Principles of Microeconomics*, 3rd ed., Mason, OH: Thomson, South-Western, p. 64.

Matsuyama, Kiminor (1997), "Economic Development as Coordination Problems," in *The Role of Government in East Asian Economic Development*, edited by Masahiko Aoki, Hyung-ki Kim, and Masahiro Okuno-Fujiwara, Oxford: Clarendon Press, pp. 134–160.

McDaniel, Bruce A. (2003), "Institutional Destruction of Entrepreneurship through Capitalist Transformation," *Journal of Economic Issues*, Vol. 37, No. 2, pp. 495–501.

Meier, Gerald M. (2001a), "Introduction: Ideas for Development," in *Frontiers of Development Economics*, edited by Gerald M. Meier and Joseph E. Stiglitz, New York: Oxford University Press, pp. 1–12.

Meier, Gerald M. (2001b), "The Old Generation of Development Economists and the New," in *Frontiers of Development Economics*, edited by Gerald M. Meier and Joseph E. Stiglitz, Oxford University Press, pp. 13–50.

Meier, Gerald M. and Joseph E. Stiglitz (2001), "Foreword," in *Frontiers of Development Economics*, edited by Gerald M. Meier and Joseph E. Stiglitz, Oxford: Oxford University Press. Menard, Claude, and Mary M. Shirley (2005), *Handbook of New Institutional Economics*, New York: Springer-Verlag New York Inc.

Mokyr, Joel (2000), "Knowledge, Technology, and Economic Growth during the Industrial Revolution," In Bart Van Ark, Simon K. Kuipers, and Gerard Kuper, eds., *Productivity, Technology and Economic Growth*. The Hague: Kluwert Academic Press, pp. 253–292.

Mokyr, Joel (2001), "The Industrial Revolution and the Economic History of Technology: Lesson from the British Experience, 1760–1850," *The Quarterly Review of Economics and Finance* Vol. 41, pp. 295–311.

Mokyr, Joel (2002), *The Gifts of Athena: Historical Origins of the Knowledge Economy*, Princeton, NJ: Princeton University Press.

Nelson, Richard R. (2002), "Bringing institutions into evolutionary growth theory," *Journal of Evolutionary Economics* Vol. 12, pp. 17–28.

North, Douglass C. and Robert Paul Thomas (1973), *The Rise of the Western World*, Cambridge, UK: Cambridge University Press. ISBN: 9780521201711.

North, Douglass C. (1994), *Structure and Change in Economic History*, Shanghai: Shanghai Sanlian Bookshop, p. 17.

North, Douglass C. (1987), "Institutions, Transactions Costs and Economic Growth," *Economic Inquiry* Vol. 25, No. 3 (July), pp. 419–428.

O'Brien, Robert (2003), *Global Political Economy: Evolution and Dynamics*, New York: Palgrave Macmillan, ISBN10: 0333689631.

Ray, Debraj (1998), *Development Economics*, Princeton, NJ: Princeton University Press.

Rosenberg, Nathan and L. E. Birdzell (1986), *How the West Grew Rich: the Economic Transformation of the Industrial World*, London, UK: I. B. Tauris & Co. Ltd, Publishers.

Song, Bingtao (2007), *The Institutional Change of Public Finance and Modern Economic Development: An Interpretation of the Puzzle of England from the Efficiency of Public Finance*, Henan, China: Henan University PhD Thesis, p. 6.

Song, Bingtao and Xin, Zhang (2007), "A Theory of the Efficiency of Public Economy," Hongkong: ACE International Conference, p. 12.

Stiglitz, Joseph E. (2004), "Information and the Change in the Paradigm in Economics," in *New Frontiers in Economics,* edited by Michael Szenberg and Lall Ramrattan, New York: Cambridge University Press, pp. 37–67.

Taylor, Lance (1998), "Growth and Development Theories," in *Theories in Growth and Development*, edited by Fabrizio Coricelli, Massimo di Matteo and Frank Hahn, London: MaCmillan Press Ltd, pp. 175–224.

Wade, Robert (1990), *Governing the Market: Economic Theory and the Role of Government in the East Asian Industrialization,* Princeton, NJ: Princeton University Press, pp. 1–32.

Wilson, C. and G. Parker (1977), *An Introduction to the Sources of European Economic History 1500–1800,* London: Weidenfeld & Nicolson Ltd., p. 122.

Wolf, Charles (1993), *Markets or Governments: Choosing between Imperfect Alternatives,* Cambridge, MA: MIT Press.

Woo-Cumings, Meredith (1997), "The Political Economy of Growth in East Asia: A Perspective on the State, Market, and Ideology," in *The Role of Government in East Asian Economic Development,* edited by Masahiko Aoki, Hyung-ki Kim, and Masahiro Okuno-Fujiwara, Oxford: Clarendon Press, pp. 323–334.

Wright, Gavin (1990), "The Origins of American Industrial Success, 1879–1940," *The American Economic Review* Vol. 80, No. 4, pp. 651–668.

3

Land Property Rights and Land Transferring in China's Industrialization Process

A Typical Traditional Rural Area Case

Mingzhai Geng

3.1 The Problems with the Process of China's Industrialization and Transformation

3.1.1 *The Industrialization of China through the Process of Social Transformation and Structural Change*

Despite being considered a hot topic in the theory of modern economic development, there is no consensus on the definition of industrialization in related literatures.

There are three different definitions of industrialization in academic works. First, some scholars stress on the change in the industrial production as the substitute of labor, the labor division, and the higher level of organization. They consider industrialization a developmental process of modern industries in which manual labor is replaced by mechanical manufacturing (Chenery and Taylor 1968, Rubberdt, 1983). In other words, industrialization is defined as the establishment of the production organizations of various industries, the basis of modern manufacturing in cities, by which manual labor is replaced by the utilization of technology and energy of machinery and electricity, characterized by specialization and labor division (Kirkpatrick, 1983). In short, industrialization is the process of the development of the machinery industry into a dominant position in a national economy (*Book of Economics in Lexical-Encyclopaedic Dictionary*, 1980).

Other scholars focus their attention on the structural change. In a sense, the industrialization process is recognized as a process by which the origin of products and the utilization of resources are transferred from agricultural activities to nonagricultural activities (Kuznets, 1989). In this regard, the characteristics of the industrialization process include the rise of the ratio between manufacturing income and the secondary industry income amongst the national income, except for the disturbance of the economic cycle.

Second, the ratio of employment in manufacturing and secondary industry to the total population also shows a rising trend in most cases. Also, the per capita population income has increased (*The New Palgrave Dictionary of Economics*, 1992). Therefore, for some experts, industrialization is the process of economic development consisting of the change in economic structure, economic mode, and economic system, for a particular term (Liu, 1992). Obviously, these scholars acknowledge that this definition also includes the change of a system in the process of industrialization.

Third, some economists have chosen to emphasize the innovation and the change of the production function. They point out that industrialization is a process of continuous change of the production function (the way of organization of production factors) from the low level to the high level organization in the national economy (Zhang, 2002). Naturally, this definition emphasizes the significance of innovation and technological advancement.

However, when discussing the ascent of industrialization in China, it is a more complicated process. Therefore, we define industrialization as a special historical moment experienced by a country or an economic area, as part of its continuous economic development, whose basic characteristics are the expansion of manufacturing, the change of structure, the increase of output, urbanization, and the modernization of agriculture (Geng, 1996). In other words, the word industrialization, at the very least, implies: (a) an improvement of the scale and organization of production and cooperation based upon labor division, (b) the application and utilization of various production technologies as the replacement of manual labor, (c) the expansion of the scale of social labor division and market exchange, (d) the continuous increase in the ratio between output and employment of the secondary and tertiary industries across all national sectors, as well as the decrease in the ratio between agricultural output and total output use, (e) the continuous transferring of population and surplus labor of the agricultural rural areas and countryside to the nonagricultural city. This helps sustain the necessary population growth during urbanization with the development of the city, (f) the radical progress in agricultural modernization and productivity, (g) the advanced education and civilization of the population, and (h) the advanced level of democracy and the legal system.

According to this understanding, industrialization is seen as a process of change in the structure of production, organization, society, policy, economy, and culture. Led by technological progress, it is a process of social transformation from the traditional agricultural civilization to the modern industrial civilization. In addition, the process of industrialization in any society, both the separation of the nonagricultural industry from agriculture as well as the transfer of the production factors from agriculture to nonagriculture, is its starting point, and China is no exception.

3.1.2   The Process of Industrialization in China

The process of industrialization in China started as early as the Westernization movement in the middle of the nineteenth century. Since then, foreign investment and private investment have been allowed, and even encouraged, to infiltrate modern industry. Modern industry began to develop outside the control of government to form a private sector (Yang, 2001).[1] However, due to the wars and social upheaval, the industrialization in Old China did not grow to the next level. By 1952, the added value of the modern industry accounted for just 20.9 percent of the total national income, while employment accounted for just 7.4 percent. The ratio of urbanization was just 15 percent (see table 3.1). Modern industry existed only in some coastal areas, such as Shanghai, Qingdao, and Tianjin. There was virtually no industrial growth in most of the inland areas and China, for the most part, enjoyed a typical agricultural economy.

In the middle of the 1950s, China initiated the first five-year plan, and started a process of industrialization on a grander scale. Up until the end of the 1970s, the total added value of the secondary industries accounted for 48.16 percent of GNP (see table 3.1, 1978). However, this kind of industrialization was a result of government dominance in the current economic system. Therefore, industrialization failed to break away from government control and the limitations of the urban system. More importantly, it set an institutional block between the agricultural and industrial sectors. It separated the rural and urban areas resulting in a typical dual economic structure by isolating agriculture and rural society from industry and urban society. In doing so, when the ratio of output of the industrial sector increased greatly, employment

Table 3.1   Comparison of industrialization in different terms for China

Year	Added Value in 1st Industry	Added Value in 2nd Industry	Added Value in 3rd Industry	Employment in 1st Industry	Employment in 2nd Industry	Employment in 3rd Industry	Urbanization Rate (%)	GDP Per Capita (Yuan)
1952	50.5	20.9	28.6	83.5	7.4	9.1	15.0	119
1978	28.1	48.7	23.7	70.5	17.4	12.1	19.4	379
2004	15.2	52.9	31.9	46.9	22.5	30.6	41.8	10,561
2010	10.2	46.8	43.0	38.0	27.0	35.0	47.5	29,678

Note: Data of 1952 come from *50 Years of China Statistics*; Data of 1978 and 2004 come from *2005 Yearbook of China Statistics*; and Data of 2010 come from *Public Report of China on National Economy and Society Development* and *Report of Government* by Wen Jiabao at fourth Conference of 11th NPC. The data of employment structure come from the calculation according to relevant information.

in the industrial sectors and the urban population hardly changed. In 1978, employment in the secondary industrial sectors accounted for only 17.4 percent of total employment, and the rate of urbanization was only 19.39 percent. At the same time, employment in agriculture accounted for 70.5 percent, while the rural residents accounted for 81.61 percent (table 3.1). As we can see, this kind of industrialization did not change the economic structure of the society or the structure of employment and population. The traditional life style and the production modes of most people remained. In other words, a real hike in industrialization did not take place.

With the reforming and opening of China at the end of the 1970s, the process of industrializing China found a new way to shake off government control and go outside of the urban areas. Especially with the reform of the rural economy, the town-owned enterprises and the private enterprises increased rapidly to become the dominant power in this new round of industrialization. The structure of the dual economy in society was broken, thereby guiding all social and economic activities onto the path of industrialization. With the reforms, the steps of structural change sped up.

For the sake of comparison, the first 26 years of the planned economy, from 1952 until 1978, show a significant decline (22.4 percentage points from 50.5 percent to 28.1 percent) in the rate of the added value of the primary industry to total economic activities. At the same time, there was only an average decline (13 percentage points from 83.5 percent to 70.5 percent) in the rate of employment in the primary industry. In the next 26 years, the term length for a market economy, there was a slower decline (12.9 percentage points from 28.1 percent to 15.2 percent) in the rate of the added value of the primary industry while the rate of employment experienced a sudden decline (23.6 percentage points from 70.5 percent to 46.9 percent) (see table 3.1). The difference in the changes of the urbanization ratios in these two terms is clearer. The first 26 years saw only an increase of 4.39 percent in the urbanization ratio (from 15 percent to 19.39 percent), while the second 26 years observed a radical increase of 22.41 percent (from 19.39 percent to 41.8 percent). This indicates that industrialization in the first 26 years of a planned economy is just a closed-door self-circulation process in an urban area. It is really the secondary industry that experienced a great change in the production structure, but experienced no change in the employment structure or the residence structure. This means that in the first 26 years, only a few people enjoyed the fruits of industrialization, with only small changes happening in the mode of production and daily life of the populace. In contrast, as a result of market economic development, the new industrialization in the second 26 years extended to all sections of society and brought many changes in employment structure and residence locations. This allowed a larger number of people in China to enjoy its benefits.

Until the end of 2010, the ratio of the added value of the primary industry, which accounted for the total added value, further declined to a low 10.2 percent. The ratio of the added value of the secondary industry decreased from its highest point to 46.8 percent. While this was happening, the ratio of the added value of the tertiary industry rose greatly to 43 percent, whereas the rate of urbanization increased to 47.5 percent (see table 3.1). China entered the process of modern transformation, both economically and socially.

3.1.3   Some Problems in the Path of Industrialization and Social Transformation in Traditional Agricultural Areas

The process of industrialization in China since the end of the 1970s holds some obvious characteristics of regional nonequilibrium. The first region to join in the process of industrialization and development was the agricultural area on the east coast and a few of the inland areas that have natural resources. We have divided the first group of industrialized areas into three groups and three models (Zhao and Huang, 1997; Geng, 2004; Liu, 2004; Zhao, 2009).

The first one is the model of the Zhujiang Triangle, which is characterized as the place of importation of capital and technology. The coastal areas of Canto province and Fujian province, due to their geographic and historic conditions as well as experience in searching cultural benefits overseas, are the homeland of Chinese nationals that live all over the world. These Chinese nationals have accumulated a massive amount of capital with the hard efforts of many generations. With the traditional education and cultural influence, especially in the regions of the homelands, these overseas Chinese nationals wished to return home. As soon as the door opened, with the approval of government policy, most of them returned to invest in homeland and to establish private companies using their accumulated capital. As a result, all sorts of enterprises were set up in these agricultural areas, which, in the short run, allowed them to begin the industrialization process.

The second is the model of the Chang Jiang Triangle, which is characterized as an extension of traditional business and a greater urban area. Since the East-Jin Dynasty, the low areas of the Yangtze River, including Shanghai, the southern area of Jiangsu province, and Zhejiang province have gradually become the richest parts of China. In particular, from the Song Dynasty to the Ming Dynasty, they were one of the richest regions in the world. The crafts industry, especially silk manufacturing, developed to an advanced stage, while related trade activities also boomed. In more modern times, since the Opium War of 1840, the most important economic aspect of the Chinese economy became importing and exporting of goods. Through this, the Chinese traditions of business were reinforced again. Even in times of a planned economy, this traditional business developed manufacturing in rural areas. After the opening and reforming of China, more and more of the social elite joined the group of entrepreneurs to establish many rural manufacturing enterprises. Of course, the development of rural manufacturing is not only the result of traditional business, but also the outcome of the influence of China's largest international city, Shanghai. For this reason, the rural manufacturing enterprises in these areas got either the technological support from the technicians in Shanghai or the market channel of Shanghai, linking up with markets all over China and the rest of the world. With the help of tradition and the influence of Shanghai, this area has become one of the most industrialized areas in China.

The third model is a little more primitive. It is founded upon the Chinese accumulation of capital based on the exploitation of natural resources. In the western areas of China, there are some places with plenty of minerals. After the opening and reforming of the country, the policy of minerals exploitation relaxed a little to approve of private capitalists entering the industry. Suddenly, many private capitalists moved into the industry of minerals, especially those minerals with a low threshold of technology and capital, such as coal and aluminum. The development of private enterprises in exploiting minerals initiated the process of industrialization in this area. Moreover, the rapid economic growth of China resulted in huge demand of energy and minerals, leading to their high prices bringing a high level of profit for these private enterprises and a great amount of capital to Chinese businesspersons. When the minerals were not produced, marginal exploitation costs rose, and the government changed policies, the Chinese investors that accumulated capital from the mineral enterprises had to look to a new area to invest. Thus, the general industries in the secondary sector gradually developed in this area. Embodied in the advanced structure of this industry, this area also got in the way of industrialization. The cities of Gongyi, Xinmi, Dengfeng, and Jiyuan in Henan province are examples of this model.

Indeed, the three models of industrialization in rural areas contributed a lot to the success of China since the end of the 1970s. However, we should note that these three kinds of models of industrialization, only took place in a small fraction of China. The industrialization success of these areas was not enough to bring about the industrialization of all rural areas in China. The data in table 3.1 shows that there was nearly 40 percent employment and more than 50 percent of the population was confined to rural areas. In fact, only if most of these employment opportunities as well as the population moved to industries in cities, is it possible to say that the industrialization of China achieved success. However, most of those people still keep their employment and life in the traditional agricultural sector and backward rural areas. Therefore, a method to push these traditional rural areas to begin the industrialization process became a significant economic topic in China.

The importance of the industrialization of these traditional rural areas and the difficulty in achieving it depend not only on the size and population of the area, but also on the absence of business tradition, the influence of a large city, the foreign direct investment (FDI), and local minerals. They also depend on the different institutions and the social and economic environments associated with those in the rapid developing times of the Zhujiang Triangle and the Changjiang Triangle. New problems and limitations appear to be the causes for the inability to begin the industrialization process in these rural areas. First, the policy of farmland protection for 1.8 billion Chinese acres places serious limitations on the location of new manufacturing establishments. Second, with advanced infrastructure and public services requirements for industry development, the new problem of how to appropriately build these types of cities or town systems crept up. Another issue was how to relocate the population and employment from rural areas to the city, and how to ensure their residence in the city in order to obtain the scaled economy of the farming business and modern agriculture.

To achieve the industrialization of traditional rural areas, many leading figures in these fields did their best to try various models of new industrialization paths. A village in Henan province, Wangzhuang, is a typical case of this. The analysis of this case follows. The purpose of its inclusion is to describe the opinions of overseas economists concerning China's recent development.

3.2   The Path of the Industrialization of Wangzhuang Village: A Case of Labors Movement and Land Transferring

3.2.1   *Industrialization Resulting from the Agricultural Product Processing Enterprise*

Wangzhuang village has a population of 70,000. It is located in the northern part of Henan province, adjacent to Anyang, Puyang, Xinxian, and Hebi. It covers an area of 110 km², including 95,000 Chinese acres of cultivated land. The fertile and flat ground and rich water resources provide Wangzhuang village a good foundation for agriculture. With the Wei River running through the land, Wangzhuang village has 20,000 Chinese acres of cultivated land guaranteed by a water-saving irrigation system, as well as the successful irrigation of about 70,000 Chinese acres. With these rich agricultural resources, Wangzhuang village is fertile for wheat, corn, peanuts, vegetables, and so on.

During the investigation, the study groups were strongly impressed by a local agricultural products processing corporation, named ZhongHe Group, that promoted the development of land property transactions in the Wangzhuang village. The development of the ZhongHe Group attracted a massive labor force, which transferred rural surplus labor to the enterprise. In addition, the agricultural product processing enterprise for land scale management provided stable market demand for labor; and the enterprise's development led to the transformation of rural residents to urban residents. The development process of the ZhongHe Group is also a way of industrializing, urbanizing, and modernizing the agriculture of traditionally plain agro-forestry areas through the interlocking of propulsive synchronous process. In Wangzhuang village's case, the study group realized that the industrialization, urbanization, and agricultural modernization were rapidly completed as a whole project. The development pattern of Wangzhuang village provides a typical case of development of plain agro-forestry areas.

The full name of the ZhongHe Group is Henan ZhongHe Agricultural Industrial Technology Group, Ltd. It started as Henan QiXue Starch Co., Ltd., located in XunXian Wangzhuang village, an industrial area of the city of Hebi. This group was founded in 1995, with a registered capital of 10.28 billion Yuan, and currently employs 3,000 people. At present, ZhongHe Group is operating a food intensive processing industrial park covering nearly 1 km² (1,400 Chinese acres). It plans to develop a new industrial park covering 5.8 km². ZhongHe Group is an agricultural industrialization company engaged in the entire industry chain operation, including trading agricultural and food storage products, wheat and corn processing, nutrition recuperation surface production, candy and bean products processing, retail, environmental protection and energy-related industries, and is a key leading enterprise of Henan province and a base for the eleventh national five-year food safety technical project.

The business pattern of the agricultural processing enterprise of controlling the whole industrial chain has already become the new direction of the Chinese food industry. The reliable and safe supplies of raw materials have become an indispensable link of food processing enterprises in the future. It is difficult to guarantee food safety for previous agricultural product processing enterprises that operate as "corporation plus farmers" management pattern. The pattern of "corporation plus agriculture products bases plus farmers" has become the mode most frequently chosen by agricultural processing corporations. It is this kind of mode that can promote a large number of farmers to participate in land transfers.

The added value of farming land is very low, which restricts the increase in the agricultural enterprise profit and prevents social capital investment from investing in the agricultural industry. Pure agricultural enterprises, especially pure grain production enterprises, are difficult to develop into large companies. Through the development of the agricultural products processing enterprise, which has expanded the industrial chain, a new way to improve the added value of agricultural products has been discovered. Providing profitability improvement and assurance for the enterprises can attract social capital investment to the industry. Therefore, the development of the industry provides conditions for a large-scale operation. This is especially true for the agriculture produce processing enterprise. When engaged in all aspects of an industry, chain operation provides development conditions for what are traditionally the plain agroforestry areas.

3.2.2   Land Transfer Conducted by the Specialized Agricultural Cooperative

In this investigation, the study group found that the cultivated land transfer process includes four types. The first of these is subcontracting. Farmers transfer their rights to use the land to others. The subcontractors can be individuals, agricultural cooperatives, or corporations, as long as they are conducting agricultural exploitation during a fixed term not exceeding their legal time limitation. This form of land transfer contains 149,512 Chinese acres, accounting for 88 percent of all land transfers.

The second is interchange. To solve the problem of scattered and fragmented landmasses, disadvantageous for exploitation, farmers exchange part or all of their land with each other. This form of land transfer contains 4,757 Chinese acres, accounting for 2.8 percent of the land transfer volume.

The third is lease. The farmers lease the rights to use their land within the valid contracting period to others, who could be individuals, agriculture collectors, or corporations, and obtain rents from the tenants. This form of land transfer contains 10,704 Chinese acres, and accounts for 6.3 percent of land transfer volume.

The fourth is being a shareholder (joint-stock cooperative). Farmers invest in cooperatives or corporations within their legal usage rights of land, and obtain their share of gains according to the cooperative (or corporation) distributable profits. This form of land transfer contains 2,568 Chinese acres, and accounts for 2.7 percent of the land transfer volume.

Among these four different land transfer patterns, the subcontract and leasing methods differ less in contract substance than in contract form. A shareholder is in a sense a cooperation organization, which is similar to a standard cooperative. Interchange is still the family small-scale operating way, constrained by scattered and fragmented landmasses, and it cannot be applied to modern agriculture production. For Wangzhuang village, the basic form of land transfer was subcontracting and leasing, and was guided by a series of specialized agriculture cooperatives invested in by the ZhongHe Group. Actually, this kind of a cooperative is not the typical model, but more like a company.

At a global level, a purely agricultural company is unusual. This is because it is difficult to control the risk and supervise the production process. In most developed countries, governments provide a wide variety of subsidies for agriculture, while in China the subsidies are few. At present, in order to promote agricultural industrialization, the Chinese government is encouraging various specialized agricultural cooperatives[2] by adopting these kinds of policies. The policies can be divided into two categories: the first is untaxed policies; the second is subsidies. An example of this is an agricultural machinery subsidy, provided to machinery cooperatives. It is in this context that the ZhongHe Group set up a Chinese capitalistic agricultural production cooperative. Through their cooperatives, the ZhongHe Group promoted land transfer and improved land management scale.

According to the ZhongHe Group development plan, a health food base of 160,000 Chinese acres will be established in the next few years, which will gradually ensure that all raw materials entering the processing of the company are supplied by that base. While establishing the 160,000 Chinese acres health food base, land transfer becomes the key point. Right now, Wangzhuang village is trying land transferring project with 50,000 Chinese acres land as a model. Through the first half of 2010, 5,000 Chinese acres of land were transferred. It is expected that there will be 30,000 Chinese acres of land transfers in 2011. The final goal is 160,000 Chinese acres of land to be transferred to the ZhongHe Group in order to control the production process.

The function of local rural leaders in land transfers is very obvious. After investigating the rural dynamics, we concluded that the local leaders in villages with specialized cooperatives or a big farming family expressed more enthusiasm, and made more effort in the advertising and promotion of the land transfer. By contrast, in villages without specialized cooperatives and big farming families, 90 percent of local leaders showed either passive or uninterested opinions about land transfers. According to the interview by the research group, the transfer of the land located by the ZhongHe Group is promoted by local rural leaders. Even the major investment constructing the specialized cooperative comes from ZhongHe. For example, in NanSuTun village, the agricultural production cooperative is financed by the ZhongHe group, including the purchase of all kinds of farming machinery and payment to the cooperative agricultural technician. Despite their control, the land transfer is finished mainly by local rural leaders. In WangSuTun village, the rule for the cooperatives is that anyone who can collect and organize 500 Chinese acres farmland will become a member of the cooperative. Finally, all members who meet the condition of admission are local rural leaders. In NanSuTun village, nearly 2,000 Chinese acres of farmland transfers are collected and organized into cooperatives run by three local rural leaders.

According to the ownership and management structure, the members of a cooperative who organize the land transfer are not permitted to distribute the income or to vote on business decisions of the cooperative. Such cooperatives are more like wholly owned companies. The main responsibility of current membership is to organize the land transfer, but whether or not a member can get some income from the company is not confirmed. However, members can often get a position in the ZhongHe group or a cooperative and participate in the process of production and business.

For villages without cooperatives and without big farming families, local rural leaders overlook the land transfers, and consider land transfers as the responsibility of the farmers and the company. They leave it to natural evolution, which results in small-scale land transfers and blocks the process of agricultural modernization in production.

3.2.3   The Price Making Decision of Land Transfers

There are a variety of different kinds of farmland in Hebi including not only the best kind of land, which once produced the biggest harvest in all of China, but also the poor land in the mountains. According to the statistical data of the agricultural agency of Hebi, there is 1,442,300 Chinese acres of farming land in Heibi, of which 1,282,400 Chinese acres of farmland can be irrigated, or 88.91 percent of the total farmland. There is 159,900 Chinese acres of land that cannot be irrigated. Additionally, 825,200 Chinese acres, or 57.2 percent, is high-harvest land, 454,300 Chinese acres, or 31.5 percent, is medium-harvest land, and 162,800 Chinese acres, or 11.3 percent, is considered low-harvest land. Different kinds of farmland have very different land transfer prices. Wangzhuang village located in XunXian of Hebi, which in ancient times was also called LiYang, was extremely expensive. There is an old saying "if the LiYang harvest is good, there is nobody hungry in all of China."

According to the county leaders, XunXian has 950,000 Chinese acres of farmland. In recent years, the wheat planting area has gone up to 840,000 Chinese acres, and the corn planting area is at 650,000 Chinese acres. The crop of wheat per Chinese acre reached 611.6 kg in 2010. Corn also reached 850 kg per acre in recent years, which basically means "one and a half tons" of grain per Chinese acre per year. Good agricultural infrastructure and production conditions make local farmland come at a high transfer price. In the cooperatives controlled by the ZhongHe Group, the transferred land is mainly two-crops per year. The price of land transfer is 500 kg of wheat, or cash no less than 1,200 Yuan. The higher of the two prices is the final one.

According to the calculation by our research group, the current price of wheat is about 1 Yuan per kg, and the corn price is about 0.9 Yuan per kg. If the crop per Chinese acre is 600 kg wheat, the gain will be 1,200 Yuan; if there is also 800 kg corn per Chinese acre, the gain will be an additional 1,440 Yuan. The total income per Chinese acre is about 2,640 Yuan. Aside from labor, all other production inputs per Chinese acre total approximately 800 Yuan. Therefore, after incorporating all labor wages and cooperative management fees into the cost, the transfer price will lead to a loss for the cooperative. According to the introduction of the agricultural scale economy from the ZhongHe Group, the integration of land will achieve a 105-acre increase of farmland by removing the field edge, the path, and the small ditch, which will increase revenue by 10 percent. In addition, integrated farmland is more conveniently plowed by machinery, which will further raise the output level and earn additional profit. At present, the ZhongHe Group can offset the loss in grain cropping with the profit in processing food. Additionally, the loss of the cooperative on new land brought creditable and healthy raw materials for the company, so overall for the entire ZhongHe Group, the current price of land transfer is still at an acceptable level.

From our survey on the land transfer in Hebi, the price of bad land on mountainous areas is about 100–150 Yuan. The price of average to good land is between 500 and 800 Yuan. The price of land transfer between farmers is 500 Yuan, and the price of land transfer between farmers and the cooperative or the company is 800 Yuan. With the relatively high price of land transfer for the ZhongHe Group comparing with other farmland, the land transfer promotes the whole industry chain, and the agricultural processing enterprise will benefit the farmers more and can promote land integration rapidly. This represents a win-win outcome for both the farmers and the company, and can certainly be easily accepted by the farmers.

3.2.4 The Bottlenecks of Industrialization: An Experiment in Financing

In the financial repression environment, the ZhongHe Group, a private enterprise, has a difficult time getting a loan from the commercial banks; especially from the large state-owned commercial banks. Financing issues are a key force restricting the corporation's development and land transfer. Considering the investment required, the study group understands that the reason that commercial banks are uninterested in giving loans to the ZhongHe Group are the following: first, as a private enterprise, the ZhongHe Group has no open, transparent financial system or statements, and lacks corresponding credit records. It is impossible for commercial banks, which avoid taking risk as a basic business rule, to provide credit loans. Second, the ZhongHe Group's fixed assets cannot be accepted as collateral. With the development of the ZhongHe Group, the corporation has accumulated a considerable amount of fixed assets, but it is difficult for these fixed assets to become available. Part of the reason is that most of those fixed assets are attached to the land. This land cannot be accepted as a collateral without the land property rights. Restricted by the state land policy, great deals of small private companies located in rural areas have no possibility of obtaining the state-owned land use rights. Most of their land is leased from local farmers. In accordance with the provisions of commercial banks, when enterprises have not obtained the usage rights of state-owned land, the entire land attachment cannot be regarded as collateral.

In absence of loan from large commercial banks, ZhongHe Group's loan is borrowed mainly from local rural credit cooperatives. According to the study group's survey, the interest rate of rural credit cooperatives, which receives 0.86–0.88 percent monthly, is higher than the large commercial banks. In fact, in order to obtain a loan from the cooperatives, the enterprises must pay a series of service charges, such as an assets valuation cost. On adding this service charge, their interest rates exceed 1.1–1.2 percent monthly. Due to this, the enterprise's ability to obtain loans from the cooperatives is still very limited, and cannot support the development of enterprise and the land transfer.

In our investigation process, the study group found that the ZhongHe Group depends more on informal finances to support its development. When a company has informal finances, it will often practice land transfers with some informal contracts. The location of ZhongHe Group, Xiaoqicun of Wangzhuang village is also the major location of industrial land used by companies, which is rented from the rural building land and farmland. The rent for the land is paid in one lump sum, at the price of 30,000 Yuan per Chinese acre by each company. At the same time, the company encourages farmers to lend this rent to the company and pay them interest at the rate of 1 percent per month. From the trade described above, we know that the informal borrowing is included in the gray area between legal and illegal actions. From the interest rate level, the 1 percent per month is not over the legal limit of 4 percent set by governments. However, from the perspective of borrowing, it is outside of regulation. Most of the farmers simply think of depositing their money in a company to receive the interest, but according to the law and regulations of China, a nonfinancial company cannot recruit deposits from the public. This is committing the crime of "illegal recruitment of deposits from the public."

3.2.5   Employment Transformation and Urbanization through Manufacturing Development and Land Transfer

The theory of Economics of Development tells us that industrialization and urbanization complement each other. Industrialization can promote urbanization; in return, urbanization can also promote industrialization. However, realizing this formation of the development pattern is a bit complicated. This approach rests upon two points. First, the industrialization process must be followed with large-scale employment; otherwise, it is difficult to promote the urbanization process. Second, industrialization must be followed with the rapid growth of the residents' income, otherwise even if we let villagers move in the rural town and live together, it is impossible to provide the large market for the development of industrialization. In China, industrialization through the method above has not been effectively realized.

During the first 30 years of reform, labor-intensive industries were the main feature of Chinese industrialization, and the industrialization process realized a large-scale employment increase. This provided the necessary conditions for urbanization. However, since there is unequal treatment between the urban and rural residents in public services, especially restrictions such as low labor wages and high cost of living in average-sized cities, the urbanization development is not being maximized. The most prominent feature of urbanizing China is that it is not effectively solving the problem of city versus rural structural characteristics. Migrant workers fail to become an integral part of the city as urban residents. Industrialization and urbanization result in peasant workers becoming industry workers while still leading a traditional social life style, thereby having a "dual identity."

If the development and achievement of industrialization is just embodied in the cities, subject to current labor wage level and living costs, current industrialization is still unable to overcome the city-rural dual structure characteristics. In addition, this dual identity of migrant workers cannot be resolved. One of the reasons a city might limit migrant workers is a result of the government's public expenditure burden. On the other hand, the low income of peasant workers cannot support the higher costs associated with living in the city. Unless the average-sized cities undergoing industrialization provide manual workers with a sufficient income level, the industrialization and urbanization coordinated development still faces significant hurdles. Considering that the Chinese economic development level faces a serious imbalance, the study group found that for the future of China's economic development, the change will also be a process. In the transformation process of the dual economic structure, Wangzhuang township and the ZhongHe Group's developmental pattern is the dual economic structure of the transformation, which provides new ideas.

The study group found that the ZhongHe Group's development is a process of constantly absorbing labor employment, which is associated with the industrial characteristics of the ZhongHe Group. Only if labor employment is constantly absorbed into industrialization, will it provide the necessary conditions for the conversion of rural labor to urbanization. Otherwise, the dualistic structure will not change and will remain in a stalemate. Take for example, Xiaoqi village and Daqi village where the ZhongHe Group is located. Most of the rural labor forces work in the ZhongHe Group. Among labor forces from Xiaoqi village, about 400 people work in the ZhongHe Group, and only 100 move out to other areas to work. Undeniably, the ZhongHe Group workers salary level is not higher than that of the moving-out workers, but, since the Group workers work and live in the local village, their cost of living is relatively low. So, to those in the lower levels of education within the general physical labor force, as well as women workers, local jobs are more attractive. According to the understanding of the study groups, more than 100 people, mostly with either advanced labor skills or heavy manual workers, are used in the company. The ZhongHe Group can gainfully employ women and workers who lack complex labor skills. In fact, this study group's research results are consistent with investigations of other researchers.

Xibao Guo and Huang Can (2009) in the Hubei province of Changyang, Autonomy County, consists of 154 villages. Amongst the 10,636 households, survey data show migrant workers to be 11,946 accounting for 45.4 percent of rural labor force resources. Of the group of farmers left behind, there are more women than men, and the percentage rises to 56.2 percent. Second, farmers who do not migrate tend to be older and between 41 and 50 years of age. Among farmers over 50 years old, nonmigrant farmers and migrant workers show a 41.4 and a 26.1 percent decline in work production, respectively. Again, the peasants' cultural level is low, but the primary and cultural level is up to 62.9 percent. As pointed out, "in other areas in China, the survey data of Changyang and the county of Hubei, is almost the same." This suggests that, in rural labor transfers lasting over 20 years, the rural qualified labor force moved out and in most rural cities the farmers who were left behind showed a tendency toward lower quality.

From the above, we observe that if one stays in the rural labor force and is recruited into the industrialization process, one will continue the traditional social production and life mode and will never realize urbanization. The spreading out of migrant workers into the cities is only one aspect of the urbanization process. Most migrant workers still fail to achieve complete urbanization. Both of these two models can cause industrialization and urbanization to develop slowly and thus, leave the structure of dual society unchanged in the long-term. In fact, traditional studies in Economics of Development do not truly depict this Chinese reality. The description of the Lewis model is different from the study group's findings. In the Lewis dual economic model, rural labor force is considered homogeneous. There are no cultural differences between farmers, nor are there gender or age differences. Their productivity is the same. In his model, when surplus rural labor began to migrate to urban nonagricultural sectors, the numbers of stay-on-the-farm workers either relatively or absolutely fell, but the model erroneously made the implicit assumption that the quality of stay-on-the-farm workers did not fall. This obviously represents a discrepancy with the reality in China.

If this problem is not resolved, China's industrialization will inevitably strengthen urban-rural dual structure problems. The decline of the size of the population in villages will mean that due to the decline of the quality of labor forces in rural areas, the rural labor force cannot move into a modern sector in the later process of industrialization. Rural land resources cannot be transited from an individual small-scale operating state to a large-scale intensive production mode, too. Resistance to land transfers will also be difficult to eliminate.

With a lower level of worker's salary than in developed areas, the ZhongHe Group absorbs a large amount of low-quality labor. The reason for this is that they can effectively transform this labor from the individual small-scale management of agricultural production to a situation whereby they can create the needed conditions for local urbanization. With the ZhongHe Group's substantial development, the size of its labor demand is increasing rapidly. Currently, the annual worth of Utah's ZhongHe Group is approximately 10 million Yuan, and the current labor of the whole group is 3,000 people, with a vast majority of Hebi locals. According to ZhongHe Group estimates, the value of the ZhongHe Group will reach 100 million Yuan in a few years. With companies like ZhongHe Group that can be local large-scale job creators, the development of local urbanization has greater potential.

Based on the ZhongHe Group's development plan, the Wangzhuang township government is planning a 100,000-person urban area. The government is trying to lead the full circulation of the rural farmland into various kinds of agricultural cooperatives controlled by the ZhongHe Group. With a significant number of local people being absorbed by industrial enterprises and agricultural cooperatives, the villagers gradually become urban residents. The government plans to concentrate all villagers into an urban area in order to share all kinds of public service facilities—to realize local urbanization. According to the current plan, the ZhongHe Group, which encompasses five villages of about 12,000 people, will soon achieve urbanization.

According to township-government plans, a building company began to build in the second half of 2010, including the first phase of the building project, covering an area of 300 Chinese acres. They will continue until the end of phase two, which covers another area of 300 Chinese acres of building land. The current residential area is up to five villages building land of 2,400 Chinese acres. Five village urbanization projects of building land occupy only 600 Chinese acres and will save three-quarters of the land for farming. Rural construction land savings provides conditions for effective utilization of the land. Wangzhuang village's final plans with the ZhongHe Group include a deep processing industrial park (including industrial enterprise, that is, the ZhongHe Group) planned to occupy a total of 5.8 km^2. According to our survey data, 12,000 people locally achieved urbanization, saving about 1,800 Chinese acre house sites used in industrial enterprises, allowing the land to be used for construction purposes.

This will allow the next 10 million people in local urbanization to save about 15,000 Chinese acres of rural construction land index, and about 22.5 km² of land for construction purposes. This completely supports the enterprises construction land index demand.

In conclusion, the developmental mode of Wangzhuang township and the ZhongHe Group plays an important role in preparing rural areas for everything, from the agricultural process and scaled management of modern agriculture to the industry characteristics—synchronization of industrialization and urbanization promotion. They also play a role in the realization of the synchronization of agricultural modernization. This is of great significance to the people it affects.

3.3   Some Remarks on the Case

The model of Wangzhuang village includes coordinated developments of three parts: industrialization, urbanization, and modernization of agriculture. These together can be described as the manufacturing enterprise of agricultural products—as the whole process contributes to the preparedness for the industrialization and the land transfers of Wangzhuang village. With higher levels of customer incomes and their newly found desire to care more for the health and reputation of food production, the manufacturing enterprises of agricultural products and food production will become a whole process enterprise. This will include all channels in the production from raw materials to the final product. The development of enterprises with the whole process requires land transfers. That is the land transfer from individual-farmer ownership to large specialized-agricultural-cooperative ownership dominated by enterprises. This kind of land transfer increases income level of local farmers as it also creates a stable supply of raw materials to the manufacturing enterprise of agricultural products. This, in turn, leads to a win-win result for farmers and enterprises. Moreover, this kind of land transfer increases the size of land farming, and achieves a scaled economy of farming production. In this model, the industrialization transformation, the land transfers, the modernization of agriculture, and even the urbanization, happen at the same time. The industrialization or the development and manufacturing of agricultural products create necessary conditions for the land transfer and the intensive running of modern agriculture. It also provides some employment opportunities for the population separated from farming. In addition, with changes in the mode of production and in the life of the local people, it raises the level of local urbanization. Therefore, the model of industrialization and land transfer appearing in Wangzhuang village is a typical way to achieve industrialization, urbanization, and modernization of agriculture based on the success of farming development.

However, even in the case of Wangzhaung, a significant portion of success must be attributed to the ZhongHe Group. The question for researchers remains as to whether or not this model of development in the traditional rural areas holds effective for all other areas. Major misgivings of this model rest on whether or not its success depends on the size of the manufacturing enterprise of agricultural products.

Development economist Chenery and his colleagues pointed out that a rise in the income level results in a change in the demand structure. The change in demand structure in turn results in a change in production structure. This theory contains three hypotheses: First, the development stage of industrialization appears as part of the obvious law of evolution. Second, each of the different developmental phases have specific dominant industries. The big countries usually experienced early, middle, and late industrialization stages in sequence. The early industrialization stage is dominated by food, leather, textile, and other industries. The middle industrialization stage is dominated by nonmetal mineral products, rubber products, wood and wood products, and petrochemical and coal products. The late industrialization stage is mainly printing, publishing, crude steel, paper products, metal products, and machine manufacturing. Their third hypothesis is that the income level promotes the change of industrial structure.

Just like the conclusion of the Chenery and Taylor theory (1968), the industrialization, urbanization, and agricultural modernization synchronized development mode led by the ZhongHe Group has not only proven significant in less developed rural areas, but it also possesses the possibility of spreading to other areas. This is precisely the requirement of less developed rural areas industrialization. At the same time, it can also be seen that the ZhongHe Group's industry development pattern cannot help throughout the industrialization phase. With the evolution of the industrialization level, the industrialization stage's progress, relying exclusively on the food industry, will be insufficient to support the requirement of further economic development.

It also can be seen that, as mentioned above, the agricultural industrialization of the ZhongHe Group, not only pursues the transverse-scale intensive running, but it also implements a vertical whole-industrial-chain business. In this sense, the development of agricultural industrialization is no longer isolated as scale-intensive running or the processing of agricultural products. The agricultural industrialization process should include both horizontal and vertical aspects. The horizontal aspect emphasizes large-scale intensive implementation in order to improve the efficiency of agricultural production, while the vertical aspect insists on the whole-industry-chain running, to ensure food safety and to avoid information asymmetry. Both the horizontal and vertical integration in enterprise theory is reflected in the practice of the ZhongHe Group. However, in recent years, as food safety issues attract more attention, food manufacturers have also increasingly focused on the construction of the agricultural raw material base, which can provide a better opportunity for the further acceleration of agricultural industrialization development. Based on the site investigation in Hebi, the study group also concluded that this kind of development mode is likely to be the general development pattern of the food industry in the future. For example, Yongda and Dayong, two food enterprises in Hebi, which cover broiler production, slaughtering, cutting, and deep processing, are also striving to strengthen the construction of their agricultural raw material base through the farming cooperative manner so that the enterprise can effectively control the whole broiler breeding process, thereby avoiding food safety problems.

Therefore, for less developed rural areas, the development of industrialization, urbanization, and agricultural modernization propelled by the expansion of the whole industrial food chain processing industry, not only is significant, but is also valuable on a larger scale. Meanwhile, it should be noticed, the entire industrial sector does not contain only the food industry. It is quite possible to apply the Wangzhuang township's development pattern to other areas.

The key point of the three coordinated development patterns guided by the ZhongHe Group is to promote the industrialization of employment. Especially, the industrialization that encourages or promotes the employment of local low-quality workforces is the basis and premise of the coordinated development of industrialization, urbanization, and agricultural modernization. Through industrialization, plenty of local labor forces are absorbed, leaving the sector of agricultural production, thereby providing necessary conditions for agricultural-scale operations and urbanization development. In a less developed area, local industrialization helps avoid the isolation of industrialization and urbanization, and then can effectively achieve the synchronous promotion of industrialization and urbanization further providing industrial land for industrialization by means of urbanization.

These three coordinates led by agricultural products processing enterprises, and one of its superiorities, industrialization, can be realized by agricultural production, processing, and sales throughout the whole industry chain. This is more beneficial to the development of agricultural modernization. As for other nonagricultural product processing enterprises, it could also satisfy most of the conditions required by the three coordinated developments, provided that the labor force can be effectively absorbed. If land transfers and agricultural-scale management can be effectively synchronized and implemented, it will be regarded as an effective approach for the development of lesser-developed rural areas.

Notes

1. [F] http://www.jjxj.com.cn/news_detail.jsp?keyno=407.
2. A nonprofit organization whose aim is to promote agricultural industrialization with members helping each other

References

Book of Economics in Lexical-Encyclopaedic Dictionary (1980), Shanghai: Shanghai Encyclopaedic Dictionary Press.
Chenery, H. and L. Taylor (1968), "Development Patterns: Among Countries and Over Time," *Review of Economic and Statistics* 50(4), pp. 391–416.

Geng, Mingzhai (1996), "A Investigation on the Path of Industrialization of Rural Areas." *Nankai Economic Research* 12(4), pp. 3–8.

Geng, Mingzhai (2004), "A Discussion on the Issues of the Industrialization of Undeveloped Rural Areas," *Zhongzhou Journal* 1.

Guo, Xibao and Huang Can (2009), "Lewis Model and the Shift of the Labor Forces in Rural Area of China," *Guangming Daily* September, 22.

Kirkpatrick, C. H., ed. (1983), *The Industrialization of Less Developed Countries,* Manchester, UK: Manchester University Press.

Kuznets, S. (1989), *Modern Economic Growth (in Chinese).* Beijing: Beijing College of Economics.

Liu, Dongxun (2004), "The Model of Economic Development of Inland Undeveloped Traditional Rural Areas," *Nankai Economic Research* 3.

Liu, Wei (1992), *Economic Development and Structure Transferring,* Beijing: Peking University Press.

The New Palgrave Dictionary of Economics (1992), Beijing: Economic Science Press.

Rubberdt, L. (1983), *The History of Industrialization (in Chinese),* Shanghai: Shanghai Translation Press.

Yang, Xiaokai (2001), "The Economic History of the People Republic of China: 1950–1978," http://www.jjxj.com.cn/news_detail.jsp?keyno=407.

Zhang, Peigang (2002), *Agriculture and Industrialization: Reconsideration of the Industrialization of Agricultural States,* Wuhan: Central China University of Science and Technology Press.

Zhao, Wei (2009), "Industrialization and Urbanization: An Analysis on the Models and their Evolution Mechanism of Three Great Regions of Coast Area," *Social Science Battlefront* 11.

Zhao, Wei and Huang Xianhai (1997), "Outside Restrains: the Major Binds of the Extension of two Regional Models of Industrialization in China," *China Industry Economy* 11.

4

Private Finance
in Modern China

Kaixiang Peng

Modern China is a paradigmatic example of an extremely controlled financial system, which has led to the development of an informal and distorted private finance sector. In recent years, researchers have begun to discuss the necessity of private finance in China. Although private financial institutions have benefited from a slight and gradual relaxation in regulation, private finance is mostly still informal or underground. Paradoxically, private finance has played an important role in financing the high ratio of investment that characterizes China's fast pace of economic growth. It is therefore important to understand private finance's relationship with the formal finance system.

In what follows, I will first present the background from traditional China. This is important to understand the mixed image of private finance. In the second part, I will look at mutual finance, which is often the starting point of regulation. In the third section, I will discuss profit finance, which is the most active component of private finance. Last, the analysis of private financial markets will offer a glimpse of the efficiency of the financial sector in contemporary China.

4.1   Background

Recent studies have led to the rethinking of traditional China's development, including its financial sector. According to Li Bozhong (2010, pp. 477–479), an integrated financial market existed at least in some regions of the Yangzi Delta. It is difficult to measure the efficiency of traditional finance exactly, but evidence suggests that financial operations had extensively worked in China before it was affected by Western influence. Most of these operations were private and informal, in the sense that no special formal rules existed. Regulation referred mainly to interest rates, but it was much milder than in contemporary Europe (Peng, Chen, and Yuan 2008).

At the end of the nineteenth century, the Bank of Great Qing, the first modern bank of China was founded incentivized by Western countries. This led to the later development of formal, government-controlled finance. In the process, the informal character of private finance was progressively strengthened. The Bank Law of 1931 constitutes a landmark. Many domestic banks and other traditional institutions could not meet the requirements of this law and became informal or, in all rigor, illegal.[1] The most important change is the nationalization of the largest banks launched by the central government of Republic of China (ROC) at the end of the 1920s (Du, 2004, pp. 109–124). Ironically, this provided the foundation for People's Republic of China's (Mainland China) (PRC's) future socialization.

Once the Chinese Communist Party (CCP) won the civil wars and the PRC was founded, they took over the enterprises run by bureaucratic capital, including the four largest banks. PBC (People's Bank of China) was founded as the new central bank owned by the state. From 1949 to 1952, private finance was remodeled: the scope of business was reduced; capital requirements increased; and the PBC became the new supervising authority. By the end of 1949, 20 percent of private banks had disappeared. During March to June 1950, two-thirds of the private banks closed (Hu, 1993, pp. 35–36). As the private economy contracted, and since state enterprises were restricted to operate with PBC, private banks got into great trouble and had to accept joint state-private management. By the end of 1952, the remodeling of private finance had been successfully accomplished.

In the countryside where 80 percent of the population resided, credit cooperatives were regarded as practicing usury (CASS and Central Archives, 2000, p. 447), which, since the 1920s and up to today is a mainstream idea in China. So, some resemblances between PRC and ROC in developing rural credit cooperatives can be found, that is, they were both led by government and aimed at increasing agricultural investment. In the 1950s, this process intensified: after the first meeting of rural credit cooperatives held by PBC in 1954, 124,000 cooperatives were founded and, only during the last three months, 90,000 of them were set up in a hurry to fulfill the annual plan (Hu, 1993, p. 128). Although some researchers commend the democratic management of these credit cooperatives, they actually functioned as exchequers of production teams rather than financial institutions.

As a consequence of institutional changes and a ban on interest, private finance shrunk greatly since the 1950s, especially in the supply side. Interest was decried as exploitation by Marxism and it was more strictly regulated than in the ROC period. Officially, this was done by lowering the state department's interest rates and the legal rates to depress usury. For example, in 1953, Guangzhou's joint state-private managed loan office lent at a 4.5 percent per month, while private pawns were allowed to lend at 9 percent[2] (PBC, 1955, p. 123). After 1964, the legal limit rate was 15 percent per month, a little below the 20 percent of ROC (Xu, 2010). In reality, legal protection of private interest was affected by ad hoc policies and enforcement. Political methods were often used to deal with usury, such as ideological education, mass displacement, and punishment (Yang and Gao, 2008). These informal methods made the meaning of legal regulation unclear, and made people mistrust financial business.[3]

As a result, private finance went underground, completely defeating the aim of eliminating usury. For example, a report of 1957 described that in Henan Province one farmer lent to agricultural cooperatives at the monthly rate of 8 percent and 15 percent. Some traders absorbed deposit at the rate of 100 percent annually (CASS and Central Archives, 2000, p. 443). Even during the Cultural Revolution, one survey of Zhejiang Province in 1974 showed that 30 percent of farmers borrowed through usury, whose monthly rates were 3–4 percent normally, while some were above 10 percent or even reached 30 percent (Hu, 1993, p. 241). The abnormally high interest rates were not only attributed to contraction of supply, but also to higher risk and transaction costs caused by regulation. Another important reason is the destruction of private property rights. This means creditors had fewer resources to lend and borrowers had less property to pledge. Land was the most important property in the countryside. In the 1950s, Land Reform and People's Commune Movement abolished traditional private land ownership, which caused one of the most profound changes in modern China, deeply felt today.

This radical attitude toward interest relaxed in 1972, in which PBC allowed savings to earn interest (Hu, 1993, p. 222). This constituted a formal acceptance of interest and change. In 1978, the famous Reform and Opening began. Gradually, the mechanisms of resource allocation were transferred from the planner to the market. Since the state-owned enterprises' reform was delayed, the private sector led this great change. However, after 30 years of nationalization they had little accumulation of capital, while banks were all state owned and had no incentive to provide capital. This led to a great increase in the demand for private finance. Regulation also relaxed to cope with the situation. In 1984, the first private domestic bank opened in Wenzhou, one of the most active regions in Reform and Opening. However, after 1986 private financial institutions again became illegal under the new rule (Hu, 2006, pp. 75, 98). Domestic banks had to operate underground or take other forms. One of them, ROSCA (Rotating Savings and Credit Association), had a particularly significant role, forming large and complex association chains in some regions. Rural cooperatives also played an important part. Many organizations of very different nature operated under this title to escape regulation (Jiang, 1996, pp. 142–168; Feng, 2006, p. 144).

Growth of the macro economy brought about the growth and demise of bubbles in private finance. Regulation was strengthened during the 1990s. The State Council and PBC separately issued decrees to ban underground finance in 1998 and 2002. Finally, in 1999 the central government decided to clear all rural cooperative foundations and attempt the creation of formal financial institutions. Private holdings of bank stock were allowed after 1996. A few forms of private credit institutions that do not handle deposits have been admitted in recent years, such as pawnshops and credit agencies. Depository institutions still face very strict regulation (Feng, 2004).

Currently the private finance sector, despite some improvements, is still very restricted by rules and regulations. Private loans are regulated mainly by contract law, where interest rates are legally limited to four times the bank rates (Xu, 2010). This incentivizes private finance to generate noninstitutional loans. At the same time reform of PBC and other state-owned banks, relaxation of interest rates and credit ratio regulation of banks, development of capital markets, and dramatic increase of foreign investment have all improved supply of capital (PBC et al., 2004). Meanwhile PBC's reduction of its commercial operations also reduced its incentive to use regulation as the competing strategy.

Besides the above factors, informal regulation at the local level cannot be neglected. Before 1978, ad hoc policies held by local governments tended to be stricter than formal regulation, but after 1978, some of them had incentives to relax regulation if they found it helpful to develop local economy. As Tsai (2001) argued, at the outset the Reform faced very different local structures. Localities such as Wenzhou that had an earlier start on decollectivization and private sector development tended to be more tolerant of local curb-market activities. Needless to say, demand for private finance was decisive. Formal and informal methods moderated financial depression to a certain extent.

Thus, private finance in modern China has a complex character. Self-organizing from grassroots and old traditions, avoidance of regulation, and rent seeking in the informal sector have all combined in the development of private finance. Policymakers' attempts to remodel private finance into a modern institutional and formal system must take into account this complexity.

4.2   Mutual Finance

In this chapter, mutual finance refers to credit that is not motivated by profit, but by family or community ties, and works as long-term reciprocal insurance. For example, loans between relatives, friends or neighbors, cooperatives, and main types of ROSCA constitute mutual finance. Its grassroots origin often causes it to be disregarded as part of the financial system, but it is in fact closely related to modern China's private finance and other financial sectors.

4.3   Proportion

Since the beginning of the twentieth century, surveys have shown that most private loans were granted by other individuals, mostly relatives, friends, or neighbors: a 1930 nearly countrywide rural sample survey showed that more than 80 percent of loans were from other individuals (Buck, 1937, Ch. 9, Tab. 14). At the end of the twentieth century, this ratio was about 70 percent (Wen, 2001). In 2005, it was 45.91 percent (Han, 2007, p. 57). In middle China the proportion in 2007 was still 60 percent (Liu, 2008, p. 35). Since these surveys use different statistic definitions and methods we cannot conclude that there is a decreasing trend. However, the surveys attest to the fact that most loans are individual. Our question is, then, how many of those individual loans are mutual? We try to answer by looking at the usage of loans index, defined as the proportion of consumption in private loans. In the above surveys this index is, respectively, 75 percent, about 40 percent and 40.86 percent.[4] Generally, people's daily life and consumption are much more similar than their productivity. If their wealth level is similar, consumption loans would also be similar between individuals. Therefore, from the above data, we can conclude that mutual loans are significant in private finance until nowadays.

4.4   Interest Regulation and Cooperatives

The importance of mutual finance has profoundly affected policies. Evidence can be found in the regulation of interest rates. Chinese Marxists define usury by the purpose of loans. If a loan is used for consumption or simple reproduction, interest on it is usury no matter what the interest rate is (Wang, 1937). This is actually another expression of the thought that interest on mutual finance is immoral. This constituted mainstream thinking during the whole twentieth century in China. Accordingly, rural private loans were mainly for consumption or simple reproduction and could be met by mutual finance, such as cooperatives. The legal limit of private loans interest is based on such consideration, although it applies to many nonmutual financial activities under today's regulation.

Modern classical economics provides an explanation for interest of mutual finance. Time preference requires positive interest and, in equilibrium, it equals productivity. If capital moves freely, there should be no difference on loans by usage. Yet, this explanation conflicts with the fact that zero interest rates in mutual finance coexist with usury interest rates. A 1937 survey of Liaoning Province reported that 63 percent of rural loans applications from farmers were interest free, while this percentage was just 26 percent for loans applications from shops (Temporary Industry Investigation, Ministry of Manchukuo Industry Bureau, 1937). Similarly, Han Jun (2007, p. 56) calculated the average interest rate of rural loans from relatives and friends and found it to be as low as 1.11 percent. Wen Tiejun (2001) uses a much smaller sample and finds the interest rate distribution to be more dispersed: nearly one-quarter of the sample exhibits monthly rates above 4 percent, and only 18 percent are interest free. Does such evidence conflict with theory? Brandt and Hosios (2010) reject the hypothesis that interest-free loans were long-term reciprocal insurance, and state that lending at zero and positive interest rates were highly segmented in the community. Based on a sample of 1930s rural China, their tests show that both market development and informational costs affect contract selection significantly. Therefore, there is no breakpoint between zero and positive interest rates. With more developed markets and lower informational costs, people will tend to select interest as repayment. At the same time, because zero and positive interest rate loans apply to the same individuals, it is reasonable to see positive interest rates as the marginal shadow price of interest-free loans. In other words, there should be a trade-off between reciprocal insurance and interest, even if the insurance function cannot be rejected.

It is also clear that interest bans cannot find support in mutual loans. On the contrary, with the development of markets, regulation of interest rates will lead to greater loss of efficiency. Peng, Chen, and Yuan (2008) analyze loan contract samples in late imperial China and find that, excluding interest-free loans and controlling for other differences, there was no significant interest difference between loans from individuals, shops, or ROSCA. They also find that transaction costs are a considerable proportion of small loans in both usury and mutual finance, even though the latter has lower informational costs. Cooperatives seem to be an effective way to save on transaction costs. However, when most transaction costs are unrelated to cash management or organization, cooperatives save little in terms of transaction costs. Rosenberg et al. (2009) indicate that microcredit is so labor intensive that scale effects cease to matter at around 2,000 clients. That is, the size of loans is more important; cooperatives can do little to increase it.

4.5   Forms and Functions

From the above discussion, we can conclude that cooperatives have more short-comings and operate less efficiently than mainstream institutions in China. During most of the life of both ROC and PRC, cooperatives were launched by the central government as a way to promote agricultural development. That is, cooperatives operated as local agencies of governments or banks and could not meet the real demand for mutual finance. On and off during the 1950s and the 1960s, management of cooperatives was left to grassroots production teams but, since they were owned by the government, more corruption ensued (Hu, 1993, p. 128).

From surveys we can see that individual loans have been the most common form of mutual finance. ROSCA exhibit the mutual trait most obviously and, in different forms, were very popular before the communist period. The diary of a Huizhou student in the 1700s shows that the writer was a member of several credit associations simultaneously (Weizhai, 1983). Even as late as 1958, we find 35 *Yao Hui*[5] and 869 members in Kaifeng City, Henan Province (CASS and Central Archives, 2000, p. 450). After 1978, ROSCA revived, especially in Zhejiang and Fujian Provinces. Currently, it exists in communities of many developing countries. Hu Biliang (2006, pp. 24–50) and Liu Mingquan et al. (2003) provide a general summary and explain the reason for its popularity. However, if we compare ROSCA to individual mutual loans we can see ROSCA's main advantage is not about information and insurance, but mostly about enhancing contract enforcement. ROSCA benefits from formal procedures, the head bears unlimited liability, and more people's involvement means more strength (Feng, 2006, p. 133).[6] Although they are informal according to the current legal system, ambiguity of land rights still makes them precious in rural China. It is not surprising that ROSCA escaped the scope of mutual finance and led to turbulence (Feng, 2006, p. 138), to which I will refer in the next section.

What form mutual finance takes is also related to its aim and function. As described above, most rural private loans cover daily needs. Consistent with many other observations,[7] Han Jun (2007, p. 59) points out that the largest items are education and medical treatment. In contrast, prior to the 1930s, food consumption was the main item (Li, 2004, p. 240). This change reflects increase of income and standards of living, but it is accompanied by high interest rates in private loans, which also reflects the inefficiency of financial control. When the shadow price of loans is high and the need for loans is mutual, ROSCA becomes more attractive. Hu Biliang (2006, p. 148–179) provides a detailed field research of ROSCA in Xiangdong villages, where more than 80 percent of residents joined in. In the 1980s, such associations expanded quickly and speculation was popular. After an initial learning process, most of them became a means to collect funds for education and medical treatment. The function of reciprocal insurance worked well by ROSCA.

Another financial form for reciprocal insurance is the local public fund, which can be set by an individual or the community. Local public funds took many forms and were also popular in traditional China.[8] Of these, the most important is Zutian, an investment on land by the clan that uses the rent to meet public expenditures and help members in difficulty. Funds destined to finance education provide an interesting comparison to modern China. The above survey of 2007 shows that education is the first use of credit, although education investment appears to be even more considerable in traditional China (Li, 2010, p. 253). Clans and local governments launched funds to cope with it, since education was related to selection of officers. *Bingxing,* a special example, is designed to subsidize the expensive journey of attending the imperial examination held at the capital. Such funds were supported by the government, but its source and management were a function of how many local gentlemen succeeded in the examination. Thus, they could be included in mutual finance and were a strong substitute of mutual loans. Their proper function was related to public affairs, such as education, irrigation works, grain storage, poverty relief, and so forth. As a consequence of socialization and the "Great Leap" in the 1950s, they have disappeared, and production teams took over some of their functions. After the reform of 1978, these functions have not been covered.

4.6   Policy

Policies on mutual finance are thought to be linked to poverty relief, but that is only partially true. As discussed above, interest regulation will depress mutual finance. Although funds are generated in the countryside, credit supply is scarce there. Legal interest rate ceilings on private lending are higher than in formal institutions, but the size of private loans is much smaller. As a result, while deposits in formal institutions remain attractive to rural residents, they are difficult to obtain. An extreme example is post saving before 2003, when it was permitted to absorb deposits and redeposit them in PBC with a favorable interest rate. Post saving is likened to a big "bloodletting instrument" of rural capital (Han, 2007, p. 16).

Besides interest regulation, the greater obstacle lies in the regulation of financial institutions. Current rules allow only financial institutions to accept deposits, and there are many limits to the creation of financial institutions. Consequently, ROSCA and other form of funds tend to be thought of as illegal, because they accept some form of deposit. This cuts the pipeline between supply and demand of mutual finance.

However, in recent years the government has been trying to develop formal insurance instruments covering all citizens, such as medical and endowment insurance.[9] They are substitutes for informal reciprocal insurance and allow more scale benefits. As urbanization is remodeling communities quickly, these attempts of substitution are valuable. However, will they squeeze out informal supply as Hoff and Stiglitz (1990) expected? The answer lies in the type of transaction costs and related scale effects. For private loans, whose scale effects depend on the size of each loan, squeeze-out effects may be small. On the contrary, scale effects of ROSCA or public funds depend on the scope of members. The more residents join in formal finance, the less attractive informal instruments become. The amount of funds provided by formal medical or endowment insurance is still very limited. This means part of the emergent need or demand of the poorest people cannot be satisfied, while it becomes more difficult to obtain money through ROSCA or local public funds.[10] Li Zhengdong's research of the urban poor in 2002 finds that they search informal credit relations when falling into persistent poverty (Li, 2009). In China, rural formal insurance lags behind urban, making the need for funds more pressing. Thus, if squeezing occurs, the rural population suffers most.

4.7   Profit Finance

Because of restructuring during the 1950s, private profit finance was depressed greatly. There were only sporadic loans mixed with mutual finance. Not until the Reform of 1978 did it revive. Formal and informal regulations relaxed, and some attempts received special permission. Since local governments and branches of banks benefit from more autonomy in management and have more incentive to increase efficiency, informal institutional change plays a much more important role. For this reason, private finance is often referred to as underground finance and reports about it read like mysterious stories. There are no reliable statistics, hence we have to analyze reports of surveys and transactions on their website.

4.8   Scale

From whatever information is available, both policymakers and researches believe the scale of private finance to be considerable, although unmeasured. Li Jianjun (2006, pp. 279–318) uses a nationwide survey in 2004 to estimate the relative scale of informal to formal finance to be 28.07 percent for the whole sample.[11] There is great geographical dispersion: from the largest percentage in Heilongjiang (over 50 percent), to the lowest in Guizhou (below 10 percent). However, there is no significant difference between east, middle, and west China. What is noticeable is the urban-rural gap: 57 percent of rural capital is provided by informal finance, well above the national average. Even for the lowest ranking province, this ratio is near 30 percent. At the same time, more than 70 percent of rural residents choose formal financial institutions as their main deposit destination. This contrast supports the view that formal finance acts as a channel to pump rural capital to push the industrialization and urbanization process (Wen, 2001; Feng, 2006, pp. 99–101).

As private finance is more extensive in the countryside, it makes sense to look at the structure of rural credit sources. Statistics based on the fixed-sample observation of the Agriculture Department covering 20,000 farmers shows that about 70 percent of rural credit came from informal finance during 1995–2003 (Feng, 2006, p. 124). This includes mutual finance, while the informal proportion of profit finance may be a little lower. However, surveys of Zhejiang, Shandong, Anhui, and Guangdong all confirm that more than half of rural private enterprises resort to informal finance as a source of funds (Feng, 2006, pp. 125–126). According to Ayyagari et al. (2008), only 20 percent of firm financing in 18 cities originates in banks, while informal channels represent 43 percent, compared to less than 9 percent in other developing countries.

Thus, private finance is the main credit source of the private sector, and its total scale is large enough to challenge formal finance. Looking at the individual size of private loans should help us judge whether they are neglected by formal finance. Feng (2006, p. 278) provided the capital structure of 24 private enterprises of Cangnan, a county in Wenzhou. For firms above 1 billion RMB Yuan, firms' own capital or equity represents the largest percentage of the total, while formal finance provides most of the borrowed capital. However, individual enterprises borrow a minimum of 720,000 RMB Yuan from state banks, while the maximum amount from private finance reaches 10 million RMB Yuan. This seems to indicate private finance is not limited to small loans.

Records on the intention of the transaction on internet provide more detailed information about the scale of private loans. I selected a "web sample" of records that I classified as demand and supply.[12] This particular site is a free information platform and its records are not limited to special mortgage terms. However, not all transaction intentions will be released on the Internet or on this site; therefore, the sample records here construct a nearly random sample. There are 2,070 records (26.3 billion RMB Yuan) of demand and 386 records (19.8 billion RMB Yuan) of supply from June 2009 to December 2010. The average amounts are,

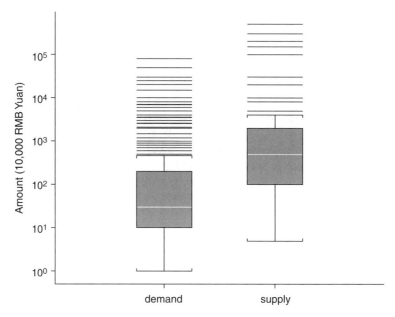

Figure 4.1   Credit amount of the web sample.

respectively, 12.7 million and 53.3 million RMB Yuan. The small credit ceiling of Postal Savings Bank of China (PSBC) is 100,000 RMB Yuan, and individual enterprise credit ceiling of Agricultural Bank of China (ABC) is 1 million RMB Yuan (cumulated).[13] Apparently, private credit has surpassed microfinance greatly. Figure 4.1 shows the box plot of outliers and averages. Although both distributions of demand and supply are biased to the left, half of the records of demand are above 300,000 and the median of supply is 5 million RMB Yuan.[14] Both of them are quite sizable compared to the quota of formal finance.

4.9   Forms and Segments

The inflow of foreign investment to China at the end of the nineteenth century contributed to the development of modern finance while traditional finance continued extending. By the early twentieth century varied forms of financial institutions coexisted. Such a complex landscape was especially dramatic in the financial center, Shanghai. Nevertheless, the main tendency was inclining toward the development of modern forms. Despite the dissatisfaction of domestic banks, the Banking Law was passed in 1931. In what followed modern banks wrestled for control of Shanghai's financial market from domestic banks. This trend reached its peak during the PRC period. Today, most private financial institutions are illegal or quasi-legal. Within this group, we find three kinds: the institutions formed to meet the endogenous financial demand; the institutions that transform to escape regulation; and the rent seekers that abide by regulation.

The first two are generated by demand, but they exhibit different legal status. Domestic banks, pyramidal investment associations, discount brokers, private foreign exchanges, and all kinds of private lending whose interest rates exceed four times the bank limit can be included in the first group, and they are underground or illegal. Some other institutions may have similar functions, but they have found a legal cover to operate. For example, pawnshops are permitted to do chattel mortgage, but it is difficult to prevent them from receiving real estate mortgage and even absorbing deposits. Recently created finance houses have similar characteristics. Their legal function is strictly to broker banks in order to crowd out informal finance and increase competition within formal finance,[15] but they have incentives to increase operating capital from other channels.[16] ROSCA, also popular, can only supply interpersonal lending under current rules. When these institutions grow, it becomes difficult to ascertain how much saving they are absorbing. In addition, it is not easy to apply regulation to their implied interest rates. However, escaping regulation is risky and has a higher cost. Related parties have to rely on verbal agreements to keep their transactions concealed, but such agreements are fragile. After the 1980s, failures of ROSCAs have led to repeated episodes of violence and unrest (Feng, 2006, p. 138). All the parties involved, including policymakers, should take this into account.

The third group changes according to regulations. During the 1980s, local governments participated in financial regulation, which opened more opportunities of rent seeking. Specifically, they were deeply involved in the demise of rural cooperative foundations. After the 1990s, regulation of informal finance became more complete, and power was concentrated in specialized departments. Reforming formal finance to substitute informal finance is regarded as a way to increase efficiency and reduce chaos at the same time. However, this intensifies rent seeking of formal financial institutions when their problems of ownership and management aren't resolved. As Han Jun (2007, p. 188) pointed out, 17 percent of investigated farmers gave up applying for loans from RCC (Rural Credit Cooperatives) because of the absence of interpersonal relationships. However, the same research also found that extra expenses, such as presents, didn't increase enterprises' opportunity of obtaining loans (Han, 2007, p. 181). According to his regression specification, extra expenses drove enterprises to informal finance. Competition from the informal sector forced the rent seeking of formal sector to combine with the second type of private finance. For example, researchers often observe that staff members of RCC play a crucial role in local private financial operations. They may act as guarantors or middlemen for private loans (Li Jing, 2006, pp. 345–347). This special relationship could explain why stricter regulation implemented after the 1990s did not result in more serious financial depression. As the Coase Theorem would predict, there were rights transactions. However, it's certainly not the best arrangement as illegal transactions bear high risk and cost. In recent years, every time a formal finance middleman has been exposed, there has been a local financial cataclysm.

4.10   Interest Rates

After 1991, the legal status of most private finance operations falls within interpersonal lending, hence their interest rate ceiling is four times that of banks.
Currently, commercial banks are permitted to float their rate around PBC's base
rate. Around 2004, the marketization of banks' interest rates was practically completed (Yi, 2009). This relaxed regulation of private finance too. However, it still
could not meet the needs of private finance whose interest rates varied widely.

The private finance monitoring report of PBC's Wenzhou branch shows
there are four types of interest rates belonging to different segments: credit of
rural farmers, operating funds' loan of microfinance houses, short-term loan of
informal finance, and public financing of informal institutions (Wu and Wang,
2010). In 2010, their normal annual rate levels were 13.37 percent, 17.74 percent,
35.65 percent, and 15 percent respectively. All of them are higher than the current bank annual base rate of 5.31 percent, but only the third type more than
quadruples it. It is also the most active and fit to be the marginal price of capital.
Wenzhou is a window of China's private finance. Wenzhou's capital from its private financial sector has ebbed to other provinces, having a considerable effect on
their capital and real estate markets. Hence, the monitoring report of Wenzhou is
quite representative of the whole market. Nevertheless, we have reason to believe
there may be sample selection problems in the monitoring, as PBC is not a neutral
observer but a regulator. In fact, after adjusting its monitoring system, the average interest rate jumped from 11 percent to 21 percent in mid-2010 (Hu, 2010).

In order to observe the real situation, we return to our web sample. Figure 4.2
shows distributions of demand and supply's interest rate. The dashed line is four

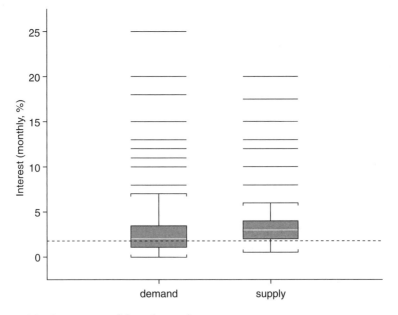

Figure 4.2   Interest rate of the web sample.

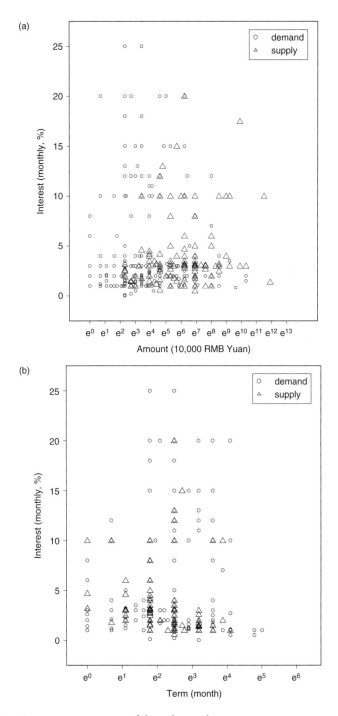

Figure 4.3 Interest rate structure of the web sample.

times the bank rate, which represents the legal ceiling rate. Interest rates of informal finance are very volatile and always exceed the ceiling. The rates required by suppliers are above demanders'. One explanation is that both suppliers and demanders don't report their reserve prices in order to gain advantage in bargaining. Yet another possibility is that the gap between formal and informal finance is wider in the supply than in the demand side. Formal financial institutions don't need to disclose their intention on the website, while demanders will try to find cheaper funds there even if they could borrow from formal finance.

It's often assumed that usury in private finance is due to the micro size of loans, which leads to scale inefficiency of suppliers and emergent needs of demanders. This logic characterizes usury as inefficient and immoral. However, it is not so obvious. In figure 4.3 (a), we plot interest rates against amount of loans. There is obviously no downward pattern in the supply side. As shown in figure 4.1, the scale of supply has clearly exceeded what we call microfinance, and it's not surprising that supply turns upwards. From figure 4.3 (a), mid-scale demanders are more tolerant of high interest rates than small borrowers. This is consistent with the nonconvexity of production, which implies there are thresholds in investment demand (Carter and Barrett, 2006). If this hypothesis is true, high interest rates will correspond to high productivity and shouldn't be abandoned.

A common criticism of private finance is that it is speculative in nature and, therefore, it is risky and constitutes usury. Some evidence supports this view. For example, the monitoring report of Wenzhou noticed that the interest rate of private finance is always negatively related to its term, which contradicts the base rate of banks (Wu and Wang, 2010). In addition, short-term loans are always correlated with speculation. Figure 4.3 (b) presents a different picture. Most of these loans aren't short term by the standard of banks, which is three months. There exists some negative relation between the interest rate and term, but it's much stronger in the supply than in the demand side. Therefore, a better explanation is the shortage of floating capital in the finance market. Although banks exhibit a lower short-term interest rate, their approval procedures are very time-consuming and make them lag behind the needs of the market. In sum, banks cannot be the effective suppliers of floating capital. This provides a natural opportunity for informal finance, which challenges regulation and is less limited by bureaucracy.

4.11   Private Finance Market

As befits the theory documented by Mckinnon (1973), China applies rather strict financial controls, while its investment and economy have developed quickly after the Reform. According to Yi Gang (1996), this is less of a paradox if we take into account the monetization after 1978 strengthened self-finance, as Mckinnon (1973) pointed out. In the previous sections, we have talked about the evolution of informal finance institutions. Formal institutional reform can't be neglected either, and we find positive evidence in Ayyagari et al. (2008). All these factors could explain why the growth of the financial sector might match the growth of total production. In this section, we will discuss the efficiency of China's informal and sizable financial market.

4.12   Integration

Development of private finance is regionally imbalanced (Li Jianjun, 2006, pp. 279–318). However, this should not lead us to conclude the whole market is inefficient, because different scales may be endogenous to demand. We could use price integration or interest rate integration by finance market as a general measure. However, systematic statistics about private interest rates are very recent. The only regional price data related closely to capital markets are the price indices of real estate in 35 large- and medium-scale cities after 2000.[17] Moreover, private capital plays an important role in interregional real estate markets. The most famous is Zhejiang's *house-frying group* active in many cities. Therefore, the integration of real estate price indices may reflect the efficiency of capital movements.

Since the sample period is too short to adopt formal time-series analysis, here I use the correlation matrix to provide a coarse observation. In order to avoid statistical problems such as spurious correlation and over difference, both link-relative and fixed-base indices are used. Table 4.1 reports the main result. It includes the correlation coefficients between each city and the four economic centers, which are Beijing, Shanghai, Guangzhou, and Shenzhen. The last row shows the coefficients of average indices. Although the result seems rather irregular, it's not difficult to find that the integration exhibits some regional pattern. Shanghai's link-relative index has little positive correlation with other cities except for the neighboring ones. In fact, the price for Shanghai and its neighbors increased dramatically in 2003 and 2004, while other cities met this problem three years later when the price of Shanghai had stopped increasing. After that, the increasing trend of prices is similar and coefficients of fixed indices are quite high. This process may be explained as the diffusion of Yangzi Delta's private capital. However, it also shows that the floating of capital is slow and not very efficient.

There are also shortcomings to using real estate price indices. Besides statistic problems, real estate prices are also affected by other factors, such as status of the city, inflation, and government intervention. Moreover, private investment in real estate originates, to a large degree, in self-finance, as defined by Mckinnon (1973), which is very different from informal financing. In order to overcome the above problems, I use the web sample again.

Figure 4.4 (a) shows a positive relation between regional supply and demand interest rates. Hence, there must be some regional market integration conducting to market equilibriums. Both demanders and suppliers adopt this information in their bargaining. Looking at the plot, we can see regional differences are quite large. It is interesting to notice that both interest rates in Shanghai are quite high, whereas in Hunan, in the hinterland, it is the opposite. Endogeneity of demand

Table 4.1   Correlations of 35 cities' real estate price indices (2000–2008)

City	Last year = 100				1999 = 100			
	Beijing	Shanghai	Guangzhou	Shenzhen	Beijing	Shanghai	Guangzhou	Shenzhen
Beijing	**1.00**	**−0.28**	**0.78**	**0.68**	**1.00**	**0.82**	**0.97**	**0.98**
Tianjin	0.51	0.41	0.58	0.44	0.95	0.95	0.94	0.96
Shijiazhuang	0.90	−0.35	0.71	0.60	0.98	0.90	0.94	0.97
Taiyuan	0.62	0.34	0.50	0.31	0.95	0.95	0.93	0.95
Hohhot	0.46	−0.16	0.76	0.61	0.95	0.92	0.95	0.97
Shenyang	0.22	0.55	0.39	0.31	0.93	0.97	0.91	0.94
Dalian	0.84	−0.20	0.87	0.74	0.99	0.84	0.99	0.99
Changchun	0.46	−0.51	0.01	0.08	0.93	0.72	0.84	0.87
Harbin	0.88	−0.18	0.59	0.46	0.98	0.90	0.95	0.97
Shanghai	**−0.28**	**1.00**	**−0.14**	**−0.19**	**0.82**	**1.00**	**0.80**	**0.84**
Nanjing	0.08	0.75	0.33	0.29	0.90	0.98	0.90	0.93
Hangzhou	0.12	0.59	0.07	−0.11	0.92	0.97	0.88	0.92
Ningbo	−0.44	0.79	−0.39	−0.36	0.87	0.99	0.82	0.88
Hefei	0.28	0.55	−0.01	−0.25	0.92	0.97	0.88	0.91
Fuzhou	0.93	−0.24	0.93	0.85	0.99	0.89	0.97	0.99
Xiamen	0.64	0.16	0.91	0.78	0.96	0.94	0.95	0.97
Nanchang	0.03	0.19	0.32	0.24	0.91	0.97	0.88	0.93
Jinan	0.48	0.35	0.40	0.19	0.95	0.96	0.92	0.95
Qingdao	−0.08	0.89	0.20	0.14	0.90	0.98	0.88	0.92
Zhengzhou	0.82	0.05	0.92	0.79	0.98	0.91	0.97	0.98
Wuhan	0.31	0.46	0.40	0.20	0.92	0.97	0.89	0.93
Changsha	0.96	−0.25	0.71	0.63	1.00	0.85	0.96	0.97
Guangzhou	**0.78**	**−0.14**	**1.00**	**0.93**	**0.97**	**0.80**	**1.00**	**0.99**
Shenzhen	0.68	−0.19	0.93	1.00	0.98	0.84	0.99	1.00
Nanning	0.87	0.12	0.60	0.44	0.98	0.91	0.95	0.97
Haikou	0.71	0.19	0.29	0.16	0.98	0.90	0.93	0.95
Chengdu	0.67	0.33	0.56	0.42	0.97	0.94	0.94	0.96
Guiyang	0.70	−0.34	0.76	0.72	0.98	0.89	0.96	0.98
Kunming	0.96	−0.33	0.63	0.55	0.99	0.77	0.96	0.96
Chongqing	−0.07	0.70	0.05	0.00	0.86	0.99	0.84	0.88
Xi.an	0.87	−0.04	0.48	0.32	0.98	0.90	0.94	0.96
Lanzhou	0.67	0.17	0.40	0.16	0.96	0.94	0.92	0.95
Xining	0.70	0.10	0.23	0.05	0.97	0.93	0.92	0.95
Yinchuan	0.41	−0.03	−0.16	−0.35	0.94	0.92	0.86	0.90
Urumqi	0.67	−0.25	0.07	0.01	0.92	0.65	0.82	0.83
Total	**0.63**	**0.44**	**0.66**	**0.50**	**0.95**	**0.95**	**0.93**	**0.96**

Source: China Statistical Yearbook.

and supply can explain this: a developed financial sector and greater financial demand support each other. This is not the same as the commonly held view that undeveloped financial sectors always lead to usury in the hinterland. Therefore, it is important to analyze the extra demand.

In figure 4.4 (b), extra demand is plotted against supply interest rates. If we compare it to figure 4.4 (a) we find that provinces with higher interest rates tend to have larger extra demand, independently from the degree of financial development. In figure 4.4 (b) we can also see that provinces form two groups: the group to the left has a steeper and lower extra demand compared with the group to the right. As we have noted above, not all demanders regard the website platform as the unique way of financing. Some demanders just use it to

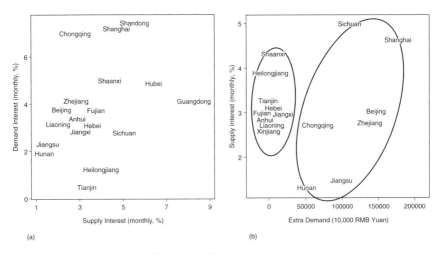

Figure 4.4   Interregional differences of the web sample.

find a better selection. It is possible, then, that the demanders in the group to the right have other selections and, therefore, their extra demand affects interest rate less. This explanation is consistent with the observation that most provinces in the group to the right have a more developed financial sector.[18] Comparing figures 4.4 (a) and (b) we can conclude that regional segments exist not only with regard to the scale of financial demand and supply but also to the structure of the financial sector.

4.13   Relationship with Macroeconomics

From the above discussion, we conclude that there exist regional markets, and their integration is still low. When private financial activities are more than spontaneous transactions, there will be an interrelation between private financial markets and macroeconomics. Policymakers often claim that private financial operations increase macroeconomics chaos and counteract the effect of government interventions. In modern China, this point is even more important than the moral purpose in government regulations of usury and private finance. Whether in PRC or ROC, financial regulation was used as a means of macroeconomic tuning.

We can trace the effects of private finance in huge-scale investments of unknown sources, in the inflow of hot money under foreign exchange regulation, and in the overshooting of capital markets. However, by responding to macro-economic variables private finance also increases the efficiency in resource allocation. In figure 4.5, because data are scarce, I use the rate of Wenzhou to show the variation of private financial rates after 1978. Bank rates refer to the base rate set by PBC, annually averaged using the valid period as weight. The inflation rate is measured by Consumer Price Index (CPI). As shown in figure 4.5,

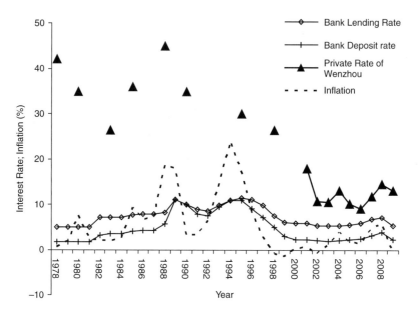

Figure 4.5   Interest rates and inflation: 1978–2009.

bank rates lag inflation, and their reaction to inflation is small. On the contrary, the response of private rates to inflation is much quicker and stronger. In other words, private finance is more efficient. Its reaction tends to stabilize inflation and the macroeconomy. However, the situation in the 1980s is a bit more complex. Usury rates in this decade were responding to inflation, and led to stricter regulation. However, they also absorbed money from the formal sector and added to the difficulties of controlling inflation. Policymakers might regard private finance as a source of trouble in the marketization reform of commodity prices, while it would be fairer to say that the troubles proved the necessity of financial reforms.

In figure 4.5, we can also see clearly that the difference between bank rates and private rates reduces greatly after 2000s. This could be attributed to the marketization reform of bank rates. Due to the reform, the current lending rates of commercial banks have no restrictions with regard to the base rate. The credit ratio regulation has also been relaxed. These policies increase the supply of capital and decrease the demand for private loans. As it has been observed, the share of private finance in Wenzhou's capital market has constricted, with its interest rate being closer to formal finance (Cheng, 2004). However, we should be careful in drawing conclusions. There is statistical inconsistency in the private rate series: data before 2000 is mainly collected from direct but incomplete surveys, while after 2000 it is reported by the monitoring system of PBC's Wenzhou branch. There may be a downward bias in the later part that is supported by the data jump of September 2010 after an adjustment of the monitoring system was made. Therefore, the real effect of Reform may be exaggerated by the evidence from interest rates.

4.14   Summary

At the beginning of its modernization, similar to other countries, private informal finance is the predominant form of China's financial institutions. At the end of the nineteenth century, however, Chinese authorities start to regard modernization as a response to Western influence, and private finance is repressed as informal and traditional. Formal finance, however, is supported and controlled by the state. This is a departure from the evolution of financial modernization in other countries, where it is an endogenous process. The result is that improvements after 1978 originate mainly in the revival of traditional private finance and the informal mixture of formal and informal finance.

However, there is still ample room for further reform. Changes in the informal sector are quite fragile and lead to social problems such as inequality and corruption. Analysis of the financial market also shows that interregional market integration is still weak. Marketization of formal finance and relaxing the regulation of private finance should be carried out together in order to improve the efficiency of financial markets and reduce rent seeking.

It is to be expected that formal financial institutions will take over traditional financial forms in the future. However, because this process is promoted by the government, one should pay attention to its side effects. One of which is the squeezing-out effect, which might decrease total financial supply of funds. This is related mainly to the type of scale effect in financial operations. As we have discussed, the poorest people depend heavily on reciprocal insurance, and should be taken care of when formal insurance takes over. Current evidence does not support the existence of strong side effects derived from the expansion of formal financial institutions in profit finance.

Notes

1. Shanghai Branch of PBC (1956, pp. 212–216).
2. These rates seem very high, because inflation was serious in the early 1950s.
3. For example, Su and Chang (2005, p. 103) described such situations in the Hubei Province around 1952.
4. All of them are calculated by loan amount. If measured by frequency, the proportion of consumption loan will be higher, especially for the last two periods.
5. A form of ROSCA in which the order of using money is decided by lots.
6. An interesting example can be found in Li Jing (2006) and Feng (2006, p. 348). It describes a creditor who always refused to provide enough funds to one borrower fearing to be his single creditor.
7. If we turn to urban loans, housing will be more important, but house mortgage finance is operated mainly by banks that do not belong to the private finance sector.
8. Detailed description of this topic can be found in Zhou Rong (2006).
9. Compulsory elementary education and subsidized higher education have also been important in reducing mutual financial demand. However, the simultaneous increase in tuition fee of higher education has offset the effect of subsidies.

10. For example, new rural medical insurance provides coverage of 100,000 RMB Yuan and its premium is below 100 Yuan. However, the treatment of some diseases costs much more than 100,000 Yuan. The patient could turn to formal financial insurance whose coverage is 300,000 Yuan at the cost of 100,000 Yuan. Such a great divergence of premium ratio leaves room for informal insurance.
11. It is a subjectively constructed weighted average, so it is not necessarily accurate.
12. In order to safeguard the identity of the website the name is not provided here. Interested readers can contact the writer for related data.
13. PSBC: http://www.psbc.com/portal/zh_CN/CreditLoans/PersonalCreditLoans /EBER/8920.html; ABC: http://www.abchina.com/cn/RuralSvc/Individuals /countypersonalloan/.
14. The scale of supply seems much larger than demand's. However, one intent to supply may be shared by several borrowers, and some of the suppliers are brokers for the totality of the capital collected. Therefore, total supply is still smaller than demand.
15. *Interim Provisions on Administering Loan Companies,* China Banking Regulatory Commission (CBRC), 2007 (6).
16. Finance houses have developed quickly in recent years. Liu Lingling et al. (2008, pp. 209–215) provide an example.
17. It has increased to 70 cities since 2007. Here, we select the 35 original cities of 2000.
18. Guangdong is an outlier not included in the two groups in figure 4.4 (b). Its extra demand is negative while its supply interest rate is quite high. As the observed sample of Guangdong is very small, it is difficult to give a reliable explanation.

References

Ayyagari, Meghana et al. (2008), "Formal versus Informal Finance: Evidence from China," *Policy Research Working Paper* 4465, the World Bank.

Brandt, Loren and Arthur J. Hosios (2010), "Interest Free Loans Among Villagers," *Economic Development and Cultural Change* 58(2), pp. 345–372.

Buck, J. L. (1937), *Land Utilization of China: Statistics,* Nanking: The University of Nanking.

Carter, Michael R. and Christopher B. Barrett, (2006), "The Economics of Poverty Traps and Persistent Poverty: An Asset-Based Approach," *Journal of Development Studies* 42(2), pp. 178–199.

CASS and Central Archives (2000), *Collection of PRC's Economic Archives: Finance (1953-1957),* China's Price Press.

CBRC (China Banking Regulatory Commission) (2007), *Interim Provisions on Administering Loan Companies* (6).

Cheng Lei (2004), "The Trend of China's Private Finance," *Economic Theory and Economic Management* 2004(3), pp. 26–30.

Du Xuncheng (2004), *Compare the History of Financial Institution Change in China and Abroad,* Shanghai Academy of Social Sciences Press.

Feng Xingyuan (2004), "Investigate Private Finance from the Case of Sun Dawu's Financing," http://www.china-review.com/gao.asp?id=9980.

Feng Xingyuan (2006), *Research of China's Township Enterprises Financing and Endogenous Institutional Innovation of Private Finance,* Shanxi Economics Press.

Han Jun (2007), *Survey on China's Rural Finance,* Shanghai Far East Press.

Hoff, Karla and Joseph E. Stiglitz (1990), "Introduction: Imperfect Information and Rural Credit Markets-Puzzles and Policy Perspectives," *The World Bank Economic Review* 4(3), pp. 235–250.

Hu Biliang (2006), *Rural Finance and Village Development: Basic Theory International Experience and Empirical Analysis*, Commercial Press.

Hu Yanlong (1993), *Financial History of PRC*, Yunnan University Press.

Hu Zuohua (2010), "Wenzhou Private Lending Rates Climbed to 11.14% in June," *Zhonghua Business Times* July 21.

Jiang Xuchao (1996), *Research of China's Private Finance*, Shandong People's Press.

Li Bozhong (2010), *China's Early Modern Economics*, Zhonghua Book Company.

Li Jianjun (2006), *Survey on China's Underground Finance*, Shanghai People's Press.

Li Jing (2006), "Reaction between Private Finance and Formal Finance," in Feng Xingyuan ed., *Research of China's Township Enterprises financing and Endogenous Institutional Innovation of Private Finance*, Shanxi Economics Press, pp. 345–352.

Li Jinzheng (2004), *Exploring Research of Rural Social-economics in Modern China*, People's Press.

Li Yilin (2010), "Does the Interest Rate of Wenzhou not Work?" *21st Century Economic Report*, January 22, p. J11.

Li Zhengdong (2009), "Survival in Poverty Dynamics in Urban Communities," *Asian Social Science* 5(10), pp. 115–127.

Liu Lingling et al. (2008), *Research of China's Rural Financial Development*, Qinghua University Publisher.

Liu Mingquan et al. (2003), "Review of ROSCA Research," *Journal of Financial Research* 2003(2), pp. 120–132.

McKinnon, Ronald I. (1973), *Money and Capital in Economic Development*, Washington, DC: Brookings Institute.

PBC (1955), *Collection of Financial Decrees in 1953*, Finance and Economics Press.

PBC (People's Bank of China), CBRC (China Banking Regulatory Commission), CSRC (China Securities Regulatory Commission) and CIRC (China Insurance Regulatory Commission) (2004), *Financial Institution Reform*, China's Fangzheng Press.

Peng, Kaixiang, Zhiwu Chen, and Weipeng Yuan (2008), "The Mechanisms of Rural Credit Market in Modern China," *Economic Research* 2008(5), pp. 147–159.

Rosenberg, Richard et al. (2009), *The New Moneylenders: Are the Poor Being Exploited by High Microcredit Interest Rates?* CGAP No. 15, September.

Su Shaozhi and Chang Mingming (2005), "A Historical Investigation of Private Financing in Rural Hubei, 1952–1954," *Contemporary China History Studies* 12(3), pp. 99–112.

Temporary Industry Investigation, Ministry of Manchukuo Industry Bureau (1937), *Farmer's Debts and Credit Relationships (South Manchukuo)*, Tokyo: Longxi Publishing House.

Tsai, Kellee S. (2001), "Beyond Banks: Informal Finance and Private Sector Development in Contemporary China," presented at the Conference on Financial Sector Reform in China, September 11–13.

Wang Yinsheng (1937), "Usury Capital," in Rural Economic Research Association ed., *China's Land Issues and Commercial Usuries*, China's Rural Economic Research Association Press, pp. 160–178.

Weizhai (1983), "Diary of Weizhai," *Historical Materials of Qing Dynasty* 1983(4), pp. 184–217.

Wen Tiejun (2001), "Research of Farmers' Credit and Private Finance: The Main Report," http://www.china-review.com/sao.asp?id=5276.

Wu Yong and Wang Kun, (2010), "PBC Issues the Monitoring Report of Private Finance in Wenzhou," *Wenzhou Daily* September 10.

Xu Defeng (2010), "Social Justice and the Rationale of Usury Law," *Law Review of Beijing Univ.* 11(1), pp. 176–209.

Yang Yidan and Gao Debu (2008), "Review of The History of Usury and Its Governance: 1957–1966," *China's Economic History Research* 2008(2), pp. 17–25.

Yi Gang (1996), "Analysis of China's Financial Assets Structure and Its Policy Implications," *Economic Research* 1996(12), pp. 26–33.

Yi Gang (2009), "Marketization of Interest Rate during the Three Decades after Reform and Opening," *Journal of Financial Research* 2009(1), pp. 1–14.

Zhou Rong (2006), *The Social Security System from Ming to Qing and the Grassroots Social of Hubei and Hunan*, Wuhan University Press.

5

Interaction and Development of Chinese Education and the Chinese Economy

Xiaomei Ji

From 1949 to 1978, the People's Republic of China employed a Soviet-style centrally planned economy. Throughout the country, private business and free enterprise were not allowed to exist. After the end of the Cultural Revolution in 1976, Deng Xiaoping and the new Chinese leadership began the reformation of the economy, moving to a market-oriented mixed economy under one-party rule. Economists now characterize the Chinese economy as a market economy, sheltered under state capitalism. With the rapid increase of enrollment in elementary and higher education, there is an expectation of exceptional prospects for China in the future.

In 1986, China set a long-term goal of providing compulsory nine-year basic education for every child. The Chinese education system was expanded under Deng Xiaoping, with the understanding that an educated population was needed for the continuous growth of a prosperous Chinese economy. The reformation process was slowed down by the Tiananmen Square incident of 1989, but thereafter it quickly regained momentum. In February 2006, the Chinese government established its basic education goal by pledging to provide a completely free nine-year education, covering expense for both tuition fees and textbooks. Before that, many poor children were unable to afford the tuition fees even though they were relatively inexpensive. Free compulsory education in China comprises of elementary school and middle school for nine grades (age 6–15 years). Almost all children in urban areas continue with 3 years of high school, which is not paid for by the government.

5.1 Chinese Literacy

Under the rule of the Communists, the population of China has become more educated and literate. Literacy rates have jumped from around 20 percent when the Communists took over in 1949 to around 91 percent today. Despite this spectacular increase, 85 million Chinese people still cannot read and write. China has developed some novel approaches to combat illiteracy. In the villages of Wiping county in Henan province in central China, visitors who cannot read a few characters on the blackboard outside the village are not allowed entry. As a result, many illiterates have enrolled in special reading classes offered in the village. When I was a little child, I knew of many children in poor families in the countryside in China that could not afford elementary education. They rarely had the chance to attend the high school or go to university because they had to work on the farm. A low education standard for the population has been one of the main obstacles to China's development and progress. In many rural areas, people who could read or write and had a middle school education, were regarded as wise and educated. Even more so, people who had a high school education and did not do manual labor, were considered intellectuals. This labeling process continues to exist in the countryside while in the cities people are generally becoming more educated.

These days, there are many Chinese citizens with university degrees who attended university abroad. However, since the year 2000, illiteracy rates in China have risen again. Between 2000 and 2005, the number of illiterate Chinese have increased 33 percent from 87 million to 116 million, essentially wiping out much of the progress that had been made over the previous decades. The Chinese population accounts for roughly 12 percent of the world's illiterate population. The increase in illiteracy was blamed on increasing numbers of poor rural children dropping out of school to find work in the cities. According to reports, as of 2007, 93.3 percent of the population over the age of 15 years is literate. In the year 2000, China's youth (age 15 to 24 years) literacy rate was 98.9 percent (99.2 percent for males and 98.5 percent for females). In March 2007, China announced the need to improve education as a national "strategic priority," and that the central budget of the national scholarships will be tripled in two years. An extra funding of 223.5 billion Yuan (28.65 billion US dollars) will be allocated from the central government in the next 5 years to improve the mandatory education in rural areas. In some of the larger cities in China before 1976, many of the Chinese people did not realize the importance of being well educated, and largely for political reasons, chose to send their kids to the army instead. Around 1976, I know of a youth in such a Chinese family who just finished junior school, and had a longing to join the army and become a soldier. His parents helped him to fulfill his wish, and in the army, he received some good training experience in the field of medicine.

After a few years, he returned to his hometown at the end of the army service. During these years, especially with the reformations and the opening of China, he began to realize that without knowledge and a degree, he cannot lead a rich and high quality life. In China and Asia, effort rather than talent and education has traditionally been seen as the key to achievement and success. An old Chinese saying goes: "If there is no dark and dogged will, there will be no shining accomplishments, if there is no dull and determined effort, there will be no brilliant achievement." With his medical training experience in the army as his foundation, he was determined to become a professional physician. He made great efforts to study fundamental medicine courses at the undergraduate level, successfully passed his exams, and eventually obtained his certificate as a professional physician. Together with his wife, he used his educational resources and set up a small hospital. Currently, he is very successful in his career, earning a fortune, buying comfortable and luxurious houses, while simultaneously many people are benefiting from his expertise, and recovering from their illnesses. As he recalled, he overcame numerous difficulties in the process of becoming a professional physician in China. It became known in China that a man, even without a good fundamental education, as long as he continued to aspire to achieve his goals and display hard work could change his personal economic status, making his idea come true, while propelling the development of the economy. There is a strong emphasis on education in China and Asia.

5.2   Economics in China's Education System

In 2007, the Chinese government announced the removal of tuition fees for primary and middle school students. In 2010, a program was announced to provide financial aid to poor rural high school students, who typically attend boarding schools away from their villages. Students that receive aid will be exempt from tuition fees. The funding would come from a number of different sources. Some of the funding would come from national sources, while some from local and province governments. The Chinese education system encourages conformity, is adult driven, and supercompetitive. Students have traditionally been expected to be diligent, silent, and obedient. For instance, in 2009, Chinese students from Shanghai achieved the best results in mathematics, science, and reading in the test of the Programme for International Student Assessment (PISA), a worldwide evaluation of 15-year-old school pupils' scholastic performance. With the development of higher and advanced education, the quality of Chinese colleges and universities is increasing considerably across the country. Among the top-ranked universities are: Peking University, Tsinghua University, Renmin University of China, Beijing Normal University, Fudan University, Shanghai Jiao Tong University, and Tongji University.

School of Economics, Peking University was established in 1985. It was formed as Department of Economics, established in 1912 by Mr. Yan Fu, after he was hired to be the president of the university. School of Economics, Peking University has one of the oldest faculties in the university and the first economics faculty among China's higher education institutions.

The academic structure of School of Economics, Peking University, synthesizes high integration of theoretical economics and the applied economics as well as the integration of the economic history and the modern economics. Not only has the school built upon and maintained their strengths in traditional fields of economics, but also, has innovatively developed and gradually advanced expertise in several new fields to adapt to the needs of China's economic development and system changes.

School of Economics, Peking University, currently has six undergraduate departments, including the Department of Economics, the Department of Finance, the Department of International Economics and Trade, the Department of Insurance and Risk Management, the Department of Public Finance, and the Department of Development Economics. The postgraduate program offers master degrees in eight majors, including Political Economics, Western Economics, Finance (International Finance, Insurance), Economic History, History of Economic Thoughts, World Economy, Public Finance, Population, Resources, and Environmental Economics. The doctoral program offers doctorates in seven majors, including Political Economics, Western Economics, Finance (International Finance, Insurance), Economic History, History of Economic Thoughts, World Economy, and Public Finance. The school also has one postdoctoral research station, which is the first of its kind ever established in China.

School of Economics, Peking University, is one of the "National Training Bases of Economics Fundamental Talents" and "National Innovative Experimental Areas of Talents Culturing Mode" assigned by the Ministry of Education. Its prominent history, renowned academic status, and innovative education mode attract the best students in China and all over the world. In 2010, School of Economics had 885 undergraduate students, 357 postgraduate and doctoral students, approximately 800 on the job postgraduate students, and about 3,500 registered students in the Continuing Education Center (including online education, advanced seminars, etc.).

School of Economics, Peking University, has a strong faculty consisting of both distinguished senior scholars and a large number of young academic leaders. In 2011, the school had 76 full time faculty members in total, including 27 professors, 35 associate professors, and 14 assistant professors. There are 81 postdoctoral research fellows in the school, as well. One-third of the faculty received their PhD overseas, and those who received a domestic PhD also have rich international academic experience through frequent visits, exchanges, and joint researches with prestigious universities and research institutes worldwide. School of Economics, Peking University, has 14 research institutes with many excellent researchers from the school and the society, which provide the institute with solid research strength. Teaching and research complement and promote each other in the School of Economics.

School of Economics, Peking University, aims at becoming one of the best economics institutions in the world. Led by its dean, Professor Sun Qixiang, the school is actively expanding its key resources and working diligently to achieve its goal through research and teaching excellence.

5.3   Chinese Education System and Economy System

As I recall from my entry into the university, it was difficult to pass the entrance examinations. Even for the very ordinary universities, there were many students who came from the countryside who were determined for the rare chance to be accepted by a university. This resulted in a very strong competition. Only very few amongst many excellent students got the opportunity to become undergraduate students. Currently, more and more Chinese people are getting richer and richer, and their value system is becoming consistent with the competitive system of the economy. Parents are urging their children to study rather than play. Many parents are highly committed to their children's education, often investing large portions of the family's income on education. Private lessons and recreational activities in foreign languages or music are popular among the middle-class families who can afford them. Based on the performance of students in top high schools and universities, Chinese students "overwhelmingly" outperformed students in both Japan and South Korea in Mathematics, Science, and English tests, even though Japan and South Korea tend to do very well in these subjects.

For the families that can afford the tuition of a higher quality education, their children will attend schools in Hong Kong, England, and the United States. The others will complete for spots in the local and national universities. The word *jiaoliu* is used to describe the stress and anxiety of everyday life, and pressure to study in China.

After such an effective investment by their parents on a valuable foreign diploma, their children usually return back to China and undertake a prosperous career. This generation is referred to as the second rich generation. However, some of the outstanding students, who originate from very poor families, are supported in Chinese universities by government and organizations, private scholarships, or student loans to receive their degrees. They, then, have to repay their education loan, which does not allow them to have as prosperous personal careers as the second rich generation.

Around 1978, a wide variety of small-scale enterprises were encouraged by the relaxed price controls and promoted foreign investment of the government to partake in these different opportunities. Foreign trade was focused upon as a major vehicle of growth, which led to the creation of Special Economic Zones (SEZs) first in Shenzhen (near Hong Kong) and then in other Chinese cities. Inefficient state-owned enterprises (SOEs) were restructured by introducing western-style management systems and the unprofitable ones were closed, which resulted in massive job losses. By the latter part of 2010, China was reversing some of its economic liberalization initiatives whereby state-owned companies were taking over independent businesses in the steel, auto, and energy industries. Due to this lack of security, the job market in China is not very optimal.

Another problem with the education system in China is that rich officers from business enterprises try to purchase their PhD degrees. An increasing number of undergraduate and PhD students are starting to do this as well. As a result, the quality of such undergraduate and PhD students is not high, which is creating problems in the labor market. The Chinese government is aware of these realities, and a series of government steps have been put in place that are meant to slow down the accelerated graduation rate of unqualified PhD and undergraduate students who have entered universities at the expense of the country.

The Chinese government also needs to deal with corruption in schools. Describing how the education system works in Foshan, a city in Guangdong province, one mother told the *Los Angeles Times* that when her son was ready for primary school she was worried about him getting in, so she found a friend who knew a senior local education official. The mother visited the official's office, left about 70 US dollars on his desk, did not say much, and left. Her son was accepted in the primary school. When it came time for her son to enter middle school she had to work harder because her son didn't do so well in his entrance exams. Friends of hers enticed key officials with wine and dine that paved the way for distributing 1,200 US dollars among education officials and making a 1,600 US dollars "donation" to the school her son wanted to be admitted to. When it was time to enter high school, she spent thousands of dollars in an attempt to get him into a first-rate school but ultimately failed and had to settle for a less prestigious school.

At the same time, the Chinese government is sending and supporting young Chinese scholars with significant scholarships to famous American universities, improving their academic studies, so that they can adapt smoothly in the everdemanding labor market.

In November 2010, output in China, surpassed Japan for the second straight quarter in the three months beginning September 2010. The Chinese economy overtook the United Kingdom as the fourth largest in 2005 and surpassed Germany at third place in 2007. In 2009, the People's Republic of China was the fourth most visited country in the world with 50.9 million inbound international visitors. It is a member of the World Trade Organization (WTO) and is the world's second-largest trading power after the United States with a total international trade of 2.21 trillion US dollars, with a breakdown of 1.20 trillion US dollars in exports and 1.01 trillion US dollars in imports. Its foreign exchange reserves have reached 2.85 trillion US dollars at the end of 2010, which is an increase of 18.7 percent from last year, making it by far the world's largest foreign exchange reserve increase over the last few years. The People's Republic of China owns an estimated 1.6 trillion US dollars of US securities while they are holding 1.16 trillion US dollars in Treasury bonds. This makes them the largest foreign holder of US public debt. China is the world's third largest recipient of inward foreign direct investment (FDI) by attracting 92.4 billion US dollars in 2008 alone. At the same time, the country itself increasingly invests abroad with a total outward FDI of 52.2 billion US dollars, which makes them the world's sixth largest outward investor. Inward FDI in 2010 was 106 billion US dollars and rose 16 percent from 2009. These new economic developments in China necessitated an expansion of the educational system to cover the costs of training Chinese students in the methods of business and finance.

China is the world's second-largest economy (IMF, 2010). The People's Republic of China's success has been primarily due to low-cost manufacturing. This is attributed to a combination of cheap labor, good infrastructure, relatively high productivity, favorable government policy, and some say, an undervalued exchange rate. The latter has been attributed to China's bulging trade surplus (262.7 billion US dollars in 2007).

In 2009, the central government approved an education fund of about 198 billion Yuan (around 21.19 billion US dollars). About 28.7 million children from poor families received financial aid for their schooling. The government plans to increase the ratio of education expenditure to gross domestic product from 3.48 percent in 2008 to 4 percent by 2012.

China's education system is plagued with problems, such as underfunding of primary and secondary schools and poor standards in higher education. In June 2010, China's leaders released the National Outline for Medium- and Long-Term Educational Reform and Development. President Hu Jintao stressed that education was the key to social development and promised to improve quality and accessibility in the coming decade. The document that highlights China's strategic goal for education before 2020 promises to reform the annual *gaokao* (entrance examination that students take to get the qualifications to enter universities and colleges in China) and force high schools, colleges, and universities to adopt more flexible enrollment policies. The plan pledges to guarantee equal access to education while improving its quality and balancing the development of compulsory education in urban and rural areas. In September 2010, Chinese President Hu Jintao, during a visit to the Renmin University of China in Beijing and its affiliated high school, called on teachers to embrace reform and innovation in teaching and enhance teaching standards. At the high school, after observing some art classes, Hu urged school authorities to respect students' individuality, tap their potentials, and help students improve their overall competence. He called on the country's teachers to learn from the model teachers, cultivate noble virtues, improve their professional standards, and make greater contributions to the scientific development of the country's educational cause.

5.4   Chinese Family in Education System

Education is seen as a family effort requiring a great deal of sacrifice, time, and money. It is not unusual for families to sell their houses and go into massive debt to send their children to university. Parents watch over their children carefully, guide, and direct them. At an early age, children are taught to memorize their textbooks. By kindergarten, they are attending a wide range of music, art, and calligraphy classes. Some of this is in line with Confucian ideas of "self-perfection" and the Maoist notion of "all-around development," with emphasis on practice, practice, and practice.

One young man who was raised only by his mother in a poor village, but managed to get into the medical school at Beijing University, told Reuters that after his father died "relatives and neighbors told me to study hard and that getting into a university is the way out." The daughter of a doctor who was brought up in a poor family told the *Los Angeles Times*, that her grandmother told her father when he was a baby, "If you don't study hard, it is worthless to have you as a son."

One of the hottest selling books in the early 2000s was *Harvard Girl*. It was written by parents who described how they prepped their little girl, beginning when she was an infant, to succeed at America's most prestigious university. The book's success inspired a dozen or so imitations: Harvard Boy, Cambridge Girl, Our Dumb Little Boy Goes to Cambridge, and Tokyo University Boy.

In many rural areas, children only attend primary school, that is if they attend school at all, and in most cases stop going after three or four years. Some rural schools do not even extend past the third grade. It is not unusual for a district with thousands of school age children to have fewer than a hundred actually in the local school, with only a handful finishing the six grades.

Textbooks are in short supply, and have been so heavily used that the paper is sometimes cracking and transparent due to age. Paper, pens, and pencils are also in short supply, and children often write on slates with broken pieces of chalk.

Many villages build their own schools, and then ask the government for a teacher. Classes are often taught in local languages, which are of little value in the major cities where most of the jobs are available and other languages predominantly spoken.

Like all parents around the world, poor villagers want their children to succeed in school, but the obstacles just to get them enrolled are enormous. Even though schools are free, the books and clothes required to attend are so expensive that they can eat up as much as a third of the villager's income.

A family that grows a cash crop may bring in 120 US dollars a year after expenses for fertilizer and pesticides while schools charge is 75 US dollars a year per student for uniforms and books. Since most families average between four and eight children, even with the father working odd jobs there is usually only enough money to send two or three children to school, at the most.

In many cases, children go to school and learn to read but fail to improve there lives. Even students that are bright and privileged to attend university, find there are no jobs waiting for them when they graduate.

When I recall how my mother and my father supported me in education, I cannot help but have tears boiling down the side of my face.

I originally had a relatively happy family before 1988. I was the only child in my family. Both, my mother and my father were professionals: a physician and an engineer, respectively, who graduated before July 1966.

Since I was a little child, my mother taught me to be an honest, upright, and decent person with credibility and trustworthiness. My father is very smart, and good in mathematics and engineering. However, in 1988, my family was completely shattered. My mother was permanently disabled in a very serious traffic accident and was forced to stay at home. Very unfortunately and very unfairly, she was mistreated and greatly harmed by people that had power and money. Under very poor conditions, my mother suffered greatly in extreme mental and body pain, until her passing away in 1997. She loved me so much that she tried her best to support me. She never delayed my study at any time, especially when

I was an undergraduate and graduate student in Peking University (PKU). She never disturbed me, even when she needed me most. Although, she did not leave any wealth for me, the lessons she taught me have had a very important effect on my success. My mother very much hoped I would be able to come to the United States, and lead the same happy life as my classmates who had left for the United States several years before me. This was her only wish before she died very tragically in 1997.

My mother also told me how to try to overcome difficulties in life. Based on the very difficult situation of my family after 1988, I had to become independent and supported myself. When I faced quite a few difficulties and huge pressures, I was taught to keep optimistic and calm, try my best to solve these difficult issues, and continue to survive. I consider my mother's suffering as a good guide for life, which has taught me how to lead a life with wisdom, courage, and confidence.

I miss my mother very much because of her great love and sacrifice. I believe that all of the pain that my mother, father, and I endured will be able to bring me a brilliant future and career.

5.5   Confucius Institute

Confucius is credited with organizing China's first educational system and setting up an efficient administration system, based on the careful selection of a bureaucracy that helped the emperor and other leaders rule. Members of the bureaucracy were trained in special schools and chosen for their jobs based on their proficiency on a civil service exam that tested their knowledge of Confucian texts. Before Confucius's time, the only schools in China were ones that taught archery. Confucius regarded government and education as inseparable. Without good education, he reasoned, it was impossible to find leaders who possess the virtues to run a government. "What has one who is not able to govern himself, to do with governing others?" Confucius asked. Under Confucianism, teachers and scholars were regarded like the elders of the communities and fathers: as unquestioned authorities. The basic principal behind Confucian education is that if you work hard, endure, and suffer as a young person you will reap rewards later in life. The strategy of Confucian education, used in China for centuries, is to memorize the moral precepts with the hopes that they will rub off and improve the character of the person who memorizes them, and will make him or her more moral. Teachers have traditionally been held in high esteem, and their power and control has been regarded as almost absolute.

Confucius Institutes (CI) are nonprofit public institutions that aim to promote Chinese language and culture, and support local Chinese teaching internationally. The headquarters is in Beijing, and is under the Office of Chinese Language Council International. Many scholars characterize the CI program as an exercise in soft power where China "sees the promotion of its culture and its chief language, standard Mandarin, as a means of expanding its economic, cultural, and diplomatic reach." Tumultuous relations between China and the

West have resulted in increasing controversy over China's relationship with the institute. The People's Republic of China has publicly supported the institution, but the universities and public school systems that incorporate the program have stressed the "total autonomy in their course materials and teachers."

The Confucius Institute is a cultural institute, but the primary focus is on the teaching of the Chinese language. Established in November 2008, the Confucius Institute at Stony Brook University (CISBU) is an educational partnership between Stony Brook University and China's Office of Chinese Language Council International, or Hanban. CISBU also maintains a partnership with its Chinese affiliate Zhongnan University of Economics and Law in Wuhan, China. The CISBU serves as a resource for Stony Brook University and the surrounding community. CISBU aims to enhance the community's understanding of Chinese language and culture. In addition, CISBU seeks to strengthen cultural exchanges and cooperation between China and the United States.

The CISBU offers the following programs to the community,

Chinese cultural performances and lectures
Chinese language classes and Chinese language library
Courses on introductory Chinese for travel and business
Training of Chinese language instructors
Preparation for the HSK examination (Chinese Proficiency Test)
Other activities related to Chinese culture.

On February 12, 2010, the CISBU held its annual Chinese New Year dinner and performance celebration in the Charles B. Wang Center. As part of the festivities, CISBU welcomed students, scholars, and the Stony Brook University (SBU) community to attend the dinner and student theater performances. The performances featured a range of traditional to modern Chinese performances, including traditional folk dances, Chinese "cross talk," and Chinese lion dance demonstrations. Liu Yandong, State Councilor, and Chairwoman of the Council of the Confucius Institute Headquarters paid an official visit to the United States, and attended the opening ceremony events held by the CISBU on April 13, 2009. After presenting 5,000 volumes of Chinese books and audiovisual materials to the institute, Madame Liu noted that language exchange is an important element of Sino-American cultural exchanges, and that it also serves as a bridge to enhance understanding and increase communications among people of different countries. Through the Confucius Institute, more and more people in the world learn about China and travel and invest in China, which helps facilitate the development of the Chinese economy.

All in all, even though there has been significant development in the interaction between Chinese education and the Chinese economy, there are still many areas in which the development remains unsatisfactory:

China spends less on education than most developing countries. Only 2.4 percent of China's GNP is spent on schools, compared to 6.7 percent in the United States and 7 percent in Taiwan. China even spends less than India. According to a survey, it is ranked 99th out of 130 counties on per capita education spending.

Free education was a hallmark of the Mao era. In the old days, people often worried about having enough money to pay school tuition. In the early 1990s, the central government began cutting off funding for rural schools.

The central government still promises free education for every child for nine years, but it provides little money to ensure that education takes place. Most funding ultimately comes from the local government. In poor rural districts in particular, schools need to charge fees or come up with money in some other way to pay for the school's expenses. Fees vary from district to district. The education system in many rural areas has virtually collapsed. Many have argued that China could better serve its people if it spent more money on education and less money on grandiose infrastructure projects such as Three Gorges Dam. In March 2007, the Chinese government announced it would increase spending on primary and secondary education by 5.02 billion US dollars over what it had spent the previous year, while also increasing funds for scholarships and doing more to help university graduates find jobs. It has also set aside more money for rural education.

We are looking forward to the better future of Chinese education and Chinese economy.

References

Chinese Education: Family, Confucianism, Marxism and Nationalism, http://factsanddetails.com/china.php.
http://www.stonybrook.edu/confucius/;

6

Mathematics Education in China

Ben Duan and Chao Zhang

B asic education plays an important part in regional development and construction. As the economy and society develop, education becomes the most fundamental and effective force for a country's production, and its significance is constantly embodied in more and more aspects. In the past decade, China has grown rapidly. It has taken great strides in economics, national defense, engineering, architecture, agriculture, and scientific research. The authors of this chapter believe that it has much to do with the Chinese government's devotion to developing basic education, and its efforts to expand investment in education and increase the overall quality of the people. In particular, its special attention to the basic education in mathematics has played a positive role in cultivating excellent talents in all walks-of-life. In China, almost every child of school age will study at least nine years of mathematics, while high school students will study 12 years. It is a matter of utmost importance. China's mathematic accomplishments cannot be achieved in many countries, even some that may be more developed. This is because mathematics is an elective course in high school in many developed countries, which means that once a student chooses not to take mathematics in high school, his/her learning of mathematics will end early, even before entering into university. In the meantime, China's constant research and practice in mathematics education, and unceasing reform and innovation in teaching methods and course contents, has also propelled its mathematics education forward. Hence, the goal of giving a detailed introduction to Chinese mathematics education in a book about China's economy will let people know that a solid basic education also brings about positive influences to a nation's economy and its other aspects.

If we can sum up the characteristics of a Chinese mathematics education in one sentence, it is "to seek students' mathematical development on a good mathematical foundation." The "mathematical foundation" here underlines the three major mathematical abilities: ability in mathematical operation, ability in space imagination, and ability in logical thinking. The "mathematical development" here refers to the ability to analyze and solve problems by using mathematical thinking and methods.

This characteristic is reflected through "two-basics teaching of mathematics" in teaching practice. "Two-basics" refer to basic knowledge and to basic skills, but "two-basics teaching" is not equal to "two basics." As a teaching thought, "two-basics teaching" is not simply to emphasize foundation; it also includes the development based on laying down a good foundation.

The modern history of mathematics education indicates, that the major reforms in mathematics education are mostly related to either "giving priority to laying a good foundation" or "giving priority to advocating innovation." For example, the United States launched "New Mathematics" movement, emphasizing innovation in the 1960s; "Returned to Foundation" in the 1970s; proposed "Problem Solving" and advocated innovative development in the 1980s; and put forward the slogan "Good Foundation for Success" in 2008. Similar cases can be seen in the history of the Chinese education.

The current mathematics education in China comprises of the following five aspects: "import of new knowledge," "teacher-student interaction and trial teaching," "variant teaching," "repeated exercise," and "refining of mathematical thinking." Below we will briefly introduce these five features, separately.

6.1   Import of New Knowledge

Mathematics teachers in China often use "old knowledge" to export "new knowledge." "Importing a new lesson" is often the part most meticulously designed by mathematics teachers. At present, "situational teaching" which is associated with a students' daily life is advocated. It is a form of "Import." However, only a few "situations" that are associated with students' daily life can be established in mathematics classes. Most of the mathematics classes, particularly systematic mathematics content about the operation rules of numbers and types, often don't have available situations. However, we may still try other ways to import them. Chinese mathematics classes have many unique import methods. In addition to "situational teaching," there are also "creating suspense," "giving a story," "reviewing old," "explaining exercises," "comparing and analyzing," and some other means of comparison. These import methods are all heuristic methods commonly used by teachers during teaching and may be used comprehensively.

In fact, direct import is a teaching method that has been most widely adopted by Chinese primary and secondary schools. The classroom teaching of mathematics in China advocates concise language. The themes of classes are clear, and the efficiency of classroom learning is high. The students in many areas in China accept this time-saving and concise teaching method, so the direct import method is often used as the main means of import. Particularly before the 1990s, it was rather popular. With the changing times, teachers gradually realized some problems in direct import teaching. For instance, due to the increase of information sources, the students are no longer able to concentrate on knowledge per se. Instead, they are distracted by the irrelevant information and can hardly focus their attention. In addition, the method of direct import is most likely too serious and can hardly arouse the students' interest. For this reason, it has been on the decline since the beginning of the 1990s. Nevertheless, this method still has a very good effect in some sections of senior high school that face large difficulty and have high density. For example, in a class teaching coordinates, the teacher writes out the definition and features of coordinates as well as the depth of knowledge and application the students should know, and then unfolds the course on this basis. Learning coordinates is a new concept in junior high school, so the teacher may often choose to adopt the method of direct import.

Import of life examples often appear as an auxiliary import in Chinese teaching. When multiple concepts are involved in a class, the teacher will import them by citing one or two circumstances in life. For example, in the teaching of junior high school geometry, if the features of a parallelogram are involved when the teacher explains the properties of a few types of quadrangles, usually they may be imported by citing the link structure of a truck trailer or the movable parallelogram structure of an automatic sliding door. These are objects that all students can associate with. These examples have been adopted for a long time. The above examples have been used in Chinese mathematics textbooks for at least ten years. Despite the availability of mathematical software and electronic courseware, it is still in the teacher's best interest to employ tangible examples. Another example of this form of teaching is with the lessons of teaching Mathematical Induction. Many students don't understand why a proposition relating to natural numbers is correct. After proving mathematical induction, the teacher may talk about a game before the beginning of a new lesson: Play "Dominoes." Playing this game should follow two rules: (1) The rule for arranging dominoes: When one domino falls, next domino must fall, too; (2) Hit down the first domino. After the teacher describes these two rules, the students are asked, "After these two steps are done, what will happen?" The students answer quickly, "All dominoes will fall." From this game, the definition of mathematical induction is deduced.

The method of import of life examples was gradually accepted by more people after the 1990s. On the one hand, people found this import method could more easily attract students' attention in the beginning, while it is very helpful to students' understanding and memorization. On the other hand, it also has some problems. For example, the students will stop at the surface of the examples and won't necessarily think any further into their studies.

The method of import of old knowledge is universally adopted in China because it has been a good supplement to the direct import method. In the teaching of secondary school mathematics in China, sometimes the lessons and information are discontinuous. For example, the concept of logarithms is taught in senior high school, but it has never been mentioned in the previous mathematics lessons, and is a difficult concept to grasp. This theory is in line with a students', often, inability to comprehend it. Therefore, before teaching logarithms, the teacher usually will spend time teaching the exponential function, and then compare the features of the exponential function with the features of the logarithmic function in order that the students will understand logarithms. Similarly, during teaching of "factorization" in a junior high school, the teacher may ask the students to do an exercise about "multiplication of polynomials." After the students get another polynomial through calculation, the teacher may say, "If we know this polynomial, how will we change it into the multiplication of two or more integral expressions? This is the issue we are going to study today—factorization of polynomial." Therefore, we may see the method of import of old knowledge often appears in the chapters and sections that are difficult and related to the content learnt before. However, it is not always easy to find the links between new knowledge and old knowledge. For this reason, some teachers in China are not used to this teaching import method, and adopt direct import method in most cases.

Practicing the import method has been tried as a new import method in China for a long time, and is applied in solid geometry in senior high school. In China, the famous teachers of some prestigious schools provide "demo classes," also known as open classes. In such classes, the teachers usually are not satisfied with ordinary direct import method or old knowledge import method. They adopt some innovations and new approaches, including the application of practice import method. In senior high school, when the concept of two perpendicular planes is taught, some students may make mistakes due to poor space imagination. Therefore, when the teachers explain concepts and methods, they will use some Do It Yourself (DIY) teaching aids. For example, to make simple stereoscopic models with cardboards and triangles, to visualize abstract images. However, as lecturing takes up a large portion of class time in China, practice import method is not often used. Another example is the introduction of the concept of a circle in junior high schools. Some teachers may give up on ordinary compasses, and adopt a makeshift compass made of a rope to let the student understand the features of a circle.

Suspense import method has been widely applied in China in the recent years. As the educational concepts of mathematics and even all natural sciences are changing gradually, and the transfer from spoon-feeding education to autonomous education is advocated, suspense import method becomes a typical method of autonomous education. In suspense import method, the teacher inspires students to think from the very beginning through designing some simple questions and situations. If necessary, the teacher may express the scenario in the form of a story. For example, when a teacher explains the relation between perimeter and area, an example will be given: Three people make a water pipe with an iron sheet of same size. The teacher for example may ask what shape of the cross section of the pipe can get the most water resource. Similarly, during study of "measuring distance by using similar triangles," it may be imported in this way: "how do you measure the width of a river without crossing it?" Nowadays, suspense import method is universal. It is also considered a typical manifestation of an interactive classroom.

Other import methods are being developed gradually in recent years. Multimedia import methods emerged in the 2000s in China. The changes in teaching infrastructure in some developed areas in China enabled the application of video and audio multimedia in classrooms. Multimedia gets more involved in the import link. After a simple investigation, we discovered that multimedia import method has a very good effect in attracting students' attention and stimulating students' interest. Meanwhile, the reactions of some students and teachers also aroused our attention. Some students that are attracted by multimedia pay so much attention to the surface of the multimedia that they are unable to enter the next stage in proper studies. In addition to the multimedia import method, some teachers have also tried game import, body import, and other more interactive import methods. For example, when teaching permutations and combinations in senior high schools, teachers may give some examples in form of games. In addition, when teaching higher-order functions, some teachers find it helpful to import the study with dance movements.

6.2   Teacher-Student Interaction and Trial Teaching

The number of students in an ordinary class in China is large. There are usually about forty students, and sometimes, even between sixty and eighty. In such large classes, the teacher-student interaction by method of "inquisition by group," "reporting by representatives," "mutual discussion," or "teacher summary" will be very difficult because it is difficult for a teacher to give general guidance to every individual student. Therefore, most mathematics teachers take "question design," "student narration," "teacher guidance," "class discussion," "writing on the blackboard," "rigorous expression," and other measures to realize the complete process of exchange between the teacher and students; a harmonious connection and formation of consensus.

When the teacher puts forth a mathematical question, a student will be asked to stand up and answer it. The student will either narrate the process in verbal mathematical language, or obtain the calculative results by method of mental arithmetic. If the answer is not complete, other students may make supplements or corrections. In the end, the teacher will refine the students' verbal expression into rigorous written mathematical language, and write it on the blackboard. In this case, by means of "loud speaking" between student and student, and between student and teacher, the thinking process of teaching is exposed, and mental arithmetic is practiced. The students correct each other during this discussion, and the teacher gives guidance and makes a summary, and in the end writes on the blackboard. This is a harmonious connection of mathematical language. The efficiency is high, the interaction between the teacher and the students is fast, and the students' ability in mathematical expression is tempered.

The optimal method of exchange and interaction in large classes has been constantly explored in the education of mathematics in Chinese primary and secondary schools. For a class of forty to sixty students, all-around interaction may mobilize the learning enthusiasm of the whole class. In China, there are many methods for interaction and exchange in large classes. Some of the methods have been used for decades and some have been adopted only in the last couple of years.

6.2.1   Q&A Dialogue Method Realizes Classroom Exchange

This interaction method originates from the "Socratic Method." As the number of students in a class is large, Chinese mathematics teachers usually adopt some special methods for question and answer (Q&A) exchange. In Chinese classrooms, a line is a natural unit and a line has six to ten students. Teachers are fond of using this natural unit. Usually, the teacher prepares a group of questions in advance, asks the students in a specific line to answer them, and then interact with the other members of the line. This method has two advantages. First, in China, primary school students and junior high school students show huge differences in their expectations of classroom interaction. When the student is in primary school, they take an active part in interaction, while in junior high school, the students' enthusiasm for interactive participation declines dramatically. This may have to do with the division of six-year primary school and three-year junior high school in China. Therefore, in order to realize interaction in a mathematics class in a junior high school, the teacher gives up individual interaction and adopts the interaction of "lines." This may effectively alleviate students' resistance and nervousness. Second, in large classrooms in Chinese primary and junior high schools, the enthusiasm for interaction usually has a vertical gradient. That is to say, the students in the front rows of the classroom readily join the interaction, while the students in the rear rows of the classroom instinctively resist the interaction. The interaction with the "line" as a unit offsets this gradient effect. In some mathematics chapters and sections, knowledge points exist in a parallel structure. In this case, they may form a group of questions, and facilitate the Q&A dialogue interaction of the "line" as a unit. For example, a group of discriminant theorems for congruent triangles and similar triangles in the geometry teaching of junior high school are very suitable to be arranged into a group of questions for interaction. Of course, this Q&A dialogue interaction with the "line" as a unit has been adopted in large Chinese classrooms for decades. Some teachers have also tried other units. This method indeed may activate classroom atmosphere to some extent.

6.2.2   Exercise-Based Interaction

In China, mathematics teachers pay much attention to solid basic skills. Particularly, in the 1950s–1990s, the consensus of teachers was that doing exercises, digesting, and understanding knowledge content in class, was the best method. Therefore, in the chapters and sections with fewer general knowledge points or with difficult content, in-class exercises are essential. These in-class exercises also contribute to an in-class discussion, and are conducive to interactive learning patterns. This interaction between the whole class helps generate a uniform learning atmosphere. There are many methods for exercise-based interaction in a classroom. For example, in the years between 1950 and 2000, the teachers in most parts of China mainly taught via the use of the blackboard, and therefore, in-class exercises also adopted the blackboard method. To sum up, the teachers set questions, the students come to the blackboard, and answered the questions on the spot. The teacher then gave guidance, and passed judgment. In this exercise, one student faces all of his peers in the classroom, so inevitably the student may feel nervous. In this case, the teacher plays a very important role. This method has been declining in the recent years, mainly because electronic courseware is replacing the blackboard and entering the mathematics classes of primary schools and junior high schools. Another way of interaction based on in-class exercises, is by employing a quiz. The "quiz" takes 5–10 min. in general, but the result of the quiz should have no influence on the students. In the chapters and sections that need to be mastered, such as: factorization, and solution of simultaneous equations of higher degree, the teacher will put aside 5–10 min. of each class to ask the students to do a unified small-scale exercise, and give a unified explanation. In addition, exercise-based interaction is very common in a review lesson and a sum-up lesson after a test, but it mostly adopts the model of "one question," "unified solving by students," and "unified explanation."

6.2.3   Situational Interaction

China has been pushing classroom reform in recent years. Much effort has been made in exploring mathematics-teaching methods, including many attempts to master the different interaction methods. Situational interaction is a classic interaction model and mostly used in the teaching of Chinese, English, and other subjects of literature and history. In the recent years, situational interaction has been utilized in the classroom teaching of mathematics. In a primary school class, the teacher may set an imagined scenario and incorporate some knowledge or exercises into it. For example, using four arithmetic operations in an example of someone shopping, or by using fractions and decimals to divide articles. In the classes of secondary schools, due to age and psychological features, situational interaction is not often employed.

6.2.4   Cooperation and Exchange-Based Interaction

In a large classroom, how to fully mobilize every student's enthusiasm for learning is one of the most important issues. That is why activities with natural "line" as a unit are often seen in Chinese mathematics classes. In addition to the abovementioned Q&A dialogue interaction with natural "line" as a unit, discussion, reporting, and other classroom interactive activities with a "line" as a unit are also adopted. For example, in a mathematics class, the teacher will set some difficult questions, and organize a discussion by group. Every group member may participate in the discussion, give a solution to a question, and exchange ideas with the teacher in form of report, or simply exchange ideas with other classmates. Of course, such cooperation and exchange-based interaction by a group cannot mobilize the learning enthusiasm of every individual, so the teacher needs to design a more detailed scheme to solve this problem.

The basic idea of the trial teaching theory is "the students may have a try, the try can lead to success and the success can lead to innovation." Its characteristic is "try before guidance, and exercise before explanation." In the long-term teaching practice, trial teaching has established a teaching model system adaptable to various teaching needs, including basic models, flexible models, and integrated models. In light of the essence of the trial teaching theory and the basic characteristic of "try before guidance, and exercise before explanation," a set of basic operating models have been gradually formed in teaching practices. The teaching procedure comprises seven steps:

The first step is to do preparatory exercises. This step is a preparatory stage for students' trial activity. The teacher asks the students to do preparatory exercises on the basic knowledge needed for solving the questions employed. The teacher then leads the trial questions from the preparatory questions by method of "leading out the new from the old," gives play to the migration effect of old knowledge, and paves a road for students' solution of the trial questions.

The second step is to put forth trial questions. In this step, the teacher sets questions, puts forth the tasks of students' trial activity, and leads the students into the situations of the questions. After the trial questions are put forth, the teacher must stimulate students' interest, and try to activate students' thinking. The teacher may ask the students to think about the questions, and discuss the solutions with each other.

The third step is self-study with the textbook. This step is to provide information to students when they solve questions by themselves in the trial activity. After the trial questions are put forth, the students become curious, and thereby, have the desire to solve them. By now, guiding the students to study the textbook by themselves becomes the immediate goal. Before self-study of the textbook, sometimes the teacher may set some reflective questions as guidance. During the self-study, if the students encounter difficulties, they may seek help from the teacher. The classmates may discuss the question with each other. Through self-study of the textbook, most students have found methods to solve trial questions. Now, it is time to go to the next step.

The fourth step is trial exercise. Trial exercise may have various forms according to disciplinary features. The teacher should be aware of success or failure of the students' trial exercise, and give individual counseling to the students with difficulty in learning. In case the students are faced with difficulties during their assignment, they may read the textbooks or seek help from their classmates.

The fifth step is student discussion. Different answers will appear during trial exercise. The students may have doubts. Now, the teacher must guide the students to have a discussion with each other. They may argue over different views. In this process, the students begin to try to be reasonable, and accepting of other possible methods of answering the trial-exercise question. After that, the students need to know whether their trial-exercise results are correct or not, and the teacher's explanation becomes the students' urgent need.

The sixth step is teacher explanation. This step is for ensuring the students systematically understand the knowledge. Some students may do trial questions, but they probably mechanically copy the examples, and don't really understand the reason. Therefore, the teacher's explanation is needed. The explanation doesn't start from the very beginning. The teacher needs only to emphatically explain the points the students find difficult, and the key points of the textbook.

The seventh step is the second trial exercise. This step offers students a chance to "shoot one more arrow."

In the first exercise, while some students may have been wrong and some students may have been correct, but they still may not have fully comprehended the exact formula of the question. After student discussion and teacher explanation, they receive feedback and do corrections. They do the second trial exercise and receive information feedback again. This step is particularly helpful to the students with difficulty in studies. The questions in the second trial exercise are different from those in the first exercise, or, at the very least, have slight changes. This change shows the application of the formula in different variances. Later, the teacher may give supplementary explanations and questions.

The above seven steps form an integral body and reflect a complete process of the students learning process. They also form an orderly and controllable teaching system. The five steps in the middle are the theme. The first step is a preparatory stage. The seventh step is an extension stage. As the teaching in reality is complex and changeable, some variants may be derived from this basic model. They are called flexible models, such as swap model, which swaps the steps in the basic model; addition model, which adds one or more steps based on the basic model. For example, you can add a student discussion after the trial questions are put forth. There is also the combination model, which means that after the students are familiar with the trial teaching, the seven steps in the basic model may not be so clear, and may be combined organically. The advance model is when the teacher may advance the first few steps in the basic model to a preclass preview, as the teaching time is limited.

During mathematics teaching, letting students "have a try" is in line with the reality of basic education. The students put forth their ideas, which may be correct or incorrect. They may be successful or unsuccessful; or may finish the question or stop halfway through. When a student is attempting a sample question, it is not necessary that the performing students discover the result themselves, but either way, they should have their own opinions, and should feel comfortable asking questions. In this way, when the teacher teaches a lesson, the students will compare the teachings with their correct or incorrect "tries." Through teacher-student interaction, they finally know the true essence of knowledge. It is an effective and operable autonomous learning method.

Below, we set a few examples to discuss the application of trial teaching in junior high school mathematics.

For example, when a teacher explains the solution set of an inequality, the students will be required to know the significance of inequalities and understand the solutions. They also need to understand the solution set of inequalities and the meaning of the concept of solving inequalities based on the size relationship of specific things. The students should be able to express the solution set of an inequality on a number axis. The content in this part may cultivate students' ability to understand and enable the students to know the relationship between the solution set of an inequality and the points on a number axis as well as to understand the exploratory nature of mathematical activities. Through self-study, the students may understand most of the content despite the combination of letters and numbers being confusing. The teacher would do well to show an example before the students begin, similar to the one below.

a. When $x = -1$, 0, 3.5, 5, or -3.2, does Inequality $x - 3 > 0$ hold?
b. Does the inequality have only one solution?
c. What are the concepts of the solution and the solution set of inequality?
d. What is the definition of solving inequalities?
e. What tools may we seek for assistance in expressing the solution set of an inequality?
f. When the solution set of an inequality is expressed on a number axis, what is the difference between a hollow circle and a solid point?

With these questions, the students will find a direction for their trial study, and their studying will become more efficient. During the study session, the teacher makes class rounds. If the teacher finds problems, the students will express their views at first, and then the teacher will make a summarization.

For another example, when a teacher teaches conditions of triangle similitude, the lesson may be designed in the following way:

The teacher may ask a few questions, as given below, to the students, and let them think about the questions during their attempt to solve them.

a. Use a piece of dark paper to partially cover two triangles (as shown in figure 6.1). Are the two triangles sole and determined? Why?
b. Measure $\angle A$, $\angle B$, $\angle C$, and $\angle D$. What have you discovered?
c. Remove the dark paper to expose the two triangles (as shown in figure 6.2). Try to know the relationship between the two triangles through measurement.

d. Change the length of segments AB and CD while keeping ∠A, ∠B, ∠C, and ∠D unchanged (as shown in figure 6.3). Measure and check the relationship between △ABE and △CDF.
e. What conclusion have you got?

Through this practice session, accompanied with the questions, the students not only can know related judgment methods, but also can more intensively understand the formation process of the conclusion through their own exploration. Compared with traditional lecture-style teachings, it can mobilize more enthusiasm of the students, and deepen their understanding of the topic.

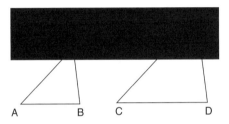

Figure 6.1   Partially covered pair of triangles.

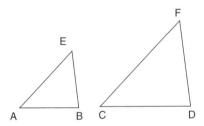

Figure 6.2   Uncovered pair of triangles in figure 6.1.

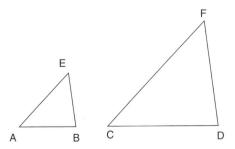

Figure 6.3   Changed lengths of segments AB and CD.

6.3   Variant Teaching

Variant teaching is adopted for all subjects in China. Its application is more popular in mathematics teaching, particularly during question's solving. It is an important feature of the Chinese mathematics education. Variant means the teacher reasonably varies a proposition in a purposeful and planned way—that is, the teacher may continuously change the nonessential features of the proposition. For example, change the conditions or conclusion of the question or vary the content and form of the question, but the essential features of the subject are not changed.

Let's see some concrete examples, in order to comprehend the method of variant teaching.

1. Change the conditions or conclusion, that is, the conditions or conclusion of the original question are changed or deepened, but the knowledge used doesn't deviate from the range of the original question.

   During the teaching of monotony of a function, the teacher may give such an example: Judge the monotony of a function in a specified interval.

   $y = x^2$, $x \in (0, +\infty)$.

   Variant 1: The teacher may ask the students to do the following question:

   $y = x^2$, $x \in (-\infty, 0)$.

   Variant 2: The teacher may remove all conditions, and ask the students the monotony of the function as in the case below:

   $y = x^2$.

   After careful consideration, the students may conclude that the function is not monotonic.

2. Generalize the conditions: That is, change the special conditions of the original question into general conditions to make the question more general. It is a method often considered during design of variant questions.

   An example of question variant design is as follows: It is known that the equation of a parabola is as given below. Please find the point M (x, y) on the curve, which is shortest to the origin.

   $y^2 = 4x$.

   Variant 1: It is known that the equation of a parabola is as given below. Please find the point M (x, y) on the curve, which is shortest to point A (a, 0).

   $y^2 = 4x$.

Variant 2: It is known that the equation of a parabola is as given below. Please find the point M (x, y) on the curve, which is shortest to the origin.

$$y^2 = 2px.$$

These variants change special conditions into more general conditions, and tally with the law of cognition from particularity to generality, so students can easily accept them.

3. Combine the practice: Combining the practice is to combine mathematical problems with the common problems in daily life. It requires the teachers to have rich life experience, and the knack for mathematical application. During teaching, the teachers should design scenarios to arouse or steer students' imagination, and let the students know mathematics is closely related to life, and many mathematical problems can be found in life's lessons. The variant teaching that combines the practice may enhance students' consciousness in the application of mathematics and their interest in learning mathematics.

For example, the teacher may ask the question: Please find the standard equation of the parabola, when it is known that a focus of a parabola is F (0, 8) and its directrix equation is,

$$y = 8.$$

It is a pure mathematical question. This question may be varied into: A bridge opening is in a shape of a parabolic arch. When the water surface is 4m wide, the bridge opening is 2m high, then after the water surface falls by 1m, how wide will the water surface be? Such variant exercise that combines the practice with mathematics can arouse students' interest in learning mathematics, thus fulfilling the purpose of teaching in a more productive way.

Variant teaching enables teachers to purposefully and consciously guide students to find "invariable" essence from "variable" phenomena, explore the law of "variation" from the "invariable" essence, and may help students thoroughly understand the knowledge points. Thus, they will be able to feel the fun of mathematics from the endless changes, and lay a good foundation for their effective study and application of mathematics.

Variant teaching plays an extremely important role in mathematics classroom teaching in the following ways:

6.3.1   *Apply Variant Teaching to Ensure Students' Consistent Enthusiasm for Participating in Teaching Activities*

To a large extent, the effectiveness of classroom teaching relies on the degree of a students' participation. This requires the students to have a sense of participation.

To enhance a students' sense of participation in classroom teaching, and make the students the real masters, classroom teaching is becoming a more popular method of modern mathematics teaching. Variant teaching is a teaching design method in which the theorems and propositions are varied from different perspectives, levels, circumstances, and backgrounds during teaching, to expose the essence of the problems, and reveal the inner links of different knowledge points. Variant teaching realizes multiple uses of one question and recombination of multiple questions, often gives people a novel feeling, and arouses students' curiosity and desire for knowledge. It can generate the motivation for active participation, and maintain the students' interest and enthusiasm for participating in teaching activities.

6.3.2   Apply Variant Teaching to Cultivate the Extensity of Students' Thinking

The extensity of thinking is another characteristic of divergent thinking. Understanding only part of the story and being puzzled by even slight changes, reflects the narrowness of thinking. Repeated exercise of one question with multiple changes is an effective method to help students to overcome narrow thinking. Discussion may be conducted to enlighten students' thinking and broaden their train of thought in solving questions. On this basis, repeated exercises may both increase students' knowledge and cultivate their thinking ability. During teaching, teachers shouldn't pay attention to calculation results only, and should carefully design the exercises at different levels, with clear requirements, and in variances, according to teaching emphases and difficulties. Through the exercises, the students should be able to continuously explore the shortcuts to questions and broaden their thinking. Through multiple progressive outward training, students are brought into a realm of broad thinking. In the current textbooks, "Think" in some examples turns examples into variant exercises. We may make use of them to effectively cultivate the extensity of students' thinking.

6.3.3   Apply Variant Teaching to Cultivate the Depth of Students' Thinking

Variant teaching refers to changing the conditions, conclusions, and forms of questions to make the essence more comprehensive. Variant teaching makes students less infatuated with the appearance of things, and enables them to consciously look at the root of the issue. Meanwhile, it also makes the students look at issues in an all-around way, and pay attention to understanding the essence of the question from the relation and contradictions between the two aspects. To some extent, it may overcome or alleviate thinking rigidly and inertia resulting from absolutization of thinking.

For example, during study of the relations between the projection of the vertex of a triangular pyramid (i.e., tetrahedron) and the "five centers" of the triangle base, the following variances may be established:

a. when the triangular pyramid is a regular triangular pyramid;
b. when the three lateral edges have an equal length;
c. when the angles between the lateral edges and the base are equal;
d. when the dihedral angles between the sides and the base are equal and the projection of the vertex is inside the triangle base;
e. when the distances from the vertex to the three sides of the base are equal;
f. when the three lateral edges are perpendicular to each other;
g. when the three lateral edges are perpendicular to their opposite sides, respectively;
h. when the three lateral edges have equal projection area on the base; and
i. when the dihedral angles between the sides and the base are equal and the projection of the vertex is outside the triangle base.

Through continuously changing the conditions of the proposition, the teacher extends and deepens the proposition, and creates many similar, yet different questions, and arouses the students' dense interest in finding fun from the challenge. It also deepens their thinking and further consolidates their knowledge on the vertical relations between a line and a line, and between a line and a plane, and in particular three perpendicular line theorems.

6.3.4 Apply Variant Teaching to Cultivate the Creativity of Thinking

Famous mathematics educator George Polya (1971) vividly pointed out that good questions are like mushrooms. They all grow in heaps. He said, "Look around when you have got your first mushroom or made your first discovery: they grow in clusters."

The success of innovation directly relies on the degree of hard work. In mathematics teaching, when we proceed from a basic issue and apply the thinking methods of analogy, association, specialization, and generalization to explore the development and changes of the issue, we may discover the essence of the issue. Teachers should combine typical examples, design stepped questions, and guide students to deepen their thinking.

Mathematics classroom teaching should introduce students' autonomous learning and subjects' intelligent involvement, as well as multidirectional and multilayered interaction in the teaching process. Only in this way, can the teaching structure have qualitative changes, and can the students become the masters of the class. Variant exercise helps students dynamically handle real problems, overcome thinking and mental block, and realize the goal of innovation.

6.4   Repeated Exercise

6.4.1   *One Question with Multiple Solutions and*
One Question with Multiple Variances

In mathematics teaching, teachers should guide students to think about multiple solutions to a question and extend the question from point to line; and guide students to think about multiple changes to a question and extend the question from line to plane. In this way, the students may understand mathematical issues from multiple layers, a broad perspective, and all directions.

One question with multiple solutions can enlighten and guide students to solve the same mathematical question from different perspectives and approaches, by employing different methods and through different operating processes. This is one of the cutting-edge approaches to problem solving. In the stage of primary school, the strategies usually include enumeration method, pattern recognition, question conversion, midway points, retreating for advancement, special to general, treating the question as a whole, and approaching from the reverse angle if a normal approach is difficult. One question with multiple solutions is the integration of many question-solving strategies. In the stages of junior high school and senior high school, this application is more extensive. In teaching, actively and appropriately doing exercises of one question with multiple solutions, and guiding students to explain their train of thought in solving questions, helps fully mobilize their enthusiasm for thinking and to improve their skills and techniques to solve mathematical problems. It not only improves students' thinking ability but also deepens their systematic understanding of the knowledge.

For example, there are at least three methods to prove the sum of the interior angles of a triangle is 180°; and applied questions may be solved directly or through setting unknown variables and writing out an equation or simultaneous equations.

One question with multiple variances can reflect certain law and associations of knowledge and help broaden students' trains of thought in thinking over questions. A series of same, approximate, or similar questions are used to cultivate students' observation competence, and make them know the exploration law of mathematics from simple to complex and from special to general. This approach not only may enlighten students to think over issues from shallow to deep but also can significantly temper their ability to reason and deduce.

For example, as shown in the diagram, it is known that AB and CD are two parallel wooden battens nailed on a wooden board. A rubber band is fixed at points A and C (figure 6.4) and point E is a point on the rubber band. Please explore the relations of $\angle$A, $\angle$C, and $\angle$AEC.

This question is too simple. All students, good or poor, can answer.

$\angle AEC = \angle A + \angle C = 180°$.

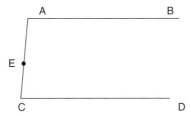

Figure 6.4   Two parallel wooden battens AB and CD connected by a rubber band AC.

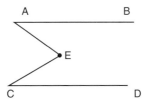

Figure 6.5   Pulling the rubber band in figure 6.4 from point E.

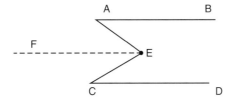

Figure 6.6   Drawing a line EF parallel to AB and CD in figure 6.5.

Now the teacher pulls the rubber band tightly from point E (as shown in figure 6.5) and then asks the students to find the relations between $\angle A$, $\angle C$, and $\angle AEC$.

With this, the students' interest is aroused. They set their wits to work, draw an auxiliary line (figure 6.6), and apply the knowledge of parallel lines to get,

$$\angle AEC = \angle A + \angle C.$$

Now the teacher may ask the students where point E may rest, as well as what the corresponding conclusion is, and whether they can draw a diagram and give the answer. The teacher encourages the students to think of as many circumstances as possible. Discussion in a group may also be conducted.

The students quickly carry out discussion in a group. Later on, the teacher asks the students from different groups to show their results on the rostrum. Five more circumstances are obtained (as shown in figure 6.7):

This setting not only increases the extensity of students' participation but also stimulates their interest in study, boosts their confidence, and cultivates their spirit.

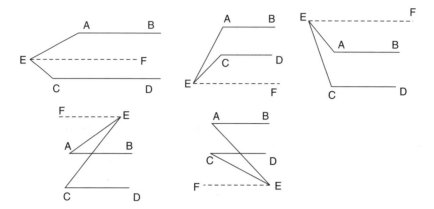

Figure 6.7   Pulling the rubber band in figure 6.6 from point E to five different positions.

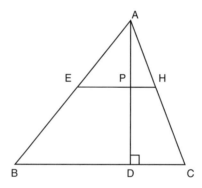

Figure 6.8   Triangle ABC with EH parallel to BC and AD vertical to BC.

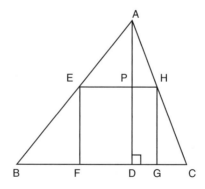

Figure 6.9   Triangle ABC with its inscribed square EFGH.

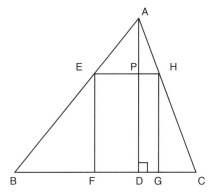

Figure 6.10   Triangle ABC with its inscribed rectangle EFGH.

Example 5: As shown in figure 6.8, it is known that in △ABC, EF // BC, and EF meets AB and AC at points E and F, respectively. Also, AD ⊥ BC, AD meets EH and BC at points P and D, respectively, EH = 50 cm, BC = 120 cm, and AD = 80 cm. Please calculate the length of PD.

> Variant 1: As shown in figure 6.9, it is known that in △ABC, AD is the height on side BC, the quadrangle EFGH is its inscribed square, BC = 120 cm, and AD = 80 cm. Please calculate the area of the square EFGH.
>
> Variant 2: As shown in figure 6.10, it is known that in △ABC, AD is the height on side BC, the quadrangle EFGH is its inscribed rectangle, BC = 120 cm, AD = 80 cm, and EH/HG = 2/3. Please calculate the area of the rectangle EFGH.
>
> Variant 3: It is known that in △ABC, AD is the height on side BC, the quadrangle EFGH is its inscribed rectangle, the ratio of its two adjacent sides is 2 : 3, BC = 120 cm, and AD = 80 cm. Please calculate the area of the rectangle EFGH.

In the above questions, the first question is a traditional question, and the length of PD may be calculated according to the theory that the ratio between the heights on corresponding sides of a similar triangle is equal to the ratio of similitude. In Variant 1, one condition is deleted, but the condition that the sides of a square are equal is hidden, so this question is not difficult, either. In Variant 2, the square is changed into rectangle, but the ratio between two adjacent sides is given, so the area can be calculated by using the principle of similitude. Variant 3 seems identical to Variant 2, but after carefully analyzing the question, you will find it doesn't have a diagram. In this case, two circumstances should be considered about the ratio between two adjacent sides. See figure 6.11.

Through this progressively designed group of questions, students can easily solve these problems. Moreover, the solution of the previous question may

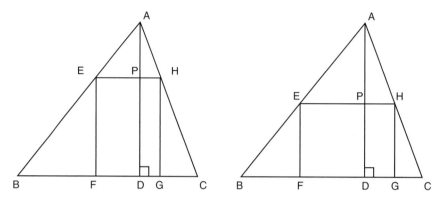

Figure 6.11   Triangle ABC with two versions of an inscribed rectangle EFGH.

provide a train of thought for the solution of the next question. The teacher may give a free hand to the students. When the students solve these questions from easy to difficult, they find the fun of autonomous learning. Even in Variant 3, the students can still comprehend the minute differences from Variant 2. The students find the difficulties, solve them by themselves, and achieve success.

6.4.2   Practice Makes Perfect

Practice makes perfect. It constitutes a part of Chinese cultural tradition, and is also one of the important concepts in Chinese mathematics education. Repeated exercise enables the students to get more perceptual knowledge and experience, and help them further establish their concepts understood by themselves.

Concretely speaking, "practice makes perfect" has the following connotation in education:

1. *Memory leads to understanding.* Understanding is the integration of memory. Without memory, there would be no understanding. Take mathematics teaching for example. The memory and recitation of the multiplication table makes it an arithmetic intuition. Recitation of the multiplication table is one of the advantages of Chinese mathematics teaching.
2. *Speed gets efficiency.* Some educational theories believe that it is fine to take a long time as long as you can eventually solve the mathematical questions. There is no need to stress on speed. The problem with this outlook is that, without necessary speed and sharp thinking, no innovation would be realized. For example, the teaching of mental arithmetic of integers, decimals, and fractions in China stresses the need for speed. We can't rely on a calculator all the time. The secondary school students show advantage in factorization, square completion, and algebraic deformations.

The establishment of these foundations may guarantee the students concentrate their attention on the advanced thinking over "the solution of questions."

3. *Rigor forms reason.* Some theories for mathematics education rely on students' daily life experience. The mathematics learning in China pays attention to the ability of reasoning. According to Chinese tradition, Chinese people fear no abstraction, and easily handle the stress of "rigorous learning." Therefore, generally speaking, Chinese students don't refuse "abstract definitions of concepts and rigorous logical expressions." Chinese students can learn Western "deductive geometry" because they have the cultural foundation.

4. *Repetition relies on variation.* Some people think the learning in China is only "repeated" exercises, and has no value. In fact, certain repetition is necessary. As mentioned above, the mathematics teaching in China pays attention to "variant exercises," finds repetition from changes, and obtains changes from repetition. Chinese research adopts many methods, such as, concept variant, process variant, and question variant. They are all important parts of mathematics teaching.

The educational concept of "practice makes perfect" has been adopted in China for a long time. For decades, proficiency and speed have dominated the mathematics education. For example, primary school students must possess certain ability in quick calculations, and recite mathematical tables. They are even required to conduct quick calculations with an abacus according to Chinese ancient abacus formulae. In the past twenty years, Chinese mathematics education is lowering the requirement on this skill. For example, the primary school students before the 1990s might have had to recite Chinese traditional multiplication table in three ways, but in the past 20 years, only two ways have been required. For another example, before the 1980s, the secondary school students were obligated to master the written extraction of a square root, but in the past 20 years, this requirement has gradually disappeared. In addition, the abacus exercise with Chinese traditional abacus formulae is no longer a compulsory subject.

However, in the mathematics education of secondary school, "practice makes perfect" is still a core concept. As mathematics examinations are difficult and the pressure from entry into a higher school is heavy in China, proficiency at mathematical skills is the key to achieving a good academic result. For example, in the mathematics education in junior high school, the proficiency at factorization and the firm memory and skillful application of Vieta's Theorem for linear equations in two unknowns are necessary skills for any student. In senior high school, some teachers may require students to learn by heart some "results of intermediate processes" to accelerate students' solution of questions. For example, Cauchy's inequality as well as some deductions met during question solving. Once the students memorize these deductions, they may greatly shorten the time of question solving.

6.4.3 Draw Inferences about Other Cases from One Instance

In mathematics teaching, drawing inferences about other cases from one instance is a technique often adopted by teachers in the chapters and sections that should be mastered. An example of this is taking "mutual conversion of fractions and decimals"—knowledge point of Chinese primary school mathematics. Chinese mathematics teachers may design the lesson in the following way:

> Step 1: Guide the students to do an exercise: How to convert 1/10, 13/100, and 19/1000 into decimals. Ask them to sum up the methods.
> Step 2: Convert 1/5, 2/5, 3/5, and 4/5 into fractions of which denominator is 10 according to the basic properties of fractions. Then convert them into decimals.
> Step 3: Convert 1/20, 2/20, 3/20, and 4/20 into fractions of which denominator is 100 according to the basic properties of fractions. Then convert them into decimals and summarize the law according to step 2 and step 3.
> Step 4: Put forth a question: Can you convert a fraction with a denominator of 50 into a decimal by a simple method? Can you convert a fraction with a denominator of 250 into a decimal via a simple method?

Through the above four steps, the students draw inferences about other cases from one instance and figure out the simple method to change denominator into 10, 100, 1000, and so on, and then convert it into decimals according to the basic properties of fractions.

> Step 5: Do an exercise—convert the following fractions into decimals: 3/40, 3/80, 6/25, and 2/50

In fact, the role of "drawing inferences about other cases from one instance" in Chinese mathematic teachings can be traced back to the thoughts of the famous mathematics book, *The Nine Chapters on the Mathematical Art*. It was written during the Han Dynasty over 2,000 years ago. The following is an example of drawing inferences about other cases from one instance in *The Nine Chapters on the Mathematical Art* (Kangshen and Crossley, 2000):

> "The circumference of the bottom circle of a cone-shaped pile of millet is 12 *zhang* (1 *zhang* = 10/3 m), the height of the pile is 2 *zhang*, what is the volume of the pile?"
> "Some beans are piled up against a wall, the semi-circumference of the bottom circle is 3 *zhang* and height of the cone-shaped pile is 7 *chi* (1*chi* = 1/3m), what is the volume of the pile?"
> "Some rice is piled up in a corner, one-quarter of the circumference of the bottom circle is 8 *chi* and the height of the pile is 5 *chi*, what is the volume of the pile?"

When we look at these three questions, we will find that there are only some small differences among them. First of all, the articles of the conditions are changed, but under general circumstances, it does not influence our thinking for solving the problem. Another change is the way of piling up the articles, which means that the shape of the pile is changed, from a cone on the ground to half a cone against a wall, and then to one-quarter of a cone in a corner. The calculation method has some slight changes, but the differences are not big. At that time, the purpose of this, to a great extent, was convenient use in practice. When using the formula to calculate volume, people can combine different situations.

Drawing inferences about other cases from one instance for practical use is also embodied in modern mathematics teaching. In the mathematics textbooks in primary school, there is a type of exercise called "application math problems," which change abstract mathematics problems into practical problems under different situations. The feature of this kind of exercises is that they are like stories, making students interested in solving mathematics problems. The exercise problems are designed with different stories and objects for the purpose of letting students learn how to draw inferences about other cases from one instance, and apply it to life. Currently, application mathematics problems in primary school are developing from "practical exercises" to "solving problems." That is to say, students are required to not only learn how to draw inferences about other cases from one instance but also find out the way of solving problems.

In China, the thinking of drawing inferences about other cases from one instance is also applied to the process of solving mathematics problems. Teachers ask students to sum up the exercises they have solved before, and remember the process or conclusions in the middle, so as to prepare for solving similar type but exercises that are more difficult.

Take the calculating of axis of symmetry of the following, as an example.

$y = \log |X|.$

This exercise is so simple that students can easily know that the axis of symmetry is $X = 0$.

Based on it, students are required to solve some slightly complicated exercises. For instance, we have known that the axis of symmetry of the function is $X = 1$. Please calculate "a."

$y = \log |ax - 2|.$

According to the conclusions learnt before, students will get that $a = 2$.

If we take a further step, we can analyze how the axis of symmetry of the following function changes.

$y = \log |ax + b|.$

6.5   Refining of Mathematical Thinking

Mathematics teachers stress the refining of mathematical thinking and methods. It is one of the important features of Chinese mathematics education.

In the 1980s, the theories for "mathematical thinking and methods" began to be directly used in Chinese classroom teaching. In addition to "analysis and synthesis," "induction and deduction," "association and analogy," and other general mathematical thinking and methods, "combination of number and shape," "reduction method," "function thinking," "equation thinking," "relation-mapping-inversion principle," "geometric transformation," "equivalent conversion," "successive approximation," "exception analysis," and other strategies for question solving are also used. As for "variable substitution," "method of undetermined coefficients," "method of cross–multiplication," and other concrete question solving methods, they have been used all the time, and are now enriched. These mathematical methods do not stop in the stage of theoretical exploration. Instead, they are put into practice and become the vehicle of Chinese mathematics teachers. The mathematics teachers have the universal teaching consciousness on mathematical thinking and method. They use mathematical thought and methods to solve questions, and methods to make summaries and introspections. This is a huge intellectual treasure. When students learn mathematics, they not only can solve questions, but also can receive the training and edification of mathematical methods, and develop their own ability in mathematical thought.

In fact, the cognitive structure of mathematics is the subjective reflection of the subjects on mathematical knowledge and structure. Just because of the existence of mathematical thought and method, mathematical knowledge is no longer an isolated single point or discrete fragment, and the method to solve mathematical questions are no longer rigid patterns and unassociated approaches. It makes mathematics more easily comprehensible and remembered. Therefore, mathematical thinking and methods play a fixed role in the cognitive structure of mathematics. However, mathematical thinking and methods are the mutual links and essence of mathematical concepts and theories. They are recapitulative concepts, which run through mathematics. In teaching, paying attention to the refining of mathematical thinking and methods is to require the students not only to learn specified knowledge, but also to master the most fundamental principles—to govern concrete knowledge and concrete question solving methods with mathematical thinking and gradually form and develop the ability in mathematical summarization.

In order that the students know necessary mathematical thought and methods, Chinese mathematics teaching exerts efforts in both textbooks and teaching methods. It infiltrates mathematical thinking and methods into textbooks, applies them in teaching methods, and pays attention to the high-degree recapitulation and hierarchy of basic mathematical thought and method. Basic mathematical thought and method have universal significance in specific teaching content and represent the spirit of this content. For example, "the thinking of elimination" (or "the method of elimination") is a basic thought that runs through the content of simultaneous equations, and is also a basic method in solving simultaneous equations. All the starting points of solving simultaneous equations rest with "elimination." Basic mathematical thought and method are obtained from high-degree recapitulation. Their recapitulation is hierarchical. Different mathematical thoughts and methods are used in different situations. Low-level mathematical thoughts and methods are the results obtained under the guidance of high-level mathematical thoughts and methods. The lowest-level mathematical thoughts and methods provide the means for the concrete solution of questions. For example, the solution of simultaneous equations:

$$2x + y + z = 3 \tag{1}$$
$$4x + 3y + z = 4 \tag{2}$$
$$4x + 5y + 2z = 5 \tag{3}$$

The basic thinking (or method) is elimination. Elimination may adopt different methods. Here it is appropriate to adopt elimination by addition or subtraction. Then you need to figure out which two expressions are added or subtracted? $(1) \times 2 - (3)$, eliminate x and z to get the value of y. Here the basic mathematical thought or method is divided into three levels: The first level is elimination; the second level is elimination by addition or subtraction; and the third level is $(1) \times 2 - (3)$ to eliminate x and z.

The textbooks regard the highest-level basic mathematical thought and method as the foundations and starting points, and unfold the content of whole secondary school mathematics on the basis of the highest-level basic mathematical thought and method. What are the highest-level basic mathematical thoughts and methods in secondary school mathematics? The answer to this question is debatable. Some people think that they are nothing but "the thinking of set correspondence" and "the thinking of contradiction transformation."

Mathematics is a subject of basic education. Basic mathematical thought and method should be gradually infiltrated into teaching, in connection with content, and shouldn't be divorced from content. Teaching may proceed from the highest-level basic mathematical thinking, and gradually turn to low-level basic mathematical thought and method, and eventually shift to concrete mathematical content. On the contrary, it may also proceed from concrete mathematical content, and gradually shift to high-level basic mathematical thought and method.

Somehow, the process of systematizing the three basic elements of the cognitive structure of mathematics—mathematical theories, mathematical skills, and mathematical experience is a process of continuously revealing the contents links. Therefore, mathematics teaching pays attention to the links of learning contents. This approach may promote or help students more effectively organize their cognitive structure, and perfect every student's cognitive structure of mathematics. It is also an important step in the development of mathematical ability.

In fact, many years ago, these links became the most natural and fundamental ideas of mathematics.

6.5.1   Infiltrate the Thinking of "Combination of Number and Shape" to Cultivate Students' Figurativeness and Creativity

Geometric questions can be solved by algebraic methods. Likewise, some algebraic questions may be studied after they are converted into geometric questions. This is the thinking of "combination of number and shape." "Number" and "shape" are two different yet associated objects in mathematical study. Highlighting the thinking of combination of number and shape helps students deepen their understanding of questions from different aspects. The combination of number and shape can intuitively and vividly present abstract and complex numerical relationships with graphs to solve the questions easily. It can also make graphic properties more complete, precise, and accurate through numerical calculation, processing, and analysis, and naturally demonstrate the harmony and beauty of mathematics. For example, use the image of a function to describe its properties; and use the equation of a curve to accurately describe its geometric properties. In fact, some knowledge in mathematics may be considered the combination of number and shape. For example, the definition of the trigonometric function of an acute angle is given with the help of right triangle. The trigonometric functions of arbitrary angles are defined with the help of rectangular coordinate system or unit circle. In the textbooks of secondary school mathematics, linear and circular schematics are used when an equation (or simultaneous equations) is written out to solve an applied question, and the content of the Pythagorean Theorem is taught in algebra and the content of Golden Section applies algebraic knowledge. All these reflect the thinking of combination of number and shape. In addition, number axis—a good carrier of the combination of number and shape—is used to vividly introduce opposite numbers, absolute values, and rational numbers. The former reduces the difficulty in the introduction of concepts. The latter makes abstract issues more comprehensible. This is a wonderful point of the combination of number and shape.

6.5.2   Infiltrate the "Thinking of Classification" to Cultivate the Coherence and Purposiveness of Students' Thinking

The thinking of classification in mathematics is to classify mathematical objects into different types according to their essential attributes. Classification is based on comparison. It can reveal the inherent law of mathematical objects, help students summarize and induce mathematical knowledge, and make the learned knowledge coherent. When mathematical questions are solved, some circumstances may be encountered. These circumstances need to be classified so that solutions are obtained and summarized. The following reasons contribute to classification:

a. The mathematical concepts involved by questions are defined by type. For example, $|a|$ is defined under three circumstances: $a > 0$, $a = 0$, and a < 0. Such questions discussed by type may be called concept-based questions.

b. The mathematical theorems, formulae, operation properties, and algorithms involved by questions are limited by range or conditions or are given by type. For example, the formula of the sum of the first n terms in a geometric progression has two circumstances: q = 1 and q ≠ 1. Such questions discussed by type may be called nature-based questions.

c. When a question containing parameters is solved, the discussion must be conducted according to the different value ranges of the parameters. For example, when ax > 2 is solved, discussion will be conducted under three circumstances: a > 0, a = 0, and a < 0. Such questions are called parameter-containing questions.

In addition, some uncertain quantities, uncertain graphic shapes or positions, and uncertain conclusions are all discussed by type to guarantee their integrity and certainty.

Classification shall guarantee no repetition and omission of classified objects. Each time, the classification shall guarantee the same standard. For example, "integers and fractions are collectively referred to as rational numbers." In this case, rational numbers are classified by its extension: "integers" and "non-integers." In fact, rational numbers may be classified by other standards. For example, by nature of numbers, rational numbers include positive rational numbers, negative rational numbers, and zero; by "integers," "non-integers," and nature of numbers, rational numbers include positive integers, positive fractions, zero, negative integers, and negative fractions. In this way, the students understand that they may classify the discussed objects into several circumstances, by different standards adaptable to the needs of the specific student, without repetition and omission. This allows them to study them one by one, thus making complex issues simple and coherent.

6.5.3   Infiltrate the "Thinking of Reduction" to Cultivate the Flexibility and Dialectics of Students' Thinking

The thinking of reduction is to convert, transform, and reduce a question into a solved, or an easily solved question, by means of observation, analogy, association, according to the subject's existing knowledge and experience. "Conversion and transformation" is the essence of the thinking of reduction. For example, the thinking of reduction is reflected by the solution of equations (simultaneous equations) and inequalities: equation of higher degree, fractional equations, and irrational equations, adopt different methods (factorization, identical transformation, and variable substitution) to reduce order, eliminate unknowns, integrate, and rationalize them. Then in the end, they sum them up into linear equations, with one unknown or linear equation with two unknowns, and solve the equations. Conversion includes equivalent conversion and nonequivalent conversion. The process of nonequivalent conversion is sufficient or necessary, and a necessary correction to its conclusion is needed. For example, as mentioned above, when an irrational equation is converted into a rational equation, the roots should be verified. It can bring forth the shining points of thinking, and find a breakthrough in the question. In order to realize the conversion, many methods are generated, such as method of elimination, order reduction method, method of substitution, graphical method, method of undetermined coefficients, and the method of completing the square. Through the use of these mathematical thoughts and methods, the students significantly enhance their ability in dialectical thinking.

6.5.4   *Infiltrate the "Thinking of Analogy" to Cultivate the Extensity and Logicality of Students' Thinking*

The thinking of analogy is to study and discover the related content from its properties, and change the law of something else, by means of association and migration. Analogy is an important inference method, as it has the nature of an educated guess. The thinking of analogy is helpful in discovering innovation, and solving questions. When we come across a mathematical proposition, we often think of the questions, conditions, forms, solutions, and other things similar to it as well. In addition, we take into account the concepts, theorems, formulae, and rules relevant to it. This broadens our train of thought, and inspires our thinking. For example, the division of integral expressions is similar to the division of integers; the definition, properties, and operation of fractional expressions are similar to the corresponding contents of fractions. The theorem of proportional division of segments by parallel lines is similar to the theorem of equal division of segments by parallel lines. The students may easily understand new knowledge, and broaden their thinking.

6.5.5   *Infiltrate the "Thinking of Function" to Cultivate the Directivity and Depth of Students' Thinking*

The thought process of a function is to observe, analyze, and handle problems by using the concepts of movement and change. Variable substitution, combination of number and shape, and solving questions by the concept of function are all the embodiments of a function. During teaching, the concepts of movement and change should be used in an all-around way, to reveal the inherent links of knowledge, and to introduce and explain mathematical concepts. The point is to incorporate functions into students' cognitive structure, and guide the students to treat mathematical knowledge while using the thought process for functions. For example, a binomial $ax + b$ may be treated as a linear function with x as an independent variable. Calculating the value of algebraic expression $ax + b$ is to calculate the function value of function $ax + b$; the solution to $ax + b = 0$ is the horizontal coordinate of the intersection between the image of $y = ax + b$ and the x axis. The solution set of $ax + b > 0$ is the value range of x when the image of $y = ax + b$ is above x axis. Generally, the thinking of a function is to set up a function and solve the question by using the properties of the function. The questions about inequalities, equation, minimum value, and maximum value may be analyzed by using the monotony, parity, periodicity, maximum value, minimum value, graphic transformation, and other properties of functions. An applied question may be translated into mathematical language and mathematical models. Function relationships may be set up, and the questions may be solved by using the properties of functions, or the knowledge of inequalities. In arithmetic progression and geometric progression, general term formula and the formula for the first "n" term may be considered as the functions of "n," and the issues of progression may be solved by method of function. The thought process that comes along with the knowledge of functions has great influence on the mathematical train of thought. However, this thought process is not established in one day, and needs exploration, refining, comprehension, and practice. During teaching, teachers should encourage students to use this "lever" to solve questions as much as possible, in order to deepen their thinking.

Chinese education attaches great importance to cultivating comprehensive and profound knowledge, logical thinking, understanding ability, and united standard in students. Teachers and parents are strict with children. In addition to regular classes, every day most students have to do a lot of homework and extracurricular exercises, while taking various tutorial classes in order to deepen their understanding of the information they have learned, as well as increase their problem-solving ability and examination skills. The following picture shows (figures 6.12 and 6.13) a test question for freshmen in British universities and one for high school students to enter into universities in China,

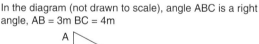

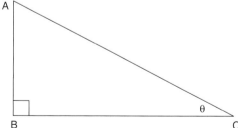

(i) What is the length of AC?

(ii) What is the area of triangle ABC (above)?

(iii) What is the tanθ of the triangle ABC (above) as a fraction?

Figure 6.12   Diagnostic test set by an English university for first-year students.

As shown in the figure, in squate prism $ABCD\text{-}A_1B_1C_1D_1$,

$AB=AD=2$, $DC=2\sqrt{3}$, $AA_1=\sqrt{3}$ $AB\perp DC$, $AC\perp BD$ and foot of perpendicular is E,

(i) Prove: $BD\perp A_1C$:

(ii) Determine the angle between the two planes A_1BD and BC_1D:

(iil) Determine the angle formed by lines AD and BC_1 which are in different planes.

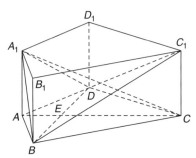

Figure 6.13   National test set by Chinese education authorities for preentry students.

from which we can easily see the discrepancy in the requirements of the command of basic knowledge and calculating ability between Chinese and western mathematics education.

As far as this author is concerned, students who receive this kind of Chinese education can thoroughly learn an enormous amount from lots of exercises, with a solid foundation, strong imitating ability, and rigorous thinking, even if the students are not quite talented. If they are engaged in research after graduating from university, and have the opportunity to make extensive communications with international colleagues to open up their mind and broaden their vision, they will achieve good research results.

However, as this kind of educational system pays too much attention to the teaching and testing of theoretical knowledge and makes relatively less cultivation of students' interest, innovation, and hands-on abilities, the purpose of doing exercises is somewhat misunderstood. Some students, under the pressure of parents and teachers, may spend the majority of their extracurricular time on repeatedly doing exercises, which easily make them lose their interest. In addition, university students majoring in mathematics also have little chance to practice independent social practices, and don't know well about how to apply the knowledge learned from their classes to society. As a result, some students are not quite enthusiastic about university studies. The author believes that there is much room for improvement. After all, "interest is the best teacher."

6.6   A Note by the Contributors

The first author of this chapter, Ben Duan, received 19 years of education, from preschool, primary school to university, in several cities in mainland China, then went to Hong Kong for further studies, and got a PhD in mathematics. Now, he is Research Assistant Professor at Pohang Mathematics Institute, Pohang

University of Science and Technology, Pohang, South Korea. When he wrote this chapter, he was a Research Fellow of Prof. Yuxi Zheng at Yeshiva University in New York, the United States.

Chao Zhang holds a bachelor's and master's degree in Astronomy from Beijing Normal University. For three years, he was an Editor of *Natural History* in Chinese National Geography. He graduated from Middle School attached to Peking University and understands science education well in middle school in China. He spent seven years to learn astronomy in Beijing Normal University. In the past six years, he wrote popular science articles for young people, and tried to introduce astronomy, astrophysics, and mathematics in astronomy for middle school students. He has written two books with coauthors on popular science.

As entrusted by Prof. Elias Grivoyannis, we wrote this article according to our own education experience, especially our elementary and secondary education experience. All of the contents of this article are the authors' and their classmates' personal experience or what they saw or heard about, and all the examples in the article are true cases used in real teaching.

References

Polya, G. (1971), *How to Solve It: A New Aspect of Mathematical Method,* Princeton University Press, 2nd edition.
Kangshen, Shen and John Crossley (2000), *The Nine Chapters on the Mathematical Art*: Companion and Commentary, Oxford University Press, USA.

7

Understanding China's Rising Saving Rate: The Role of Higher Education Reform

Binkai Chen and Rudai Yang

Substantial empirical studies show that households in China have strong precautionary saving motive; however, few studies explore the microfoundation and underlying reasons accounting for this phenomenon. Comparative analysis of household education expenditure and household consumption behavior before and after the higher education reform suggests that the reform has remarkable impacts on household consumption. Based on the life cycle hypothesis, a theoretical model is constructed with education being introduced in. Simulation results indicate that higher education reform is one of the most important reasons that account for the strong precautionary saving motive and thus the sluggish consumption demand in China. Based on household-level data collected by Chinese Academy of Social Sciences in 1995 and 2002, we test the relationship between the higher education reform and household consumption quantitatively. Cross-sectional regression demonstrates that the higher education reform in 1999 had a significant effect on household consumption. The marginal propensity to consume (MPC) of households with members attaining higher education had decreased by 12 percent from 1995 to 2002.

7.1 Introduction

Since the economic reform, China has undergone rapid economic growth. However, China's economic expansion disproportionately depends on rising investment expenditures and expanding trade surplus in recent years. Since the late 1990s, investment and export grew vigorously, while the share of household consumption in GDP has fallen dramatically, from over 60 percent in 2000 to 48.6 percent in 2008. Meanwhile, national savings have continued to rise (Modigliani and Cao, 2004).

It should be noted that, however, consumption demand tended to rise before 2000. The consumption/GDP ratio increased from 58.1 percent in 1995 to a peak of 62.3 percent in 2000. However, it has dropped continuously from then on. What has given rise to the decline in the consumption ratio? Substantial studies have focused on the increasing precautionary savings caused by rising income and expenditure uncertainties during economic reforms (Chamon and Prasad, 2010). The reforms initiated in the late 1990s on education, housing, medical, social security systems, and state-owned enterprises are, naturally, to be taken into consideration. Studies based on the data of China (See Shi and Zhu, 2004; Yi et al., 2008) suggest that precautionary saving motive became stronger since 2000. What's more important, this change is nationwide, including both rural residents and urban residents. Since, reforms on medical, housing, social security systems, and state-owned enterprises are basically related to urban residents, it is hard to explain the increasing precautionary motive of rural residents. Among the main reforms started in the late 1990s, only the education reform directly involves both rural residents and urban residents. Therefore, it is quite reasonable to conjecture that education reform may be the main force that accounts for increasing precautionary saving in China.

Based on the precautionary saving theory (Kimball, 1990; Caballero, 1990; Carroll, 1994; Kazarosian, 1997), many empirical studies try to explain the high saving and low consumption phenomena in China. Song (1999) concludes that precautionary saving has substantial impacts on Chinese consumer behavior. Shi and Zhu (2004) investigate the intensity of Chinese consumer's precautionary saving motive. Yi et al. (2008) suggests that rural residents in China have strong precautionary saving motive. However, most existing studies on precautionary saving in China are restricted to two areas: (1) analyzing the impacts of precautionary saving on China; (2) investigating the intensity of precautionary saving motive. However, few studies focus on the causes of precautionary saving. Although some qualitative analysis suggests that precautionary saving motive has been intensified in China mainly due to increasing uncertainty resulting from market-oriented reform, little quantitative analysis on the causes of precautionary saving has been conducted. This chapter contributes to this literature, and studies the effects of higher education reform on household consumption quantitatively.

The rest of this chapter is arranged as follows: Section 7.2 outlines some descriptive statistics about the education reform and the unbalance growth pattern in China during 1995–2005. A theoretical model is constructed in section 7.3 to investigate the long-term effects of education reform. Section 7.4 tests the impacts of higher education reform on household consumption. Section 7.5 provides conclusion and possible extensions.

7.2   Empirical Observation

China has been confronting sluggish domestic demand characterized by decreasing consumption share since the late 1990s. China's vigorous economic growth in recent years has been accompanied by an explosion in the household saving ratio, which has reached an impressive level. Meanwhile, the scale of high school and college education has quadrupled, and private education expenditure has decupled mainly as a result of the education reform initiated in 1999.

7.2.1   Imbalance in Growth of Consumption and Income

Before the Asian financial crisis, China's domestic demand was very strong, while investment and export was maintained at a moderate level. However, since the late 1990s, China's consumption/GDP ratio went down continuously, and private saving increased dramatically. As is shown in figure 7.1, consumption/GDP ratio increased from 58.1 percent in 1995 to 62.3 percent in 2000, and fell down to 49.9 percent in 2006.

There are at least two reasons that can be accounted for insufficient consumer demand and growing precautionary saving in China. First, with economic reforms deepening, the share of transitory income in total income goes up significantly, and income uncertainty is intensified. As a result, although income level of Chinese people has substantially increased since the late 1990s, the consumption/GDP ratio went down continuously due to increasing income uncertainty. Second, consumption depends not only on future income, but also on future expenditure. Market-oriented reforms on education, medical, and housing in the late 1990s added great uncertainty to household expenditure, which inevitably prompted people to cut down their current consumption and put more money aside.

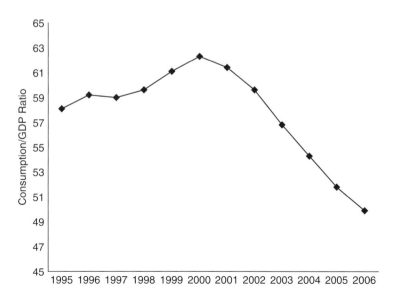

Figure 7.1   Consumption/GDP ratio: 1995–2006.

7.2.2   Higher Education Reform in 1999

When we think about the causes contributing to consumer demand downturn, it is natural to take into consideration the massive reforms on education, medical, social security systems, and state-owned enterprises initiated in the late 1990s. Key elements of the higher education reform were to expand the scale of China's higher education and to end the free higher education system. Before 1999, higher education in China was almost free. Chinese central government was in charge of the higher education, and little burden was loaded on families. Under such a policy, the scale of higher education in China grew slowly. Figure 7.2 shows that university/college recruitment increased from 570,000 in 1986 to 1,080,000 in 1998, an increase of 89 percent. In addition, university/college enrollment increased from 1,880,000 in 1986 to 3,410,000, an increase of 81 percent. In fact, the development of higher education lagged far behind the rapidly increasing education demand during this period. Fortunately, things changed thanks to the higher education reform launched in 1999; and higher education in China advanced rapidly from then on. By 2005, university/college recruitment and enrollment had reached 5.05 million and 15.62 million, respectively, increasing 368 percent and 358 percent, respectively, as compared with those in 1998.

Expenditure on higher education increased rapidly as its scale expanded. It had increased from 59.8 billion Yuan to 266 billion Yuan over the period 1998–2005, a rise of about 345 percent. Such an enormous amount of spending challenged the previous free higher education system. Although input from Chinese central government increased from 35.7 billion Yuan to 109 billion Yuan during this period, it was much less than needed. Money from other sources was required

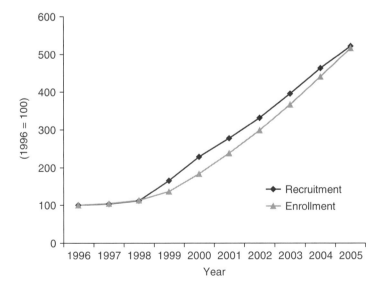

Figure 7.2   University/college recruitment and enrollment: 1995–2005.

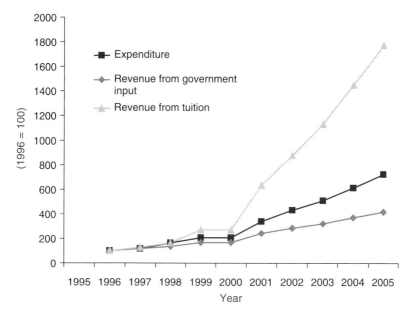

Figure 7.3   Expenditure and revenue of higher education institutes in China from the state's finance and tuition: 1996–2005.

to offset the deficit. Starting in 1999, higher education institutes in China began to charge tuitions as they expanded their scale. Revenue from tuition of higher education institutes increased from 7.3 billion Yuan in 1998 to 79.2 billion Yuan in 2005, about tenfold increase. As a result, expenditure on higher education of households increased dramatically. With the deepening of the reform, the burden of higher education has given rise to far-reaching impacts on household consumption and saving behavior, and expenditure on higher education has become a primary consideration for household decision on consumption (figure 7.3).

7.2.3   The Relationship between Private Consumption and Education Expenditure

There should be a great deal of reasons that account for the imbalance in growth between consumption and GDP since the late 1990s. However, it is widely believed that the market-oriented reforms on housing, education, medical, and social security systems initiated in the late 1990s are the main forces. There is no doubt that these reforms have substantial impacts on residents' expectation of their future expenditure. However, it is worth noting that all these reforms mainly involve urban residents, and have little direct effect on the rural residents except for education reform. Compared with the other reforms, higher education reform has a nationwide impact. Therefore, we expected the higher education reform initiated in 1999 to be closely related to the change in private consumption and saving behavior.

Higher education reform started in 1999 has two far-reaching consequences on household consumption. First, the expanding higher education scale enables more students in China to attain higher education. Second, education-expense burden on families is increasing. This chapter tries to cast light on their impacts on private consumption. First, increasing expenditure on higher education directly decreases other consumptions. Second, nonfree higher education and easier access to it prompt people to put more money aside for possible higher education expenditure.

Macrodata of private consumption confirm our hypothesis. The share of food and clothing expenditure in aggregate consumption is decreasing, and the share of education expenditure is rising. For example, the share of education expenditure in total consumption of urban residents has increased from about 9 percent in 1995 to 15 percent in 2002, while that of rural residents has increased from 8 percent to 12 percent. By now, we can draw a preliminary conclusion that actual and expected expenditure increase on education have substantial impacts on individual consumption and saving behavior.

7.3   Theoretical Analysis

Theoretically, the impacts of education reform on consumer behavior are very complex. We need to consider many economic factors, such as the return on education, the opportunity cost of education, etc. What's more important, the effects of education reform on consumption are a dynamic continuous process. In order to study the dynamic effects and explore the underlying mechanism, we construct a dynamic theoretical model to evaluate the effects of higher education reform in this section. The model is closely related to the precautionary saving literature (Deaton, 1991; Carroll, 2001, etc.). Based on life cycle hypothesis, we present a standard model with borrowing constraint, incorporating education fee as a lump-sum expenditure at certain age.

$$\max \ E_t \sum_{s=t}^{T} \beta^{s-t} u(C_s),$$

s.t. $W_{s+1} \leq R_{s+1}(X_s - C_s)$ if no education fee is paid at time s,

$W_{s+1} \leq R_{s+1}(X_s - C_s - E_s)$ if education fee is paid at time s,

$Y_{s+1} = P_{s+1}\varepsilon_{s+1},$

$P_{s+1} = GP_s,$

$X_{s+1} = W_{s+1} + Y_{s+1},$

$X_s \geq 0.$

Where beginning-of-period wealth, W_{s+1}, is equal to unspent resources from period s accumulated at a gross interest rate R_{s+1}; the resources spent in period s depend on whether the education fee, E_s, is paid at period s. Y_{s+1} is labor income in period $s+1$, which is equal to "permanent labor income" P_{s+1} multiplied by a transitory shock ε_{s+1}, $E_s(\varepsilon_{s+1}) = 1$; permanent labor income grows by a factor G between periods; and "cash-on-hand" in period $s+1$ is equal to beginning-of-period wealth W_{s+1} plus the period $s+1$'s labor income Y_{s+1}; people cannot borrow to finance their consumption and education.[1]

For computation simplicity, we define $c_s = C_s/P_s$, $w_s = W_s/P_s$, $x_s = X_s/P_s$, $y_s = Y_s/P_s$, $e_s = E_s/P_s$ (Carroll, 2001). Let the utility function be CRRA,

$$u(c) = (c^{1-\theta}-1)/(1-\theta).$$

The value function of the model can be reduced to:

$$v_t(x_t) = \max\ u(c_t) + \beta E_t[G^{1-\theta}v_{t+1}(x_{t+1})]$$

$$s.t.\ w_{t+1} = R/G(x_t - c_t)\ \text{if no education fee is paid at time } t$$

$$w_{t+1} = R/G(x_t - c_t - e_t)\ \text{if education fee is paid at time } t$$

$$x_{t+1} = w_{t+1} + \varepsilon_{t+1}$$

$$x_t \geq 0$$

The next step in solving the model computationally is to choose values for the parameters that characterize consumers' tastes and the income uncertainty that typical households face. For the simulation results presented in this chapter, we follow a traditional calibration in the macroliterature, choose a time preference factor of $\beta = 0.96$ implying that consumers discount future utility at a rate of about 4 percent annually, and we make a symmetric assumption that the interest rate is also 4 percent per year. The coefficient of relative risk aversion is chosen to be $\theta = 2$, the low end of the range from 1 to 5 is generally considered plausible. The growth rate of permanent income is set to be 9 percent per year that coincides with the average growth rate of China from 1978 to 2006. Similar to Carroll (2001), the transitory shock is assumed to be distributed lognormally with a mean value of one and a standard deviation of $\sigma_\varepsilon = 0.2$. We then follow the procedure described in Deaton (1991) and Aiyagari (1993) to approximate the stochastic income shock with a nine state independent and identically distributed (i.i.d) process.[2] Suppose the agent enters the labor market at age 20, retires at age 60, and thereby we set the life period as 40. We can use backward deduction to solve the consumption function. In order to explicitly investigate the dynamic relationship between household income,

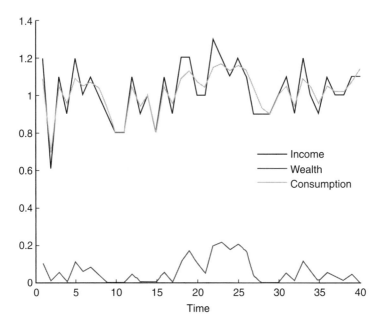

Figure 7.4   Simulations of income, consumption, and wealth without education expenditure.

consumption, and saving, we conduct simulations on household consumption-saving behavior.

Figure 7.4 shows a 40-year period simulation. Income, consumption, and wealth level are drawn to the same scale. Income is simply 40 random drawings from *lognormal (1, 0.2)*. Consumption is smoother than income: its standard deviation is 0.149 as opposed to 0.2082 for the income process. Wealth level shows repeated reversions to zero, although wealth is more often held than not. Only along the "flats" at zero, consumption is equal to income, something that happens relatively rarely. Note that the level of assets is typically quite low, usually less than 10 percent of income, which implies that the precautionary saving is relatively lower when there is no education expenditure.[3]

We now introduce the education expenditure into the model. As mentioned in the previous sections, the education reform launched in 1999 has raised the probability of college education, at an expense of higher household education expenditure, and these facts will be accounted in our model. The household faces a stochastic expenditure on education at some age, that is, an educational expenditure E_s with a probability p. The stochastic future educational expenditure will give rise to precautionary saving for the household. The probability of college education is chosen to be $p=0.52$, which is the matriculation ratio in 2002. Some anecdotal evidences show that the four-year college educational expenditure is about 40,000 Yuan, and the per capita GDP in 2002 is 9,398 Yuan. We set the average educational expenditure–permanent income ratio to be $e_s = E_s/P_s = 4$. College education has private return in that it raises the household's permanent income at a rate of δ. Substantial empirical evidences show that private higher education return in China is about 40 percent (Gao, 2007), and we set $\delta = 0.4$. For simplicity, we assume the education fee will be paid at a certain age, say, $t_e = 20$. The consumption function after t_e is similar to that without education expenditure. However, the consumption functions before t_e are quite different. We simulate the dynamics of consumption and wealth accumulation during the household's lifetime under different circumstances, which is shown in figure 7.5.

For comparison, the consumption/wealth path after reform is only depicted for the households who have expectations on future education expenditure that does not eventually occur.[4] From figure 7.5, we find that consumption and wealth after the reform are almost the same as those before the reform in the first and the last ten periods, which implies that the effects of educational reform are concentrated in the periods around educational expenditure. Before educational expenditure ($t < 20$), consumption after the reform is much lower than that before the reform, which results in higher wealth accumulation. The accumulated wealth after the reform is almost 30 times higher than that before the reform! The huge difference in household saving behavior reflects strong precautionary saving motive caused by the educational reform. After the amount of educational expenditure is realized to be zero ($t > 20$), both the wealth and consumption smoothly decrease to the same level as those without education expenditure.

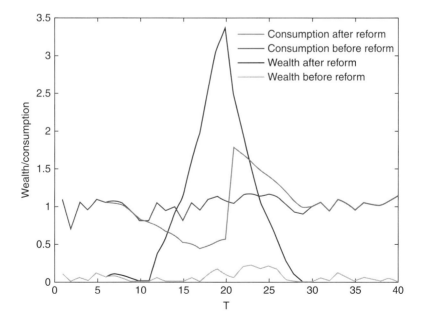

Figure 7.5   Consumption and wealth before/after reform.

<h2 align="center">7.4   Empirical Test</h2>

The period during the late 1990s represents a turning point for China's economic reform in the recent years. Deepening reforms on housing, medical, education, and social security systems in this period have brought about great changes in socioeconomic life in China. From then on, despite of all kinds of proactive fiscal and monetary policies, such as cutting down taxes, China's consumption demand continued to slow down. The theoretical analysis indicates that the higher education reform initiated in 1999 may account for the sluggish consumer demand. Based on detailed microdata, we try to test this hypothesis in this section.

<h3 align="center">7.4.1   Data Description</h3>

Our data come from two surveys conducted by the Institute of Economics, Chinese Academy of Social Sciences, with the assistance of the State Statistical Bureau in Beijing.[5] The 1995 survey covers 14,932 households (among which 6,934 are urban households,[6] and 7,998 are rural households) distributed in 19 provinces (including municipalities and autonomous regions), involving 21,696 urban residents and 34,739 rural residents. The 2002 survey covers 16,035 households (among which 6,835 are urban households, and 9,200 are rural households) distributed in 22 provinces (including municipalities and autonomous regions), involving 20,632 urban residents and 37,969 rural residents.

<h3 align="center">7.4.2   Methodology</h3>

The greatest difficulty in testing the precautionary saving theory lies in the measurement of exogenous uncertainty (Engen and Gruber, 2001). Existing literature always measures uncertainty in two ways. One way is to measure the income or expenditure uncertainty directly. For example, Kazarosian (1997) uses the next 15 years household income variance as a measure of household income uncertainty. The second way is to construct proxies for individual income and expenditure uncertainty based on individual educational level, nature of work, and other information (Carroll, 1994). The biggest flaw of these methods is that the indicators of uncertainties may be a reflection of the household preferences, and the preferences of the household may have a direct effect on household saving behavior. In other words, most of the uncertainty indicators in the existing literature are endogenous, and it will lead to inconsistent estimation. A possible solution is to find exogenous policy shocks. For instance, Engen and Gruber (2001) take advantage of the US unemployment insurance system reform to identify the strength of household precautionary saving motive. Similar to Engen and Gruber (2001), China's education system reform provides a very good chance to test the theory of precautionary saving. For the household, the education system reform can be regarded as an exogenous policy shock, and it has a direct effect on household spending uncertainty. To study the effects of higher education reform on household precautionary saving motive, the household data before and after the higher education reform at 1999 is required. Fortunately, the household survey of income and consumption data in 1995 and 2002 meets such conditions well.

To study the impacts of the higher education reform, we are interested in the consumer behavior change of households with members attaining college before and after the higher education reform. In addition, we adopt MPC as the indicator that measures this behavior change. We expect that the reform of higher education system will increase the household expenditure uncertainty, which will lead to a decline in MPC; meanwhile, households without college students will not be impacted by the higher education reform. Based on the data of 1995 and 2002, our method is to test whether decline in MPC due to higher education reform exists in households with college students.

Let C represent current consumption expenditure, and Y denote current disposable income. *Stu_college* is a dummy variable and its vale of 1 means the relevant household has members attaining college/university education, while a value of 0 means it does not have. X stands for other control variables, and ε stands for error term. Thus, the regression equation is defined as follows:

$$C = \alpha + \beta Y + \theta Y * stu\_college + \gamma stu\_college + \eta X + \varepsilon \qquad (1)$$

We need to test whether the coefficient θ is statistically significant and negative, which means that households with members attaining college/university have lower MPCs. In other words, the higher education reform has significant impacts on household consumption expenditure. Based on equation (1), cross-section regressions can be conducted using both the 1995 data and the 2002 data.

7.4.3   Definition of Relevant Variables

The two surveys include both household data and individual data, and we treat household as a unit in this chapter. All the data, such as consumption expenditure, income, and household asset, are measured by per capita value of the family. Education expenditure includes expenditure on education for both adults and children. According to the definition of Chinese National Bureau of Statistics, consumption expenditure includes eight categories, and they are expenditure on food, clothing, household appliances and services, transport and communications, housing, education and culture, health care, and other terms, respectively. However, consumption expenditure in our regression equations excludes education and medical expenditure.[7] Total household income includes wage of all family members, family business income, property income, transfer income, and equal market value of some nonmarket goods. Moreover, rent of land is also treated as income for rural families. Taking into account

Table 7.1   Descriptive statistics for main variables

Year	Variable Name	Definition of Variable	Observation	Mean	SD	Min	Max
1995	Consumption	Consumption expenditure	14,426	2,115	1,838	100	9,992
	Income	Income	14,426	3,226	2,312	302	14,677
	Stu_college	Has or has not members attaining higher education	0 (has not): 13,028; 1(has): 1,400				
	Total_asset	Aggregate asset	13,960	7,189	11,432	8	26,4300
	Edu_payment	Education expenditure	11,751	154	327	0.12	9,022
	Med_payment	Medical expenditure	11,600	135	442	0.14	40,059
	Avg_edu	Education attainment	14,108	6.90	2.85	0.17	20.50
	Pop_number	Family size	14,426	3.79	1.25	1	10
	Hholder_gender	Gender of household head	0 (woman): 2,578; 1 (man): 11,850				
	Hholder_age	Age of household head	14,428	44.95	11.07	16	95
	Hholder_married	Marital status of household head	0 (no spouse): 548; 1 (has spouse): 13,880				
	Hholder_edu	Education attaint of household head	14,276	8.23	3.66	0	24
2002	Consumption	Consumption expenditure	15,512	2,275	1,834	4	13,187
	Income	Income	15,517	4,773	3,746	555	22,798
	Stu_college	Has or has not members attaining higher education	0 (has not): 13,266; 1 (has): 2,251				
	Total_asset	Aggregate asset	14,806	17,455	23,798	0.90	620,051
	Edu_payment	Education expenditure	10,104	625	952	0.15	20,288
	Med_payment	Medical expenditure	14,411	247	593	0.13	18,014
	Avg_edu	Education attainment	15,456	7.64	2.75	0.33	20
	Pop_number	Family size	15,515	3.65	1.23	1	12
	Hholder_gender	Gender of household head	0 (woman): 2,517; 1 (man):13,000				
	Hholder_age	Age of household head	15,517	47.06	10.72	16	92
	Hholder_married	Marital status of household head	0 (no spouse): 740; 1 (has spouse): 14,769				
	Hholder_edu	Education attainment of household head	15,517	8.71	3.34	0	23

Note: Variables such as consumption expenditure, income, aggregate asset, education expenditure, medical expenditure, and education attainment are average value of each family. Adjustment has been made on values of variables in 2002 based on the price in 1995.

measurement error, we exclude 1 percent of the lowest- and the highest-income families from our sample.

In addition, other variables are introduced in our regressions, such as household asset, medical expenditure, education attainment of family members, family size, ownership of consumer durables, character of household head, and household location. Of these, household asset covers household financial asset, estimated value of housing, fixed productive asset, and so forth. Medical expenditure includes spending on hospitalization, surgery, and medicine. Education attainment of family members is average years of schooling of all members. Ownership of consumer durables covers motorcycles, cars, color television sets, refrigerators, and washing machines. Character of household head includes gender, age, marital status, and education attainment. Furthermore, noting that there are significant differences in income and consumption between urban and rural residents as well as among households in different provinces, we set a dummy variable in order to distinguish rural household from urban household and use dummies for provinces.

Table 7.1 provides descriptive statistics for some main variables. Relevant adjustment has been made on the values of variables in 2002 according to the price in 1995. As it is shown in table 7.1, per capita family income increased by 48 percent from 1995 to 2002, while per capita family consumption only increased by 7.6 percent, which confirms the unequal growth between consumption and income based on the macrodata. By contrast, education expenditure increased rapidly and per capita expenditure on education tripled. Moreover, average years of schooling rose from 6.9 years in 1995 to 7.64 years in 2002 with a decline in its standard deviation, which might well reflect the increasing emphasis on human capital investment in China.

7.4.4   Results

Table 7.2 provides the regression results. In particular, it presents: (a) results based on equation (1) using data of 1995; (b) results based on equation (1) using data of 2002. For the sake of simplicity, results for consumer durables and the dummy variables of province are not provided.

Result (a) suggests that in 1995 there was no significant difference in consumer behavior between household with and without college/university students. While result (b) indicates that in 2002 MPC of households with college/university students is almost 11.5 percent (a difference of 0.03) lower than MPC of households without college/university students. In other words, the higher education reform has negative impacts on household consumption.

Aforementioned analysis argues that the higher education reform impacts household consumption behavior from two aspects. First, it costs families more to afford a college/university student. Second, the reform increases the probability of a senior high school student to go to a college/university. With more children being sent to senior high schools, families will not only be spending more on education but also save more money for possible higher education expenditure. However, the foregoing regressions only test for the first impacts. Nevertheless, it is easy for us to test the second proposition by changing the definition of the variable stu_college. In the foregoing regression equations, we define that a family has college/university students if it has members attaining over-12-year education. When we test the second proposition by just changing that to be over-9-year education, we find that the results are similar when we change the definition of stu_college.

Table 7.2   Main results

Variable	(a)		(b)		(c)	
	Coefficient	t-value	Coefficient	t-value	Coefficient	t-value
Income	0.3493***	63.07	0.2603***	74.86	0.3877***	78.95
Income*stu_college	0.0203	1.49	−0.0299***	−4.12	0.0082	0.60
Income*stu_ college*year					−0.0315**	−2.03
Year*income					−0.1374***	-26.63
Year*total_asset					0.0002	0.20
Total_asset*stu_ college*year					0.0060**	2.07
Year*stu_college					263.10***	3.84
Year					96.52***	4.48
Total_asset*stu_ college	−0.0028	−1.07	0.0026**	2.39	−0.0030	−1.11
Stu_college	−315.41***	−5.52	57.49	1.42	−257.37***	−4.52
Total_asset	0.0028***	3.33	0.0038***	8.45	0.0036***	4.23
Medical_payment	0.0265	1.27	0.0888***	6.00	0.0479***	3.94
Education	39.19***	7.07	47.65***	9.25	48.14***	12.63
Pop_number	−127.64***	−15.75	−99.72	−12.43	−107.65***	−18.86
Urban	1,031.48**	31.03	571.06***	18.94	911.56***	44.38
Hholder_gender	26.75	1.08	108.90***	4.43	89.21***	5.06
Hholder_age	4.01***	4.69	−5.13***	−6.16	−0.57	−0.95
Hholder_married	87.83**	1.95	24.20	0.62	42.08	1.41
Hholder_edu	2.49	0.63	6.20	1.63	6.60**	2.39
Constant	442.01***	4.65	1220.12***	13.46	822.77***	12.29
Obs.	10,087		13,323		24,843	
Adj. R^2	0.7086		0.7125		0.7031	

Note: The dummy variable year is 0 when it is year 1995 and is 1 when it is year 2002.
*** represents 1% significant level; ** represents 5% significant level; * represents 10% significant level.

Regression results also show that the total household asset and the average years of schooling has significant impacts on consumption, which accords with conclusions drawn by other studies based on Permanent Income Hypothesis. Moreover, MPC of the urban consumers is higher than that of the rural consumers, which may be due to the fact that the rural consumers have stronger precautionary saving motive than urban consumers have (see Liu, 1999). However, that part of rural residents' consumption on their own products is hard to be included in their consumption expenditure may also be on account of lower MPC of rural residents. In addition, family size has a significant negative effect on household consumption, which may be due to the fact that marginal consumption is decreasing as one more member is added in.

In order to verify the consistency between our model and the empirical results, we take advantage of numerical simulation methods. We simulated 600,000 samples with different wealth levels, different income levels, and different ages (300,000 samples with education expenditure and 300,000 samples without education expenditure, respectively). Based on these simulated samples,

Table 7.3 Regression results of the simulated samples

Variable	(a)		(b)	
	Coefficient	t	Coefficient	t
Income	0.2137***	77.01	0.1822***	61.30
Wealth	0.1980***	665.40	0.1884***	591.47
Constant	4.1247***	554.54	4.1956***	526.59
Obs.	300,000		300,000	
Adj. R^2	0.7668		0.7793	

Note: *** represents 1% significant level.

we did the same econometric analysis as that in the empirical part. In comparing the results of the empirical part and those of the simulation exercise, we can justify the validity of this model. The regression results of the simulated samples are shown in table 7.3.

Model (a) is the regression results when there is no education expenditure, and model (b) is the regression results when education expenditure exists. Similar to the empirical results in the previous section, the higher education reform leads to a decline in MPC. We find that the MPC decreases from 0.2137 to 0.1822, a decrease of 14.7 percent, which strongly supports our results.

In a nutshell, the empirical results reinforces our theoretical analysis: the educational reform in China has led to strong precautionary saving motive, which can account for the increasing saving rate and decreasing consumption-GDP ratio after the educational reform was launched in 1999.

7.5   Conclusion and Remarks

Despite rapid economic growth, consumption demand in China has slowed down since the late 1990s. Many studies suggest that strong precautionary saving motive is the main reason. However, few studies explore the microfoundation and underlying reasons accounting for this phenomenon. This chapter studies the impacts of the higher education reform on consumer behavior in China. Two main conclusions can be drawn. First, a theoretical model is constructed to study the micromechanism and dynamic effects of the higher education reform. According to simulation analysis of the theoretical model, the higher education reform is one of the most important reasons that accounts for the strong precautionary saving motive, and thus, the sluggish consumption demand in China. Second, based on the household data, our empirical results demonstrate that the higher education reform in 1999 has a significant effect on household consumption, and the MPC of households with members attaining higher education had decreased by 12 percent from 1995 to 2002. These empirical findings are consistent with the simulation results based on the theoretical model.

Market-oriented reform has changed consumer behavior remarkably in China. This chapter takes a preliminary step to evaluate the effects of the higher education reform. However, many further investigations are needed. First, household consumption and saving are dynamic choices; therefore, the results based on two-year pooled cross-section data in this chapter are quite restrictive, and panel data analysis may provide more precise results. Second, the higher education reform not only affects residents' consumption and saving behavior but also their decision on education investment, labor supply, and so forth, which needs further exploration. Last but not the least, more quantitative studies are needed for other market-oriented reforms, such as reforms on health, housing, social security system, and state-owned enterprises.

Notes

1. This assumption is used to simplify our numerical analysis. There are many assumptions about the borrowing constraint, such as no borrowing, the natural borrowing constraint, and so on. However, It is very hard to justify which one is valid in a theoretical model, so we choose the simplest one. Relaxing this assumption will make our numerical analysis much more complex, but will not change our basic results.
2. We divide the real line into nine intervals as follows: $I_1 = (-\infty, 1-7/4\sigma_\varepsilon)$, $I_2 = (1-7/4\sigma_\varepsilon, 1-5/4\sigma_\varepsilon) \ldots I_9 = (1+7/4\sigma_\varepsilon, +\infty)$. The state place of ε is taken to be the finite set $\{1-2\sigma_\varepsilon, \ldots, 1+2\sigma_\varepsilon\}$.
3. Of course, the results are impacted by the parameters, that is θ and σ, which controls the degree of prudence and the income uncertainty, respectively. However, the qualitative results do not change when higher degree of prudence and more risky income are used.
4. The income process of the households who failed in gaining college education is the same as that of the households with no education expenditure (i.e., before reform), and therefore, their consumption-saving behavior is comparable. For the households who have expectations on future education expenditure, the consumption behavior is the same as before $t_e = 20$. After t_e, however, consumption for the households who succeeded in gaining college education is different from those who failed, because educational expenditure and permanent income level are different.
5. For more information, see, Li and Luo (2007) and Luo (2004).
6. There are only 6,931 urban households available for individual data.
7. We choose this definition due to our research purpose. Education expenditure and medical expenditure are not regular consumption goods, and they only occur at some specific time for the household. From this perspective, they are more close to durable consumption goods, and we choose to leave them in the control variables. Including education and medical expenditure, does not change our basic results.

References

Aiyagari, S. Rao (1993), "Uninsured Idiosyncratic Risk and Aggregate Saving," Working Papers 502, Federal Reserve Bank of Minneapolis.

Caballero, R. J. (1990), "Consumption Puzzles and Precautionary Savings," *Journal of Monetary Economics* Vol. 25, pp. 113–136.

Carroll, C. D. (1994), "How Does Future Income Affect Current Consumption," *Quarterly Journal of Economics* Vol. 109, pp. 111–147.

Carroll, C. D. (2001), "A Theory of the Consumption Function, With and Without Liquidity Constraints (Expanded Version)," NBER Working Paper No. W8387.

Chamon, Marcos and Prasad, Eswar (2010), "Why Are Saving Rates of Urban Households in China Rising?" *American Economic Journal—Macroeconomics* Vol. 2, No. 1, pp. 93–130.

Deaton, A. S. (1991), "Saving and Liquidity Constraints," *Econometrica* Vol. 59, pp. 1121–1148.

Engen, E. M. and Gruber, J. (2001), "Unemployment Insurance and Precautionary Saving," *Journal of Monetary Economics* Vol. 47, pp. 545–579.

Gao, M. (2007), "Estimation on the Return of Higher Education—Evidence from three Western Cities in China," *Statistics Research* Vol. 24, No. 4, pp. 69–76.

Kazarosian, M. (1997), "Precautionary Savings—A Panel Study," *Review of Economics and Statistics* Vol. 79, pp. 241–247.

Kimball, M. S. (1990), "Precautionary Savings in the Small and in the Large," *Econometrica* Vol. 58, pp. 53–73.

Liu, Jianguo (1999), "The Reasons for the Low Propensity to Consume in Rural China," *Economic Research Journal* (Chinese), Vol. 3, pp. 52–65.

Luo, Chuliang (2004), "Uncertainty during economic transition and household consumption behavior in urban China," *Economic Research Journal* (Chinese), Vol. 4, pp. 100–106.

Modigliani, Franco and Shi Larry Cao (2004), "The Chinese Saving Puzzle and the Life-Cycle Hypothesis," *Journal of Economic Literature* Vol. 42, No. 1, pp. 145–170.

Shi, Jianhuai and Haiting Zhu (2004), "Household Precautionary Saving and Strength of the Precautionary Motive in China: 1999–2003," *Economic Research Journal* (Chinese), Vol. 10, pp. 66–74.

Song, Zeng (1999), "Studies on the Saving Behavior of Households in China," *Financial Studies* (Chinese), No. 6, pp. 46–50.

Yi, Xingjian, Junhai Wang, and Junjian Yi (2008), "The Flucturation and Regional Difference of the Strength of Precautionary Saving Motive," *Economic Research Journal* (Chinese), Vol. 2, pp. 119–131.

8

The Dynamics of
Urban Income Distribution
in China (1995–2007)

Hao Zhou

This chapter investigates the income distribution among different Chinese cities using GDP data from the period 1995–2007. We use a city-level dataset covering all of mainland China, and provide an outline of Chinese urban growth. Nonparametric kernel-density estimation is employed to describe the evolution of the entire cross-sectional distribution of real per capita GDP over time. The main conclusions are as follows: (1) the urban income distribution structure of China has changed substantially from a unimodal pattern to a bimodal pattern between 1995 and 2007; (2) the dynamics of income distribution of prefecture-level cities is somewhat different from that of county-level cities; and (3) the ratio of people living below the absolute poverty line ($1/day) has dramatically declined in cities of all levels.

8.1   Introduction

Rural-urban migration is a main feature of modern economic growth. Significant changes in income distribution have been evidenced in many countries and regions during the path of urbanization and economic transition. The Industrial Revolution in the late eighteenth century, created a new era in the history of urban development. The socialization of economic activity and the specialization of production stimulated quick mobilization of capital, population, knowledge, and firms into the cities, and therefore, cities gradually became the flagship of growth in modern economic development. Kuznets (1966) suggests that the percentage of urban population tends to increase with the economic growth in some rich countries. Chenery and Syrquin (1975), using cross-sectional data, also prove that the percentage of urban population rises with per capita GNP. Lucas (1988) emphasizes that human capital and its externalities are the engines of growth, and that cities play an important role in accumulating human capital, and exerting its external effects as much as possible. China is experiencing fast growth and a dynamic transition that may have a drastic influence on income distribution. Therefore, we investigate the income dynamics at a city level to shed light on the sources of national income evolution.

China's economic performance has been remarkable since the beginning of its economic reform in the late 1970s. The real per capita GDP growth has averaged nearly a 10 percent increase. Since the early 1990s, the center of Chinese economic reform and development has been gradually transferring to urban and industrial sectors, resulting in the increasing urban population from 350 million in 1995 to 600 million in 2007, while raising the share of urban population from 29 percent to 45 percent (NBS, 2008). However, the urban-rural income disparity has been widening. According to the statistical results published in *Green Book of China's Rural Economy*, the income ratio between urban and rural residents increased from 2.5 in 1996, to 3.22 in 2005. However, the increase of residents' income across cities remains unbalanced. The Gini coefficient of per capita GDP in cities remained above 0.35 during 1995–2004 (Zhou, 2007). Income disparity across the different cities has become the main source of Chinese regional income inequality. However, most studies are based on macro- and provincial-data (Cai and Du, 2000; Aziz and Duenwald, 2001; Wang, 2004; Peng, 2005), and very little microdata about the economic transition and income dynamics has been used at the city level.

This chapter presents an empirical study of income convergence across China at the city level during the years 1995–2007 using the distribution dynamics approach to economic convergence proposed by Quah (1993, 1996).

This chapter provides several findings about the urban income distribution. First, the urban income distribution structure of China has changed substantially between 1995 and 2007. Second, the dynamics of income distribution of prefecture-level cities is somewhat different from that of county-level cities. Third, the ratio of people living below the absolute poverty line ($1/day) has dramatically declined at city level.

The remainder of this chapter is organized as follows: Section 8.2 summarizes the related literature. Section 8.3 discusses some stylized facts of Chinese urban economic growth and income gap within cities during the period of 1995–2007. Section 8.4 focuses on the dynamic evolution of per capita GDP at the city level, based on the Gaussian kernel-density methods, and the investigation of the urban poverty ratio and its changes. The concluding remarks come in the final section.

8.2   Related Literature

The neoclassical theory of economic growth (Solow, 1956; Swan, 1956) provides the foundation for most empirical studies on income disparity across countries/regions. Abramovitz (1986) and Baumol (1986), in their pioneering analysis, first applied the growth regression method to explore the evidence of convergence of economic growth and per capita income across countries. Following the leading work of Mankiw, Romer, and Weil (1992) and Barro and Sala-i-Martin (1992), growth regression based on cross-sectional data has been the workhorse of empirical growth literature. Since the convergence hypothesis emphasizes a long-term relationship between the growth rate and initial level of output, regression based on cross-sectional data is subject to substantial estimation problems induced by measurement biases, omitted variables, autocorrelation, and variable endogeneity. Henceforth, it cannot provide convincing empirical estimation on economic growth and income distribution. Thereafter, many researchers use modern econometric methods to modify the traditional growth convergence regression from every side. Some use time-series data to systematically test the across-region growth convergence (Bernard and Durlauf, 1995; Evans, 1996). Some apply cross-country growth regression to investigate the convergence across regions within a particular country (Cai and Du, 2000; Johnson and Takeyama, 2001). While, others apply the spatial econometric method used in economic geography to examine the growth convergence across regions (Rey and Montuori, 1999; Arbia and Basile, 2005). Panel data, time-series data, and spatial econometric estimations have been widely used regression approaches in economic growth and convergence (Bernard and Durlauf, 1995; Islam, 1995; Caselli, Esquivel, and Lefort, 1996; Rey and Montouri, 1999).

Quah (1996, 1997) and Durlauf and Quah (1998) challenge the regression approach. They argue that conclusions based on the conventional regression can only shed light on the behavior of the representative unit, and provide no information on the intradistribution dynamics in the process of growth convergence. Therefore, they propose the distribution dynamic approach as an alternative. This method takes income distribution across countries or regions as probability distribution, examines how the cross-sectional distribution of per capita output changes over time directly through the shape and the intradistribution dynamics of income distribution. As a nonparametric estimation method, it represents a radical departure from the traditional regression approach. Recently, many researchers have been adopting the distribution dynamic approach, to examine income distribution across countries, and offer new explanations to cross-country income gap (Jones, 1997; Bourguignon and Morrisson, 2002; Kumar and Russell, 2002; Sala-i-Martin, 2002; Beaudry, Collard, and Green, 2003; Leonida and Montolio, 2004; Quah, 2006). These studies show much progress in the field of empirics of income distribution and long-term economic growth.

Across region, the urban-rural income disparity tends to increase with the rapid growth of the national economy. What is the best way to measure and analyze the extent of income inequality? What is the best way to find Chinese evidence of across-region convergence or divergence in the path of economic transition? These questions have long attracted academic attention worldwide. Under the framework of "conditional convergence" and "club convergence," some researchers classify Chinese provinces as several growth clubs and test the speeds of convergence in developed groups and developing groups (Cai and Du, 2000; Dayal-Gulati and Husain, 2000; Aziz and Duenwald, 2001; Demurger et al., 2002; Wang, 2004; Peng, 2005; Xu and Li, 2006; Zou and Zhou, 2007a). Other researchers use the decomposition approach to investigate the effects of different growth factors (physical capital, human capital, infrastructure, economic openness, etc.) on growth and the per capita income gap across region (Li, Liu, and Rebelo, 1998; Chen and Feng, 2000; Xu and Shu, 2004; Zou and Zhou, 2007b).

However, since income disparity across China's provinces is a very complex issue, and not a single overall pattern, and varies with distribution patterns in different places, it is difficult to use conditional convergence to analyze the results of regression to capture this complexity (Raiser, 1998). There is, therefore, a need to find new ways to study various areas of the convergence issues in China. More and more researchers have begun applying the method of distribution dynamics in studying the issue of regional convergence in China. Aziz and Duenwald (2001) estimate the probability density of China's provincial-level income distribution for 1978–1997 based on the per capita GDP, and they suggest that in the initial stage of the reform, the income gap has declined. However, China's interprovincial income distribution is a bimodal distribution of development. Xu and Li (2004) use the kernel-density function method for 1978–1998, and estimate China's provincial-level income distribution based on the GDP per labor. Their findings are in line with Aziz and Duenwald (2001) that the formation of a single peak changes to twin peaks in the evolution of the trend, but their density map indicates the more obvious trend than that of Aziz and Duenwald (2001). Sakamoto and Nazrul (2008) study the convergence issues of China's provinces between 1952 and 2003, using the Gaussian kernel-density distribution for selected years to describe the shape of the graph of the provinces' per capita GDP. They also use the Markov transition matrix to reveal the dynamic changes in distribution of shape, offering the most reasonable interpretation of the convergence issues of China's provinces, thus far.

However, there are two drawbacks to the current growing literature on Chinese income inequality and growth. First, most studies adopt the growth regression approach to examine across-region income gap, and explore its sources from different perspectives. Using the scalar index to measure inequality, these studies tend to be static, and thus cannot give comprehensive information on national income distribution and its evolution. Only a few chapters (Aziz and Duenwald, 2001; Xu and Shu, 2004; Zou and Zhou, 2007b; Sakamoto and Nazrul, 2008) use the distribution dynamic approach to investigate China's growth difference across regions, but they only focus on the period between the mid-1970s and the mid-1990s. Very little research has been done on the income dynamics since the mid-1990s, a time period with fast economic growth and a widening income gap. Second, many of the current studies concentrate mainly on the provincial level, and few attempt to compile microdata to take into account the effect of urbanization. As Zhou (2007) found out, urban industrial sectors have become the driving force of economic reform and growth during the last 20 years. The accelerating urbanization and the enlarged income gap of urban residents should play an important role in income dynamics nationwide. In addition, the city is a relatively complete basic space unit in China. Based on city-level data, a study would be able to provide more detailed information and in-depth reliable conclusion.

8.3   China's Urban Economic Growth: Descriptive Evidence

Many regional growth studies of the Chinese economic growth are based on data related to Chinese province-level divisions. However, China is a large country, and many provinces in mainland represent very large geographic units and experience various economic policies and growth paths. A lower level of aggregation may be regarded as a natural choice for an analysis of regional growth patterns. In addition, few attempts have been made to use microdata to account for the effect of urbanization.

As Zhou (2007) points out, urban industrial sectors have become the driving force of economic reform and growth. The accelerating urbanization and the constantly enlarging income gap of urban residents should perform an important role in income dynamics nationwide. Therefore, the analysis of this chapter focuses on the distribution and evolution of per capita GDP at city level over the 1995–2007 period. The urban data on per capita GDP is compiled from *China City Statistical Yearbook (1996–2008)* published by NBS. It is well known that per capita GDP may not be a perfect proxy for income. However, to the best of our knowledge, there is no alternative to using per capita GDP to cover the whole of mainland China. Thus, we follow the previous literature to focus on this variable. The yearbook classifies all cities into four groups: municipalities under direct control of central government (*Zhixia Shi*), subprovincial cities (*Fushenji Shi*), prefecture-level cities (*Diji Shi*), and county-level cities (*Xianji Shi*).

Before beginning our analysis, it is useful to provide a brief explanation of the administrative structure of mainland China. The mainland is divided into 27 provinces and 4 municipalities. This makes up the first administrative level. Since 1983, the government has implemented a new administrative format setting up the "prefecture-level cities" by assigning adjacent rural counties under the city's administration. Therefore, the prefecture-level cities form the second level of the administrative structure, ranking right below the provinces. As urbanization progressed, some rural counties became "county-level cities", which forms the third level of the administrative structure. County-level cities are usually governed by prefecture-level divisions, but a few are governed directly by province-level divisions. Below the county, there are towns, which form the lowest level of administrative structure.

With this special structure, "cities" in Chinese terminology do not refer to only the urban areas, because often, rural counties and towns are attached to them. In the data released annually, information on urban area (Shiqu) and the overall administrated territory (Diqu) is available for prefecture-level cities and municipalities, but the overall administrated territory is only available for county-level cities.

Therefore, in this study, the data of prefecture-level cities only covers its urban area, while the data of county-level cities covers the entire administrated territory.

In order to maintain a large sample size without generalizing, this chapter classifies all cities into two groups, prefecture-level cities and county-level cities. Due to the particularly large size of the four municipalities, Beijing, Shanghai, Tianjin, and Chongqing, we have dropped them from the sample. In addition, all subprovincial cities are included in prefecture-level cities. According to the annual data, the city numbers of each year may be different, because each administrative region may vary with time. The number of cities is 632, 653, 639, 643, 658, 656, 687, 651, 643, 649, 654, 656, and 650 in the annual sample of 1995–2007, respectively. For consistency, this chapter adjusts GDP based on the price level of 2000.

8.3.1   China's Urban Per Capita GDP (1995–2007)

In this section, the trend of urban economic growth is discussed. At the national level, the per capita GDP of the urban sector rose to 24,949 Yuan (RMB) in 2007 from 7,877 Yuan in 1995, a growth rate of 217 percent. At the same time, per capita GDP of prefecture-level cities increased to 29,432 Yuan from 11,165 Yuan, and per capita GDP of county-level cities went up to 21,492 Yuan from 6,310 Yuan—growth rates of 164 percent and 241 percent, respectively. County-level cities GDP are growing at a higher rate as well. Interestingly, it turns out that the per capita GDP ratio of prefecture-level cities to county-level Cities is narrowing (see table 8.1). The per capita GDP ratio between these two subgroups of cities is declining from 1.77 in 1995 to 1.37 in 2004—a decrease of 22.6 percent. In addition, according to provincial data from *China Statistics Yearbook*, the average per

Table 8.1   China's urban per capita GDP (1995–2007) in Yuan (RMB)

Year	All cities	Prefectural-level cities	County-level cities	Ratio of Prefectural-to-County-level cities
1995	7,876.93	11,165.08	6,309.68	1.77
1996	8,354.45	11,813.10	6,794.22	1.74
1997	8,940.96	12,308.67	7,172.71	1.72
1998	9,618.60	13,051.15	7,796.07	1.67
1999	10,095.97	13,678.77	8,157.73	1.68
2000	10,810.81	14,125.21	8,675.96	1.63
2001	11,776.23	15,081.86	9,375.91	1.61
2002	12,523.77	15,635.57	10,276.35	1.52
2003	13,175.60	15,081.50	11,714.77	1.29
2004	16,307.98	19,823.09	13,623.90	1.46
2005	18,504.50	22,926.21	15,173.41	1.51
2006	21,295.43	26,224.59	17,555.61	1.49
2007	24,948.79	29,432.15	21,491.59	1.37

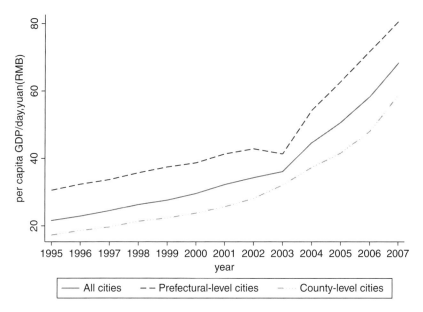

Figure 8.1   Chinese urban per capita GDP/day (1995–2007).

capita GDP in 2007 was 16,993 Yuan. Apparently, per capita GDP in cities of all levels is much higher than the national average.

Figure 8.1 illustrates the trend of per capita GDP at the city level during the period of 1995–2007. It shows that the time series of per capita GDP is, basically, a line. This is not only true for the big cities, but also at prefecture-level cities and county-level cities. This means that urban economic growth is stable and smooth during this period. However, there is one small kink in 2003. This most likely corresponds to the situation in the year when national economic activities suffered due to disasters, such as SARS and a series of natural disasters, including typhoon and drought. Shortly after this, macroadjustments helped the economy recover. It should be noted that per capita GDP of county-level cities did not experience the shock that year. To some extent, the reason is that the central government implemented exemption of taxes and charges in rural area to relieve peasant's burden and stimulate agricultural economy in that year.

8.3.2   Changes in Percentile of Urban Per Capita GDP (1995–2007)

In this section, we use percentile comparisons to show several prominent features of the per capita GDP of the urban population. The deviation of per capita GDP is calculated from the given years mean in order to emphasize changes in these percentiles.

First, we find that the interpercentile range expanded quite substantially between 1995 and 2007. This movement is documented in table 8.2 which reports

Table 8.2 Changes in the interpercentile ranges

		Ranges			Changes		
		1995	2001	2007	1995–2001	2001–2007	1995–2007
All cities	05–95	2.0091	2.1457	2.3796	0.1366	0.2339	0.3704
	10–90	1.6286	1.6671	1.7872	0.0385	0.1201	0.1586
	15–85	1.3035	1.3971	1.4496	0.0936	0.0525	0.1461
	20–80	1.0720	1.1207	1.2417	0.0487	0.1210	0.1697
	25–75	0.8527	0.8974	0.9875	0.0448	0.0901	0.1349
	30–70	0.6508	0.6698	0.7562	0.0189	0.0865	0.1054
	35–65	0.4599	0.4970	0.5577	0.0370	0.0608	0.0978
	40–60	0.3123	0.3702	0.3880	0.0579	0.0178	0.0757
Prefectural-level cities	05–95	2.0645	2.2571	2.3627	0.1926	0.1056	0.2982
	10–90	1.5147	1.6393	1.7907	0.1246	0.1514	0.2760
	15–85	1.2272	1.3493	1.4248	0.1221	0.0755	0.1976
	20–80	1.0243	1.0698	1.1642	0.0454	0.0944	0.1398
	25–75	0.7834	0.8681	0.9224	0.0847	0.0543	0.1390
	30–70	0.6049	0.6983	0.7226	0.0934	0.0243	0.1177
	35–65	0.4009	0.4397	0.4577	0.0388	0.0180	0.0568
	40–60	0.2684	0.2475	0.2703	−0.0209	0.0228	0.0019
County-level cities	05–95	1.8702	1.9661	2.1723	0.0959	0.2062	0.3021
	10–90	1.4162	1.5198	1.7023	0.1036	0.1825	0.2861
	15–85	1.0985	1.2500	1.3931	0.1515	0.1431	0.2946
	20–80	0.8850	0.9636	1.1657	0.0786	0.2021	0.2807
	25–75	0.7152	0.7593	0.9594	0.0441	0.2001	0.2443
	30–70	0.5433	0.6348	0.8021	0.0915	0.1673	0.2588
	35–65	0.3988	0.4477	0.5870	0.0489	0.1393	0.1882
	40–60	0.2635	0.2394	0.3782	−0.0241	0.1388	0.1147

the interpercentile range of the urban populations per capita GDP in 1995, 2001, and 2007, as well as the changes that took place over each subperiod. The interquartile range increased by about 0.135 for all cities over the period, and the widening was also found at other percentile ranges. An example of this is at the 20–80, 30–70, and 40–60 percentile differences. At the same time, both the per capita GDP of prefectural- and county-level cities show the same feature. In particular, the interquartile range increases by about 0.139 and 0.244 for prefectural- and county-level cities, respectively. Second, the widening of interpercentile ranges accelerated for all cities in 1995–2007. Table 8.2 shows the changes of interquartile range over two subperiods of 1995–2001 and 2001–2007 as 0.045 and 0.09, respectively. In other words, the interquartile range increases by about 5 percent from 1995 to 2001, and increased by slightly more than 10 percent between 2001 and 2007. Apparently, this pattern is found as well at other percentile ranges, for example, at the 10–90, 20–80, and 30–70 percentile differences. However, at the 40–60 percentile difference, the interquartile range increased by 18.5 percent between 1995 and 2001, and increased by 4.8 percent between 2001 and 2007. If we classify all cities into two subgroups, the prefectural- and county-level cities, we find the difference in the movements of these two subgroups. For

Table 8.3   Mass around mean

		Mass around the means			Changes		
	Δ	1995	2001	2007	1995–2001	2001–2007	1995–2007
All cities	0.5	0.5396	0.4454	0.4031	−0.0941	−0.0423	−0.1365
	0.6	0.6313	0.5298	0.4662	−0.1015	−0.0637	−0.1652
	0.7	0.7009	0.5881	0.5400	−0.1129	−0.0481	−0.1609
	0.8	0.7832	0.6710	0.6015	−0.1122	−0.0695	−0.1817
	0.9	0.8434	0.7234	0.6492	−0.1199	−0.0742	−0.1941
	1.0	0.8908	0.7875	0.7015	−0.1033	−0.0859	−0.1893
Prefectural-level cities	0.5	0.5931	0.5467	0.4664	−0.0464	−0.0803	−0.1267
	0.6	0.6667	0.6055	0.5371	−0.0611	−0.0684	−0.1296
	0.7	0.7353	0.6574	0.6148	−0.0779	−0.0426	−0.1205
	0.8	0.7941	0.7232	0.6643	−0.0709	−0.0589	−0.1298
	0.9	0.8186	0.7682	0.7208	−0.0505	−0.0473	−0.0978
	1.0	0.8627	0.8166	0.7739	−0.0461	−0.0428	−0.0889
County-level cities	0.5	0.6168	0.5653	0.4823	−0.0515	−0.0830	−0.1345
	0.6	0.6916	0.6709	0.5613	−0.0207	−0.1095	−0.1303
	0.7	0.7827	0.7312	0.6376	−0.0516	−0.0936	−0.1451
	0.8	0.8388	0.7915	0.7330	−0.0473	−0.0585	−0.1058
	0.9	0.8832	0.8568	0.8011	−0.0264	−0.0557	−0.0821
	1.0	0.9229	0.8869	0.8474	−0.0360	−0.0395	−0.0755

the latter, its per capita GDP experienced a pattern similar to all cities. For the former, in general, the interpercentile ranges showed an expanding tendency that weakened over time, as can be seen at the 25–75, 30–70, and 35–65 percentile differences.

Since the widening of the interpercentile range can arise in many different forms, it is useful to look at how a fraction of the cities located within a given window around the mean fluctuate over time. For example, let us take a window of ±50 percent (i.e. 0.5 log-points) around the mean and examine the fraction of cities within that band in 1995, 2001, and 2007. We find that the fraction of cities located around the mean decreases quite substantially between 1995 and 2007. Table 8.3 reports these numbers. In 1995, 54 percent of cities fell into the ±0.5 log-points window, while in 2007 only 40 percent of cities fell within the same window. This phenomenon is also found in other windows. Moreover, this observation holds true at the prefectural- and county-level cities. These numbers—when taken together with the percentile differences—indicate a widening process that has taken place around the interpercentile range and corresponds to a divergence mode.

8.4   Gaussian Kernel-Density Distribution

The results from the previous section, which provided only summarized information about the change of Chinese urban per capita GDP, while useful, do not show a complete picture of the relative income distribution, never mind how it has evolved over the years. In this section, approximation of the per capita GDP in Chinese cities will be examined. We are interested in the change of the structure of the distribution. If the income distribution becomes concentrated around the average level, it can be interpreted that absolute convergence exists. If not, income convergence does not exist, and income divergence will exist in some cases. Therefore, for the detailed distribution-change situation, it is more effective to examine the density function through estimation (Quah, 1996; Sakamoto and Nazrul, 2008). To do so, the *kernels* of the actual relative urban income in different time periods are estimated so that their shapes and intertemporal dynamics can be depicted.

Gaussian kernel-density distribution is commonly used for estimating distribution. It is a nonparametrical estimation method. We only have discrete income data for each economy. Estimating the density function means transformation from discrete data to a continuous curve. As an approach of expressing the discrete income distribution as a continuous curve at each stage, the kernel-density estimation is broadly adopted. If the width of the discrete income distribution becomes fine enough, the distribution could be expressed by a continuous curve.

Let x_i denote per capita GDP of city i in 2000 prices, and $\bar{x}$ be the cross-sectional population weighted average of x_i. To make the comparison over time easier, we first subtract from the shift in the mean of distribution as reflected in the secular movement in $\bar{x}$. Therefore, we normalize the data of different years by their respective cross-sectional means, and take the log of the ratio of x_i to $\bar{x}$ as the variable that we are analyzing. We denote this variable by z_i, so that:

$$z_i = \ln\left(\frac{x_i}{\bar{x}}\right) = \ln x_i - \ln \bar{x} \ .$$

We begin by estimating the actual distribution of z_i for selected years using the Guassian normal kernel. Mathematically, the kernel estimator $f(z)$ is defined as,

$$f(z) = \frac{1}{h}\sum_{i=1}^{}\frac{w_i}{\sqrt{2\pi}}\exp\left(-\frac{1}{2}\left(\frac{z-z_i}{h}\right)^2\right),$$

where z_i is an observed value of the variable. In this case, the actual relative urban per capita GDP, w_i is the population weight of sample i, and h is the window width. A crucial point in nonparametric econometrics is the choice of the window width h. The larger the value of h, the smoother the density estimate. Among several possibilities to select, we choose the smoothing parameter to be $0.9 * sd * N^{-0.5}$, where sd is the standard deviation of relative per capita GDP, and N is the number of observations. This window width criterion has been recommended by Silverman (1986), and has been used in almost all related studies.

In addition, the kernel density graph of urban per capita GDP describes the proportion of the population with certain levels of income in total population in an accurate and visual way. Hence, we apply income distribution dynamics to measure urban poverty in China. In 1985, the World Bank defined the poverty line as the one-dollar-a-day ($1/day) line. Based on this standard, we calculate the corresponding years' poverty lines respectively[1], and plot these lines into the distributions. After that, the fraction of distribution below poverty line represents the poverty rate.

Figures 8.2, 8.3, and 8.4 depict the distribution dynamics of per capita GDP in Chinese cities. Figure 8.2 illustrates the approximated distributions of all cities for years 1995, 2001, and 2007. Figures 8.3 and 8.4 correspond to the distributions of prefectural- and county-level cities in the same three years, respectively. In addition, we add three years' vertical lines, which correspond to $1/day poverty line.

As we can see, figure 8.2 displays that the form of income distribution of all cities has changed remarkably over time. Three features in the evolution of the distribution are evident.

First, the distribution has changed from a unimodal pattern to a bimodal one. In 1995, the distribution of relative per capita GDP looked similar to a unimodal distribution with its peak at around −0.36. In the following years, the distribution had changed substantially to a bimodal pattern. In 2001, some cities tended to congregate at lower relative income levels than the national average, and some cities tended to congregate at higher relative income levels than the national average. This "emerging twin-peaks" proposed by Quah (1996) in the cross-city data suggests a tendency of stratification in income distribution of cities. At the same time, the entire distribution seems to be more compact in 2001 than it was in 1995. This reflects the theory that income inequality within cities decreased somewhat. Furthermore, comparing the distribution for 2001 and 2007, figure 8.2 shows that both relative income levels corresponding to low-income peak and high-income peak declined from −0.29 to −0.99 and from 0.21 to −0.217, respectively. Apparently, the gap between the two peaks increased from 0.5 in 2001 to 0.77 in 2007. An interesting observation is that the distribution seems to be more "dispersed" in 2007 than it was in 1995 or 2001. This reflects the well known increase in income inequality within China.

Second, the subsection of income distribution differs in the extent and patterns of changes over time. We classify the sample into two groups, high-income group with a log of relative income greater than zero and low-income group with a log of relative income less than zero. During the period 1995–2001, the fraction of high-income group increased to 0.396 in 2001 from 0.365 in 1995, a growth rate of 8.5 percent. This means that the proportion of urban residents with relative incomes above the national average increased during the period 1995–2001. Between 2001 and 2007, this shift did not continue, but rather, moved in the opposite direction. The fraction of the high-income group declined to 0.348 in 2007 from 0.396 in 2001. This means that more urban residents joined the low-income group during the process of enlarging income inequality.

Third, the $1/day poverty line moved to the left gradually, and the fraction lying to the left of the poverty line declined dramatically over time. Figure 8.2 shows three vertical lines corresponding to the poverty line. The right one located at around −0.5239 represents the real gap between $1/day in 1985 values and the national average of Chinese urban per capita GDP for 1995. Similarly, both the middle line and the left line located at −1.0938 and −1.771 correspond to 2001 and 2007, respectively. This situation suggests that the whole density function in terms of real per capita GDP shifts to the right over time, and reflects the fact that Chinese urban incomes have increased substantially. In addition, an interesting point worth emphasizing is that the fraction below the one-dollar line in 1995, 2001, and 2007 were about 36.31 percent, 11.08 percent, and 2.31 percent, respectively. This means that the fraction of poor people declined dramatically. If we use the one-dollar definition, about 36.31 percent of the Chinese urban residents in 1995 lived in absolute poverty, and the fraction of poor declined to 11.08 percent in 2001 and to 2.31 percent in 2007. Apparently, China has made great achievements in urban poverty alleviation.

To summarize, during the period 1995–2007, the urban per capita GDP of the Chinese grew, the poverty rate reduced dramatically, and income inequality across all cities increased.

Corresponding years' distributions in the case of the prefectural- and county-level cities are shown in figures 8.3 and 8.4, respectively. They somewhat display the similar evolution from a unimodal pattern to a bimodal one, but still show some different features as well.

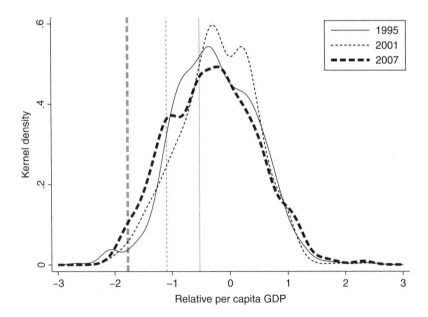

Figure 8.2   Income distribution of Chinese urban per capita GDP.

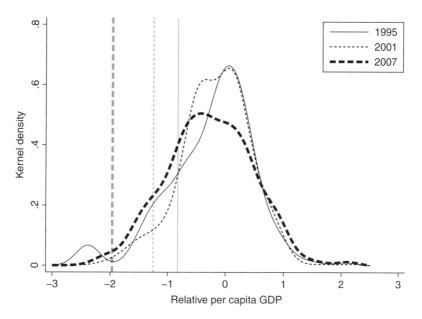

Figure 8.3 Income distribution of Chinese prefecture-level cities' per capita GDP.

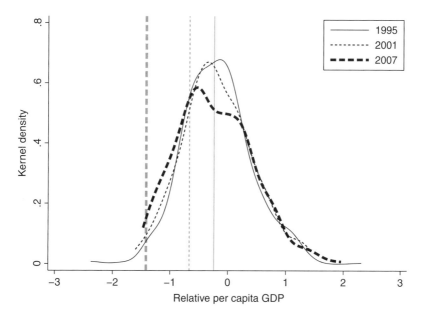

Figure 8.4 Income distribution of Chinese county-level cities' per capita GDP.

Likewise, figure 8.3 shows the evolution of distribution of the per capita GDP for the prefecture-level cities over the period 1995–2007. First, we notice that the distribution for 1995 was almost a unimodal pattern, whose single peak was located at around 0.07. In addition, there is a small peak at the lower tail of the distribution, which is located at around −2.394. Six years later, the income distribution changed to a bimodal situation whose peaks are about −0.395 and 0.07, while the small peak at the lower tail disappeared. This situation is similar to that of all cities. After this, the distribution did not change much, and still kept a bimodal pattern. The result in 2007 was similar to that of 2001. Figure 8.3 displays that the density below −0.8 rose, though the position of the two peaks did not change. As a result, the entire distribution process extended. Second, an interesting observation to notice is that the main change of distribution over time happened on the left—the fraction of low-income group with relative income less than zero. On the right hand side, distribution remained stable during the period of 1995–2001. Instead, the left side of distribution experienced more changes. In 2001, a peak appeared in the fraction between −0.8 and 0. In addition, the size of the fraction increased between 1995 and 2001, followed by a decrease during the period of 2001–2007. On the contrary, the fraction less than −0.8 decreased during the first period, and increased during the second period. In general, in the left of distribution, changes were more dispersed, which suggests that more people lived with low relative income. Third, the fraction below $1/day poverty line declined dramatically over time. In figure 8.3, the right side corresponding to 1995 is located at around −0.8257. Similarly, both the middle line and the left line are located at around −1.2511 and −1.9653, which correspond to 2001 and 2007. In other words, in 1995, about 19.2 percent of the Chinese prefecture-level cities' residents lived in absolute poverty, a number that declined to 5.82 percent in 2001 and to 1.4 percent in 2007.

Figure 8.4 shows the evolution of distribution of per capita GDP for the county-level cities over the period of 1995–2007. As can be seen, the distribution in 1995 is hump-shaped with the mode at −0.135. In 2001, the distribution did not change much, and kept the original shape, except that the mode moved to −0.338. Over the following years, the distribution experienced a significant change, and formed a bimodal pattern gradually. In particular, the original peak kept moving to the left, and formed a significant left peak, located at around −0.69. At the same time, an insignificant hump appeared, located at 0.128. An interesting point about the distribution of county-level cities must be noted. The distribution of county-level cities is more compact than those of all big cities and prefecture-level cities. This reflects the income disparity within county-level cities, and gives us a few moments of optimism during the period of 1995–2007. In addition, figure 8.4 also displays that the $1/day poverty line is located at around −0.2358 in 1995, −0.663 in 2001, and −1.4154 in 2007, respectively. In other words, about 47.72 percent of the Chinese county-level cities' residents in 1995 lived in absolute poverty, a number that declined to 22.25 percent in 2001 and to 3.39 percent in 2007.

In general, the discussion above shows that the distribution of county-level cities for the period 1995–2007 is more stable than that of prefecture-level cities, especially between 1995–2001. This situation somewhat reflects the history and path of Chinese economic growth. Since the mid-1990s, urban industrial sectors have become the crucial engine of economic growth. Since it is the location of most industrial sectors, the divergence in growth occurs among prefecture-level cities due to differences in initial conditions, infrastructure, and human capital accumulation as well as government policies. This in turn, should result in a tendency to have stratifications and local polarizations in income distribution. However, there is no significant difference in initial conditions and low proportions of industry in county-level cities. Hence, there is no significant tendency for stratification or twin-peak distribution before 2000. As a result, we conjecture that the driving force of the change of income distribution of all cities in the period 1995–2001 originated from the income inequality in prefecture-level cities.

With the deepening of economic growth, a pattern of gradient development from big cities to small and medium cities emerged gradually. Therefore, the prefecture-level cities diffused economic effects to county-level cities around them, and played a more important role in pushing the economic development of county-level cities. Since the prefecture-level cities are different in economic development, the income inequality in county-level cities increased gradually. Hence, there is somewhat of a stratification or twin-peak distribution in county-level cities.

8.5   Conclusion

Income distribution dynamics approach, proposed first by Quah (1993, 1996, and 1997) and Sala-i-Martin (2006) provided a new view in exploring growth convergence and income evolution across regions of economic growth. The distribution density approach facilitates analysis of entire distribution, and not just its mean and/or dispersion. Especially, the approach has the advantage of establishing income distribution based on kernel-density function, investigating its shape and change over time in a more explicit way.

This chapter applies an income distribution dynamics approach to investigate the shape and evolution of Chinese per capita incomes at city levels in 1995–2007. We find the following conclusions.

First, the income distribution structure of all cities has changed greatly between 1995 and 2007. In particular, the distribution of per capita GDP across-city changed to a "twin-peak" distribution in 2007 from an apparent unique-peak in 1995. The driving force of the apparent change originates from prefecture-level cities' growth gap.

Second, during the period 1995–2007, the dynamics of income distribution of prefecture-level cities is somewhat different from that of county-level cities. The prefecture-level cities have evolved to an apparent "twin-peak" distribution from single-peak one, while the county-level cities have evolved to an emerging "twin-peak" distribution with a significant left-peak and an insignificant right-peak. In addition, the distribution of county-level cities does not change much, and keeps the original shape during the period between 1995 and 2001.

Third, the ratios of people that live under absolute poverty line have dramatically declined at all levels, including big city, prefectural- and county-level city.

The policy implications from our research are straightforward. First, we should accelerate urbanization orderly. Although the income disparity and polarization of prefecture-level cities drove the expansion of national urban income gap, the entire income distribution of county-level cities is more stable and compact than that of prefectual-level cities. Therefore, developing small- and medium–county-level cities further has important significance in promoting the improvement of traditional agriculture, and raise residents' income. Second, although we make great achievements in urban poverty alleviation, the proportion of urban population living in absolute poverty is still large, especially in county-level cities. Therefore, along with promoting urbanization, we should emphasize the construction of urban infrastructures and social security system to alleviate urban poverty.

Notes

The author thanks the National Foundation of Social Science (09CJL041) for financial support for this research. The views expressed are those of the author and do not necessarily reflect the views of the Institute of Industrial Economics, Jinan University. Of course, the author is entirely responsible for all the remaining errors.

1. In particular, we change $1/day in 1985 values to 4,835 Yuan(RMB)/year in 2000 values in our data set, adjust the number from different years by their respective cross-sectional means of per capita GDP, $\bar{x}$, and take the log of the ratio of 4835/ $\bar{x}$.

References

Abramovitz, M. (1986), "Catching Up, Forging Ahead and Falling Behind," *Journal of Economic History* 46, pp. 385–406.

Arbia, G. and R. Basile (2005), "Spatial Dependence and Non-Linearities in Regional Growth Behaviour in Italy," *Statistica* LXV(2), pp. 145–167.

Aziz, J. and C. Duenwald (2001), "China's Provincial Growth Dynamics," IMF Working Paper 01/3, January, www.imf.org/external/pubs/ft/wp/2001/wp0103.pdf.

Barro, R. and X. Sala-i-Martin (1992), "Regional Growth and Migration: a Japanese-US Comparison," *Journal of the Japanese and International Economy* 6(4), pp. 312–346.

Baumol, W. (1986), "Productivity Growth, Convergence, and Welfare: What the Long-Run Data Show," *American Economic Review* 76(5), pp. 1072–1085.

Beaudry, P., F. Collard, and D. A. Green (2003), "Changes in the World Distribution of Output-Per-Worker 1960–98: How a Standard Decomposition Tells an Unorthodox Story," mimeo.

Bernard, A. and S. Durlauf (1995), "Convergence in International Output," *Journal of Applied Econometrics* 10(2), pp. 97–108.

Bourguignon, F. and C. Morrisson (2002), "Inequality Among World Citizens: 1820–1992," *American Economic Review* 92, pp. 727–744.

Cai, Fang and Yang Du (2000), "Convergence and Divergence of Regional Economic Growth in China," *Economic Research Journal* 35(10), pp. 30–37 (in Chinese).

Caselli, F., G. Esquivel, and F. Lefort (1996), "Reopening the Convergence Debate: A New Look at Cross-country Growth Empirics," *Journal of Economic Growth* 1(3), pp. 363–389.

Chen, B. and Y. Feng (2000), "Determinants of Economic Growth in China: Private Enterprise, Education and Openness," *China Economic Review* 7(1), pp. 1–15.

Chenery, H. B. and M. Syrquin (1975), "Patterns of Development: 1950–1970" London: Oxford University Press.

Dayal-Gulati, A. and A. M. Husain (2000), "Centripetal Forces in China's Economic Take-off," IMF Working Paper 00/86.

Demurger, S., J. D. Sachs, W. T. Woo, S. Bao, G. Chang, and A. Mellinger (2002), "Geography, Economic Policy and Regional Development in China," NBER Working Paper No. 8897.

Durlauf S. N. and D. Quah (1998), "The New Empirics of Economic Growth," NBER Working Paper No. 6422.

Evans, P. (1996), "Using Cross-Country Variances to Evaluate Growth Theories," *Journal of Economic Dynamics and Control* 20, pp. 1027–1049.

Islam, N. (1995), "Growth Empirics: A Panel Data Approach," *Quarterly Journal of Economics* 110(4), pp. 1127–1170.

Johnson, P. and L. Takeyama (2001), "Initial Conditions and Economic Growth in the US States," *European Economic Review* 45, pp. 919–927.

Jones, C. (1997), "On the Evolution of the World Income Distribution," *Journal of Economic Perspective* 11(3), Summer, pp. 19–36.

Kumar, S. and R. Russell (2002), "Technological Change, Technological Catch-Up, and Capital Deepening: Relative Contributions to Growth and Convergence," *American Economic Review* 92, pp. 527–548.

Kuznets, S. (1966), *Modern Economic Growth*, New Haven, CT: Yale University Press.

Leonida, L. and D. Montolio (2004), "On the Determinants of Convergence and Divergence Processes in Spain" *Investigationes Economicas* 28, pp. 89–121.

Li, Hong, Zinan Liu, and I. Rebelo (1998), "Testing the Neocalassical Theory of Economic Growth: Evidence from Chinese Provinces," *Economics of Planning* 31, pp. 117–132.

Lucas, R. (1988), "On the Mechanics of Economic Development," *Journal of Monetary Economics* 22, pp. 3–42.

Mankiw, G. N., D. Romer, and D. N. Weil (1992), "A Contribution to the Empirics of Economic Growth," *Quarterly Journal of Economics* 107(2), pp. 407–437.

NBS (National Bureau of Statistics of China) (2008), *China City Statistical Yearbook (1996–2008)*, Beijing: Statistical Publishing House of China.

Peng, Guohua (2005), "The Disparity of Income, TFP and the Convergence Hypothesis in Chinese Provinces," *Economic Research Journal* 40(9), pp. 42–50 (in Chinese).

Quah, D. (1993), "Galton's Fallacy and Tests of the Convergence Hypothesis," *Scandinavian Journal of Economics* 95, pp. 427–443.

Quah, D. (1996), "Twin Peaks: Growth and Convergence in Models of Distribution Dynamics," *Economic Journal* 106, pp. 1045–1055.

Quah, D. (1997), "Empirics for Growth and Distribution: Stratification, Polarization, and Convergence Clubs," *Journal of Economic Growth* 2(1), pp. 27–59.

Quah, D. (2006), "Growth and distribution," Sir R. Stone lecture, Bank of England, refer to: http://econ.lse.ac.uk/staff/dquah/.

Raiser, M. (1998), "Subsidizing Inequality: Economic Reforms, Fiscal Transfer and Convergence Across Chinese Provinces," *Journal of Development Studies* 34(3), pp. 1–26.

Rey, S. J. and B. D. Montuori (1999), "US Regional Income Convergence: A Spatial Econometric Perspective," *Regional Studies* 33(2), pp. 143–156.

Sakamoto, H. and I. Nazrul (2008), "Convergence across Chinese Provinces: An Analysis Using Markov Transition Matrix," *China Economic Review* 19(1), pp. 66–79.

Sala-i-Martin, X. (2002), "15 Years of New Growth Economics: What Have We Learnt?" Columbia University Discussion Paper No. 0102-47.

Sala-i-Martin, X. (2006), "The World Distribution of Income: Falling Poverty and…Convergence, Period," *The Quarterly Journal of Economics* 121(2), pp. 351–397.

Silverman, B. W. (1986), *Density Estimation for Statistics and Data Analysis*, New York: Chapman and Hall.

Solow, R. M. (1956), "A Contribution to the Theory of Economic Growth," *Quarterly Journal of Economics* 70(5), pp. 65–94.

Swan, T. W. (1956), "Economic Growth and Capital Accumulation," *Economic Record* 32(November), pp. 334–361.

Wang, Zhigang (2004) "My Doubt about the Condition Convergence in China's Economic Growth," *Management World* 126, pp. 25–30 (in Chinese).

Xu, Xianxiang and Xun Li (2004), "The Chinese City's Convergence of Economic Growth," *Economic Research Journal* 39(5), pp. 40–48 (in Chinese).

Xu, Xianxiang and Yuan Shu(2004), "Growth Dynamics in Chinese Provinces (1978–1998)," *China Economic Quarterly* 3(3), pp. 619–638 (in Chinese).

Xu, Zhaoyuan and Shantung Li (2006), "Analysis on the Trend of Regional Income Disparity in China," *Economic Research Journal* 41(7), pp. 106–116 (in Chinese).

Zou, Wei and Hao Zhou (2007a), "The Classification of Growth Clubs and Convergence-Evidence from Panel Data in China (1981-2004)," *China & World Economy* 15(5), pp. 91–106.

Zou, Wei and Hao Zhou (2007b), "The Calculation and Analysis of Origin of the Differences in China's Provincial Economic Growth (1978–2002)," *Management World* 126, pp. 37–46 (in Chinese).

Zhou, Hao (2007), "On Club Convergence, Source of Growth and Income Dynamics of China Economy" Dissertation, Wuhan University, China (in Chinese).

9

International Implications of China's Transition into an Open Market Economy

Elias C. Grivoyannis

Global business interaction makes countries important to each other because of anticipated benefits. Some countries, though, might become more important than others as a result of their business interaction with the global community. Paraphrasing what was attributed to Japan at the beginning of the twentieth century (Whelpley, 1913, pp. 247–248), "There was a time when all the countries around the world hoped to find their chief field of commercial enterprise in the 'west'; but today, at the beginning of the twenty-first century, the mind of all the countries around the world is all toward China as the commercial hope of their future." This was not so before 1979 when the Chinese economy was still dominated by central planning.

9.1   China's Transition into a New Economy

During the period of the Cold War (1946–1991), the world was divided into two blocs, eastern and western. China joined the eastern bloc in 1949. The two blocs were dominated by the same motivation, the achievement of rapid economic growth, but by different political systems and economic strategies that led them to isolation from each other. This division of the world imposed a heavy economic burden on countries of both blocs, and prevented the establishment of a mutually beneficial world order. Each bloc visualized a desirable world order under its own terms and strategies. The desire of the eastern bloc countries was to see the rest of the world transformed into centrally planned national economies blessed by rapid economic growth. Just the opposite was the desire of the West. By the turn of the twenty-first century it became obvious that market economies were growing faster than centrally planned economies, and the dominant countries of the eastern bloc gradually adopted some type of a market economy on their own.

Before its transition into an open market economy with "Chinese characteristics," China was feared because of its adherence on central planning, and Western countries didn't want to share any economic benefits with her. Today China is feared only to the extent that its successes are achieved at the expense of other countries within a competitive market environment. China's successes are welcomed, though, when they are shared with the West. China's transition into a market economy and its advancement into an economic giant has been a blessing for many foreign firms and countries, albeit at a small cost for others.

By 2025, China is expected to overtake the United States to become the largest economy in the world (Maddison, 2006). Today, she is one of the largest trade partners for many countries, and holds $3.1 trillion in foreign exchange reserves. These reserves represent China's immediate claim on the GDP of other countries. However, power with money corrupts. China is now feared because of her money and her international market power, which can be transformed into political power. A corrupted China, from money and power, can potentially disturb a desirable world order. China's openness to globalization and its interaction with other economies created country interdependences. Market interdependences can be best managed by money, market power, and political intervention. A world order could be significantly influenced by the way the new China uses its newfound economic power and financial wealth.

9.2   A Sample of Victims and the Beneficiaries

Many authors have discussed recent world implications of China's openness and adoption of export-led growth strategies (see Ahearne, Fernald, Loungani, and Schindler, 2003, 2006; Eichengreen, Rhee, and Tong, 2004; Ianchovichina and Walmsley, 2005; Rodrik, 2006; Feenstra and Wei, 2008; Fukuda and Kasuya, 2010). Increased international trade with China was substantial in the 2000s, and supported the recovery of the Japanese economy from both the demand and the supply sides (Fukuda, 2008, Fukuda and Kasuya, 2010). In 2005, China was the fourth largest export destination of the United States, and is now the second-largest US trading partner after Canada. It also had a positive effect on Hong Kong, Korea, Singapore, and Taiwan due to increased exports of high-technology products to China. However, for countries such as Vietnam, the Philippines, Thailand, Indonesia, and Malaysia, the effect of China's increased international trade was detrimental due to declines of export competitiveness among labor-intensive manufacturers in these countries.

9.3   China's Exports and Their Impact on the Volume of Output and the Price of Inputs in Other Countries

China's exploitation of her comparative advantage in the production of labor-intensive commodities, such as textiles, apparel, footwear, toys, and laptop computers, has two important implications for the world economy. It affects the volume of output and the price of inputs of foreign firms. Some of the labor-intensive manufacturers in other countries might lose their export competitiveness after China's entry and reduce their volume of their output. Such an output adjustment will eliminate profits for domestic firms and employment opportunities for unskilled labor workers. It will also reduce the volume of sales of the input supply companies to those affected firms. For example, the excellent infrastructure along with China's high labor productivity and low labor cost have increased China's apparel exports at the expense of producers in Africa, in Latin America, and countries in South and Southeast Asia, such as Vietnam, the Philippines, Thailand, Indonesia, and Malaysia.

Other labor-intensive manufacturers in other countries, in order to retain their export competitiveness after China's entry, will have to keep the average wage of hourly workers from rising, as the United States did during the last decade. Stagnation in the growth rate of unskilled labor and the prices of other inputs in countries such as the European Union and the United States benefits consumers, but contributes to an increasing income inequality among the citizens of those countries.

9.4   China's Imports and Their Impact on Other Countries

The geographic distance of China from the consumer markets around the world is not a considerable obstacle for its exports. For a long period, the cost of transportation represented only a few percentage points of a country's international sales (Leontief, 1973). As a result, during the last thirty years, Asian firms from technologically advanced countries used China as an export platform. In the process, China acquired appropriate technology from neighboring countries, and made advances in the manufacturing of sophisticated export goods for the world markets. Proximity created supply-side linkages and reliance on imports of machinery and components from the region's more advanced economies—Japan, Korea, Taiwan, and Singapore. It also expanded its demand for imports of advanced technology from the United States and Europe.

As a result, China's exports of consumer electronics products and information technology hardware have been supported by foreign companies. China provides low-wage assembly services with the high-tech inputs imported from other countries. It imports high-technology inputs such as semiconductors, operating systems, hard drives, and microprocessors from countries such as Japan, Malaysia, Singapore, and Taiwan. These imports are then assembled with domestic cheap labor into laptops, DVD players, and cell phones, and shipped back as exports to countries around the world. In 2005, 60 percent of the total global semiconductor output was sold to China. In 2005, China was the largest importer of semiconductors and microprocessors in the global economy, and the fastest growing exports destination for the United States of America. This created a relationship of complementarity and a virtuous circle of further transactions for inputs from countries with advanced technologies. China's high value-added imports create profits for foreign manufacturing firms along with employment and high income for their employees. This helps power the economic growth throughout the countries that export advanced technology inputs, and benefits consumers in the rest of the world.

China's growing demand for imports also covers low technology items such as agricultural products, for example, soybeans from Brazil, and commodity inputs, such as petroleum products, iron ore, nickel, copper, and aluminum from various countries. China's demand for such commodities during the 2000 to 2005 period accounted for 45 to 100 percent of the increased global demand. Today, China consumes twice as much steel as Europe, Japan, and the United States combined do. Population growth and urbanization will increase the need for public transportation in China and the per capita consumption of iron, aluminum, and other metals in the years to come. This supports the demand for exports and employment, and increases the supply of foreign exchange reserves for many developing countries around the globe.

9.5   Breeding "Flying Geese" on China's Feeding Ground for the Economic Development of Other Countries

There is an interesting presentation and interpretation of the "Flying Geese" theory of economic development in the economics literature (see Akamatsu, 1961, 1962; Korhonen, 1994, Bernard and Ravenhill, 1995; Kojima, 2000; Ozawa, 2001; Ozawa, 2003; Tung, 2003; Ginzburg and Simonazzi, 2005). This model argues that economic development and industrialization can spread from advanced economies to developing countries as the labor cost in advanced countries rises, and multinational corporations move their operations through direct investment to countries with lower labor cost. In the process, developing countries change their patterns of comparative advantage, and the composition of their tradable commodities, as they catch up with more advanced economies and acquire from them better technologies through foreign direct investment (FDI) and international trade.

In the original presentation of the model, the "flying geese" are developing countries aligned behind economically advanced ones and ready to receive their old technologies as the leading countries become more sophisticated and advanced. In our interpretation of the model, the "flying geese" are the "light feet" multinationals that move their production facilities to "better feeding grounds" attracted by lower input cost when the labor cost in the hosting country rises, and they start losing their international competitiveness. According to our view, a developing country can passively receive FDI and technology to speed up its economic growth, or it can actively attempt to attract FDI and advanced technology by reducing business obstacles and facilitating higher profitability for multinationals.

In our view, China receives and is now breeding an increasing number of export-oriented manufacturing multinationals in her vast area of low-labor-cost geographic regions. This growing number of low-labor-cost manufacturing firms will soon start "flying" to the lower labor cost countries of Africa and other developing countries of the world as soon as the labor costs in China rise to a critical high level.

In order to attract the migrant "flying geese" of low-labor-cost manufacturing firms, the central planners of China established "safe feeding grounds" for these firms in their special economic zones (SEZs). The Chinese government secured respectable profitability for those firms in the form of low-cost labor by facilitating the flow of excess underemployed labor supply from China's agricultural sector. It also cleared the feeding ground of the SEZs from the "parasites" of tariffs and taxes by providing a duty-free environment for all imports of raw materials to be used in the production of goods for export by the foreign manufacturing firms. In addition, joint ventures of foreign companies with Chinese firms and wholly foreign-owned companies were allowed to import capital goods duty free (Lardy, 2002, p. 36; Branstetter and Lardy, 2008, p. 636), and thus, establish and maintain international competitiveness. Now, China is increasing its sophisticated manufacturing capacity by attracting intellectual property sensitive technology from foreign investors. The FDI of the United States firms increased in China from $9.4 billion in 1999 to $49 billion in 2009. This more advanced FDI is replacing the old one as a moving force of the country's economic growth.

As the labor cost in China rises, labor-intensive manufacturing becomes more expensive, and some of this manufacturing is expected to "fly" into lower labor cost countries in Southeast Asia, Latin America, or Africa. It is reasonable though to expect that before the "migrant geese" of labor-intensive manufacturing firms fly to Africa they will first rest for a while in mainland China. There is still plenty of rich feeding ground of low-cost labor in newly established SEZs for them over there. There is also an institutional safety that the Chinese government is progressively securing for its multinational "migrant" firms, even at the expense of its own national "domesticated" enterprises. "Domesticated" enterprises enjoy fewer business benefits in China than the "migrant" ones. When this labor-intensive manufacturing "flies" into the newly developed SEZs in mainland China it will reduce labor unemployment and underemployment there, until time comes to do the same in other parts of the world. As more and more such companies are growing in China, more and more of them will be "flying" into other low-income countries to stimulate their development in the future.

In our interpretation of the "flying geese model," FDI in export-oriented labor-intensive manufacturing with low cost of labor in developing countries of the world creates a successful division of labor, and can lead the way toward rapid economic development in those countries. Incomes are eventually rising, and export-oriented manufacturing skills are acquired. This enables a developing country to adopt more advanced technologies, and acquire new comparative advantage. As new skills are developed and labor cost rises, the labor-intensive manufacturing will "fly" to other low labor cost developing countries of the world, and get replaced by more sophisticated and advanced types of manufacturing and services.

An unskilled-labor-intensive manufacturing can lead a developing region into industrialization and development by introducing older, labor-intensive technologies, and eventually enable the region to replace those technologies with more advanced ones. In the process, we will have spillover beneficial effects to other parts of the world and global economic progress.

9.6   Anticipated Global Benefits from Chinese Innovation

In the recent year, China relied on imported foreign technology for its speedy economic growth. As the new China pursues upgrading of its economy, it encourages indigenous innovation to develop advanced technology domestically, rather than importing it. China's new "indigenous innovation" policies promote the development, commercialization, and purchase of Chinese products and technologies. Chinese innovations are advantageous to domestic and foreign firms by introducing new products, increasing sales at a lower cost, or creating new opportunities for FDI abroad by Chinese corporations. Domestic research and development capabilities are facilitating Chinese firms' innovative capacity and increasing the value that domestic companies add to the global economy. The savings rate is high enough in China to finance capital accumulation necessary to turn discoveries of research and development into new marketable products. This is an important anticipated contribution of China's openness to global welfare. The indigenous innovation "web of policies" in China is also expected to inspire and create incentives for foreign companies to become more innovative, and compete for the income of the Chinese and the international consumer.

9.7   Preventing the Appreciation of the Yuan

For a long period of time, the Chinese currency has been undervalued, and the Chinese government is supporting it. This creates trade imbalances with global implications. It makes Chinese exports more price competitive for foreign buyers, and China's imports more expensive for domestic consumers. This increases China's exports, decreases China's imports, and increases China's accumulation of foreign currency reserves.

Since many multinational manufacturing firms are using China as an export-support base, the ultimate beneficiaries of the growing Chinese exports are the foreign stockholders of those firms. Appreciation of the Yuan could undermine the competitiveness of export-oriented investments by foreign corporations. Cheap exports benefit foreign consumers, and making them more expensive will reduce social welfare, along with the reduction in profits of foreign firms who invested in China to serve the foreign consumers. So even when China's currency is not properly aligned, it still generates welfare benefits for the rest of the world.

The appreciation of the Yuan is associated with a trade-off. The global economy stands to lose welfare benefits for its consumers or gain welfare benefits for its producers. International consumers benefit from the low prices of Chinese exports, but some of them also benefit from employment with companies that produce Chinese imports.

9.8   China's Fixed Investment

Unlike Asian firms, European and US firms invested in China in order to serve the local market. The growth of China's domestic market benefits both, foreign firms that produce in China and those that import their products in China from their overseas operations.

The recent growth in China's economy was fueled by net exports and fixed investment. In 2010, China's expenditures on fixed investment were approximately 50 percent of its GDP, more than double the under-20 percent world average and the 15 percent US rate. China needs a solid infrastructure for economic growth such as airports, highways, bridges, ports, factories, offices, and housing.

The government in China is recently forcing state firms to invest and directing state-owned banks to lend more on investment projects. A high ratio of investment to GDP is a good sign for a successful developing economy. America's capital per worker is 20 times higher than in China. Government-influenced investment accounted in 2009 for about three-fifths of the growth in market-based investment. The fastest expansion in government spending has been in railroads, highways, electric power grids, and running water. In 2008, fixed investment in infrastructure rose by twice as much in the less-developed western regions of the country than in the more-advanced eastern provinces. All these activities facilitate the expansion of domestic markets, both in the short and in the long run, and benefit foreign producers. All this investment will yield high long-term returns by allowing China to sustain rapid growth, increasing per capita income, and rising domestic consumption per capita.

It is expected that after this infrastructure is in place China's fixed investment will decline in order to avoid an increasing maintenance cost of a massive amount of overcapacity and an accumulation of nonperforming loans in the banking system. A record high of a $2.7 trillion of loans were extended recently in China over a two years period to finance spending on fixed investment. China's economy will be eventually forced to reduce fixed investment spending to 20 percent of its GDP, which is the world average, and replace the difference by an increase in domestic consumption of approximately 30 percent of its GDP if its economy is going to maintain its current performance. This would be a relatively easy task for policymakers to perform if the government provides a social safety net (heath care, unemployment, and retirement age benefits) that could encourage reduction in personal savings and increased spend on consumption.

Government sponsored fixed investment is a stepping-stone toward higher consumer spending in the long run. It creates jobs and higher family incomes in the short run, and better infrastructure to support jobs and consumer spending in the long run. Without roads and bridges, people will not buy automobiles and producers will not have easy access to consumer markets. Supply of running water and electricity induces people to buy washing machine, refrigerators, and personal entertainment electronic products. Foreign producers will benefit in the long run from the recent government sponsored fixed investment in the country. China is becoming the destination of a growing number of American and European products and one of their largest trade partners.

9.9   The Environment

High economic growth is associated with environmental concerns. China's impact on the global environment has been addressed by the signing of many technology partnership agreements with the United Kingdom, Germany, Spain, and France on low-carbon advanced European technology for sustainable development of Chinese industries.

A mutual desire to promote communication and further economic cooperation has been evidenced by an increased exchange of visitors between China and the other countries not only for the purpose of increasing business and trade, but also in the fields of education and culture for further enhancement of trust and mutual respect of people, nature, and its resources.

9.10   Lending to Your Customers to Buy Your Exports!

The market economy in China is still, in a number of ways, very communistic. It naturally developed and still maintains a Chinese style of forced "collective savings" that create "collective benefits" for its citizens through an interesting sequence of global interactions. Chinese exports are sold at world market prices, but Chinese workers producing those exports are paid wages that are below the marginal value product of their work. The value addition of Chinese labor that is not paid to the Chinese workers helps China become globally competitive in commodities markets and accumulate foreign exchange reserves that reached the astonishing level of $3.1 trillion by 2011.

Foreign exchange reserves enable China to interact in global financial markets and become, among other things, the biggest overseas holder of US Treasury bonds. US Treasury bonds enabled recently the US government to stimulate the US economy and support American jobs that generate income which enable American citizens to buy Chinese products. Exports of Chinese products create and support jobs in China in this interdependent paradoxical way. "Forcing" its low-income citizens to "save collectively," by receiving low wages, China is able to lend to its relatively rich customers in the United States, and help them buy its exports that support employment and income for its low-wage citizens in China.

By using its foreign exchange reserves to buy EU and US bonds, China has certainly supported the recovery process of the global economy during its post-2008 recession. It is not China's responsibility to stabilize the global economy, or the global financial system, but China was supportive indeed of the US and the EU governments when they "socialized private debt" by buying from their banks "toxic assets" to enable them neutralize the deleterious effects of those assets on domestic and international financial markets.

Internally generated economic problems by countries around the world, cannot be solved by China. China, though, can still prove instrumental in helping them stabilize and stimulate their economies in more than one ways. It can use its foreign exchange reserves to buy their bonds, and thus, finance their debt. It can accelerate the increase in the purchasing power of the Chinese citizens, and thus, enable them to buy imports from those countries. It can invest productively in these deficit countries, and thus, enable them to earn themselves out of their debt. The last two options appear to be more attractive for a long-term global economic growth and benefit. The second one is more beneficial for the 150 million poverty-stricken Chinese population. Acceleration in the increase of their labor wages will reduce the international competitiveness of China's exports. This would replace exports demand with consumer domestic demand, and reduce the welfare of foreign consumers while increasing the exports to China of foreign producers generating employment and income for their employees.

9.11   Summary

China's transition into an open market economy increased competition in the commodities markets and benefited consumers around the world. It increased the global demand for commodity and high-technology inputs and benefited producers in other countries. China's SEZs, along with its increased labor productivity, competitive wage rates, and consumer demand of foreign products, increased investment opportunities for foreign producers and benefited their stockholders and employees. Noncompetitive producers were forced to abandon wasteful production processes and identify for themselves a new comparative advantage. China's accumulation of foreign exchange reserves has been used to stimulate the global economy and possess the potential for more attractive global economic benefits in the future. China's driving forces of economic growth are expected to rebalance from exports and investment toward domestic consumption and from manufacturing toward services with overall positive global implications. China's transition into an open market economy has benefited, both, her citizens and citizens in the rest of the world.

References

Ahearne, Alan G., John G. Fernald, Prakash Loungani, and John W Schindler (2003), "China and Emerging Asia: Comrades or Competitors?" *Seoul Journal of Economics* summer, special issue on The Post-Crisis Macroeconomic Adjustment in Asia.

Ahearne, Alan G., John G. Fernald, Prakash Loungani, and John W. Schindler (2006), "Flying Geese or Sitting Ducks: China's Impact on the Trading Fortunes of Other Asian Economies," Board of Governors of the Federal Reserve System, International Finance Discussion Papers #887.

Akamatsu, Kaname (1961), "A Theory of Unbalanced Growth in the World Economy," *Weltwirtschaftliches Archiv* Hamburg, 86, pp. 196–217.

Akamatsu, Kaname (1962), "A Historical Pattern of Economic Growth in Developing Countries," *The Developing Economies* Tokyo, 1(Preliminary Issue, March–August, 1962), pp. 3–25.

Bernard, M., and J. Ravenhill (1995), "Beyond Product Cycles and Flying Geese: Regionalization, Hierarchy, and the Industrialization of East Asia" *World Politics* 47(2), pp. 171–209.

Branstetter Lee and Nicholas Lardy (2008), "China's Embrace of Globalization" in Loren Brandt and Thomas G. Rawski, eds., *China's Great Economic Transformation*, New York: Cambridge University Press, pp. 633–682.

Eichengreen, Barry, Yeongseop Rhee, and Hui Tong (2004), "The Impact of China on the Exports of Other Asian Countries," NBER Working Paper No. W10768.

Feenstra, Robert and Shiang-Jin Wei, eds. (2008), *China's Growing Role in World Trade*, Chicago: University of Chicago Press.

Fukuda, Shin-ichi (2008), "The Rise of China and Sustained Recovery of Japan," Discussion Papers, CIRJE-F-589, University of Tokyo.

Fukuda Shin-ichi and Munehisa Kasuya (2010), "The Rise of China and the Japanese Economy: Evidence from Macro and Firm-level Micro Data" Bank of Japan Working Paper Series, No. 10-E-1, March.

Ginzburg Andrea and Annamaria Simonazzi (2005), "Patterns of Industrialization and the Flying Geese Model: The Case of Electronics in East Asia," *Journal of Asian Economics* 15(6), January, pp. 1051–1078.

Ianchovichina, Elena and Terrie Walmsley (2005), "Impact of China's WTO Accession on East Asia," *Contemporary Economic Policy* 23(2), pp. 261–277.

Kojima, Kiyoshi (2000), "The 'Flying Geese' Model of Asian Economic Development: Origin, Theoretical Extensions, and Regional Policy Implications," *Journal of Asian Economics* 11(4, Autumn), pp. 375–401.

Korhonen, P. (1994), "The Theory of Flying Geese Pattern of Development and Its Interpretations," *Journal of Peace Research* 31(1), pp. 93–108.

Lardy Nicholas (2002), *Integrating China into the Global Economy*, Washington, DC: Brookings Institution.

Leontief, Wassily (1973), "Explanatory Power of the Comparative Cost Theory of International Trade and Its Limits" in H. C. Bos, ed., *Economic Structure and Development: Lectures in Honor of Jan Tinbergen*. Amsterdam, North-Holland: Elsevier Science Publishing Co Inc, pp. 153–160.

Maddison, Angus (2006), "Asia in the World Economy, 1500–2030," *Asian Pacific Economic Literature* 20(2), pp. 1–37.

Ozawa, Terutomo (2001), "The 'Hidden' Side of the 'Flying Geese' Catch-Up Model: Japan's Dirigiste Institutional Setup and a Deepening Financial Morass," *Journal of Asian Economics* 12(4), pp. 471–491.

Ozawa, Terutomo (2003), "Pax Americana-Led Macro-Clustering and Flying-Geese-Style Catch-Up in East Asia: Mechanisms of Regionalized Endogenous Growth," *Journal of Asian Economics* 13(6), pp. 699–713.

Rodrik, Dani (2006), "What's So Special About China's Exports?" NBER Working Paper No. 11947.

Tung, An-Chi (2003), "Beyond Flying Geese: The Expansion of East Asia's Electronics Trade," *German Economic Review* 4(1), pp. 35–51.

Whelpley, James D. (1913), *The Trade of the World*, New York: Century Company.

Index